PLANNING AND SOCIAL SCIENCE

A Humanistic Approach

D0289896

Gerald A. Gutenschwager

University Press of America,® Inc.
Lanham · Boulder · New York · Toronto · Oxford

Copyright © 2004 by
University Press of America,® Inc.
4501 Forbes Boulevard
Suite 200
Lanham, Maryland 20706
UPA Acquisitions Department (301) 459-3366

PO Box 317
Oxford
OX2 9RU, UK

Library of Congress Control Number: 2003110867
ISBN 0-7618-2664-5 (paperback : alk. ppr.)

Πάσα επιστήμη χωριζόμενη δικαιο-
σύνης και της άλλης αρετής πανουρ-
γία, ου σοφία φαίνεται.

Πλάτων, *Μενέξενος*

All science without justice and any
other virtue must be seen as mere
cunning and not wisdom.

Plato, *Menexenos*

CONTENTS

FIGURES

TABLES

PREFACE

The story of this book begins in the mid 1950's when I entered the graduate program in city and regional planning at the University of Chicago. Positivism was in its heyday in the social sciences at that time, and, as planning was seeking to distinguish itself from architectural design, we were given the benefit of all the latest in this from of scientific thinking. There was a serious disjuncture between the accomplishments in the classroom and those of the profession in the City of Chicago, as I was to learn from my subsequent employment there, but this did not seem to trouble the academic program very much. Since then I have worked in other practical planning situations, first with a large international consulting firm, Doxiadis Associates, where I researched the planning problems of cities and regions in Africa, Asia and North America, and, subsequently, with the City of Athens, Greece.

In the meantime, I continued my academic training in the doctoral program in city and regional planning at the University of North Carolina, which was an excellent all around program in its own right. Here, however, I was challenged by a chance enrollment in a course in the philosophy of social science, where I was introduced to phenomenology. Marxist urban theory subsequently introduced me to structuralism, and to a different set of epistemological and ontological presuppositions, which were as distinct from positivism as were those of phenomenology. Finally, academic teaching helped me to clarify the role of communication in every aspect of human existence, and encouraged me to become familiar with language and its sociodramatic uses as an invaluable dimension of planning theory.

Gerald Gutenschwager
Milies, Mount Pelion, Greece
May 2003

ACKNOWLEDGMENTS

I would like to thank the Department of Planning and Regional Development at the University of Thessaly, and especially Byron Kotzamanis, Director of the Laboratory of Demographic and Social Analysis, for support during the writing of this book. I would also like to thank and, indeed, dedicate this book to my wife, Mary, for all her help, academic and emotional, in the preparation and organization of the book.

CREDITS

The quotation by Lawrence Durrell on pp. 11-12 is reproduced with permision of Curtis Brown Ltd., on behalf of the estate of Lawrence Durrell. Copyright © Lawrence Durrell, 1963.

Cover Design: Erica Gutenschwager

INTRODUCTION

When planning in the U.S.A. shifted from a design activity to a technocratic process after World War II, it sought a *scientific* basis for its new professional approach. The academic climate in the United States at that time would permit no other concept of social science than that inspired by positivism, along with the ontological and epistemological presuppositions that it carried with it from the natural sciences. Subsequent developments, both inside and outside academia, have raised doubts about how sufficient positivism is for comprehending society in all its complexity, especially to the extent that it differs from nature in important respects. This is not to say that positive social science should be abandoned in any sense of the word, but rather that there are important additional dimensions of society that cannot be understood from such a perspective. Thus, borrowing a term from Thomas Kuhn, an attempt is made here to explore the limitations and potential of not only positivism, but also of two other 'paradigms', phenomenology and structuralism, in the hopes that a more comprehensive social scientific basis for planning could be articulated.

Phenomenology addresses important dimensions of society missing in nature, such as consciousness and intention, and attempts to formulate a paradigmatic or meta-theoretical framework for understanding human behavior as not just a succession of facts and events, but as the outcome of thought and purpose. This immediately poses the question as to how consciousness and intention come into being in the absence of a biogenetic program, assuming that human behavior is characterized by the absence of such ultimate determination. Here important social processes, such as habitualization or routinization of behavior, leading to its typification and ultimate institutionalization, come into play, all in a social context that directs this process without determining it in any causal sense. Of importance here is the dialectical relationship that characterizes the association between the individual and the collectivity. The collectivity socializes the individual into its rules and roles, while the individual always may select which of these to accept, which to oppose, and which to doubt, all with potential effects back on that collectivity. There is, therefore, an ambiguity to the social order that postmodernists have observed (and often exaggerated for their own reasons). This gives an uncertainty to many of the positivist explanations of social phenomena, which cannot be washed away with reservations having to do with probability, etc.

The chapters on structuralism explore other dimensions of the social whole, suggesting forms of regulation that also cannot be reduced to mechanistic causal formulations. Here concepts of wholeness (the totality more that a mere sum of the parts), self-regulation and transformation are discussed. When these concepts are formulated in more than static and descriptive terms, they once again raise the question of the dialectic: How is the whole constituted? How do self-regulation and transformation take place? Etc. All the authors discussed here place emphasis upon the structuring process rather than upon structures, as such. That there are isomorphisms, topological, and other mathematical features of structures, etc., is less important than how they have come into being. Piaget bases his discussion on the formation of psychological and intellectual structures. Giddens emphasizes institutionalizing processes, very much like those described by the phenomenologists. Burke finds explanation in the narrative, and more specifically dramatic form, as the master metaphor for understanding how humans create and maintain (or change) social structure.

By placing emphasis on communication as the 'cause' of social structuring, we can begin to extend the traditional engineering concept of planning to encompass new insights into its actual role in society. Planning is an *intervention* in society, as is all social science in a less formal way. Engineers see as their role to control and manipulate. Is this the proper role of planning? If so, in whose interests is society (or nature) to be manipulated and controlled? Can planning simply relax and assume that 'political processes' will ensure a democratic formulation of priorities? All scientists and engineers have been under a form of ' house arrest' since the time of Galileo, to a large extent self-imposed (perhaps to avoid the fate of Giordano Bruno). They have made historic compromises, first with the church and now with the hegemonic bourgeoisie, to insure their social benefits and (circumscribed) freedom to pursue their intellectual interests. This 'attitude toward history (society)' is self-imposed because it has become institutionalized, i.e., taken for granted. In short, this is a socially constructed form of 'imprisonment'. However, (communicative) planning actions which seek to overstep the bounds of this institutionalized order can be 'dangerous'; there is security in political apathy.

Thus, planning as a scientific activity faces a double challenge. First, it must understand its social reality (as differentiated from the reality of nature). Second, it must understand its own role in constituting that socially constructed reality, which is also its object of study. This is not an easy challenge, and it carries planning well beyond its traditionally defined role, both as an academic as well as a professional activity. These boundaries were transgressed briefly in the 1960's, so there is a glimpse of what could be done. But planning would have to sharpen its understanding, not only of the society into which it is intervening, but also of its own rhetorical resources for intervening in socially and politically responsible ways.

PART ONE

PARADIGMS IN SOCIAL SCIENCE

CHAPTER 1

POSITIVISM AND ITS 'DISCONTENT'

> The central idea of the consilience world view is that all tangible phenomena, from the birth of stars to the workings of social institutions, are based upon material processes that are ultimately reducible, however long and tortuous the sequences, to the laws of physics. . .
> I admit that the confidence of natural scientists often seems overweening.
>
> E.O.Wilson, *Consilience*

> He's a scientist. He does not think of defending his actions. He is not weakened with a conscience. . . Christianity he regards as no more than a poetic conceit. He doesn't even bother to criticize it, or to mock it or to disavow it.
>
> E.L.Doctorow, *The Waterworks*

The authority of scientific planning is based on its association with positive science. That is, it will generate and/or use knowledge according to the accepted principles of the scientific method. It will thus also accept the ontological and epistemological presuppositions of positive science, irrespective of whether they are applied to natural or social phenomena. Indifference to this distinction has, as I shall hope to demonstrate, important implications for the definition of planning as a social and professional activity.

Positivism

The characteristics of positive science are well known. They include an assumption that only those phenomena that can be observed will constitute the proper subject matter of science. Closely associated with this is the imperative that all observations be reduced to operational, hence measurable form, which then allows their manipulation in mathematical terms. It is further assumed that those things that are to be observed exist apart from the scientist and independent from her or his volition or action. In addition, intuition is not a proper form of scientific knowledge, and, in fact, ideas generally are suspect until placed within a proper theoretical framework and tested empirically through rigorous controlled experimentation. Knowledge is thus defined as inductive or deductive thought about objects and events that has been subjected to empirical testing. The scientist is privileged to stand outside (and usually above) reality and hence to be able to manipulate the observed phenomena so as to test suspected relationships among them. This 'objectivity' gives the 'certainty' to knowledge and to the 'bureaucratic rationality' that is associated with science.

Reality (whether natural or social) is viewed as a mechanism, operating essentially without intention or purpose. Objects and events are believed to exist in linear (and multi-linear) causal relationships and are thus determined by the natural laws that govern their motion. These relationships, which give rise to and are determined by the mechanism, are assumed to be timeless (even when the mechanism is an evolutionary one), and thus allow for prediction of future states that might derive from manipulation of the variables within the known relationships. Engineering of nature (and society) is both possible and likely, once the laws governing the mechanism are uncovered.

It must be remembered, of course, that positive science was invented to transcend the dogmatism and mysticism of religion and to overcome the limitations of 'lived praxis' (Gellner 1984, pp. 576 ff). Positive science is seen to work within a carefully articulated framework of abstract logic, posing hypotheses that are tested (and testable) under precisely controlled and replicable experimental conditions. It is by nature a critical and public activity with conclusions that can always be validated (or invalidated) by other scientists. It is intercultural, using the universal language of mathematics to communicate with anyone willing and able to undergo the difficult and extended training that gives access to this language and its attendant specialized concepts.

Positive science is seen as progressive and cumulative, and has in any case extended human control over nature to a degree unknown or unthinkable prior to the nineteenth century. The growth of scientific knowledge has now, in fact, far exceeded the ability of ordinary human beings to comprehend, let alone exercise any democratic control over it. Even fellow scientists are restricted to only general understanding because of the high degree of specialization that characterizes modern scientific research. As a result, for every intelligent technological advance based in science there is a mindless incremental increase in the means of destruction, ranging from (inadvertent) chemical pollution to laser-guided 'smart' bombs.

One might well ask whether a positive *social* science could not better direct or give intelligence that would allow only 'positive' use of scientific knowledge. It is, indeed, within such a framework that positivism was introduced into the social sciences. Halfpenny (1982), whose excellent survey of the evolving meanings of positivism in social science over the past two centuries, provides the basis for the discussion that follows. He identifies twelve different stages or meanings for the term positivism in the social sciences. He begins with Aguste Comte, who claimed that positivism could provide 1) a theory of historical development, 2) a theory of knowledge, and 3) a unity of science. Comte meant to overcome the mysticism of religion and metaphysics which were unchecked and unsubstantiated by empirical evidence. He sought to improve society by replacing the authority of the church with a moral order based in the predictive wisdom of a positive social science. As a fourth meaning, positive science would thus provide a "religion of humanity" (Halfpenny 1982, p. 20), with scientist-priests administering this new temple of wisdom (a not unseemly portent of the self-appointed social status of a large number of 20th century positivist scientists). Thus, there was a clear moral purpose in these early formulations of positivism directed toward a conscious improvement in the human condition.

Influenced by Darwin and Spencer a fifth conception of positive social science took an evolutionary form based upon the idea of the survival of the fittest among competing individuals, subsequently to be embodied in a semi-normative form as social Darwinism. This form of positivism was discredited in sociology by the end of the nineteenth century because it was clearly not attaining its goal of improving society. It has, however, continued to maintain its status in neo-classical economics (and in popular prejudice) under the banner of the so-called 'free-market system', because of its normative importance to capitalism. It was also revived in sociology once the restriction was lifted that science be directed to the improvement of society, as in the logical positivist form discussed below (Runciman 1997, 1998, also Rustin 1999 and Runciman 1999)

Positivism next took an empirical quantitative turn in its sixth form under the influence of Emile Durkheim, and came to be associated with the ". . .collection and statistical analysis of quantitative data about society" (Halfpenny 1982, pp. 24-26). An attempt was to be made to establish (natural) social laws through this analysis, based largely on probability theory. Three kinds of statistical analysis were developed to further this goal: 1) a descriptive statistics which are used to summarize distributions of social phenomena as well as their measures of central tendency: mean, mode, median, etc.; 2) inferential or inductive statistics which are used to extrapolate quantitative data about a population based upon a (mathematically) random sample drawn from it; and 3) multivariate statistics which are used to establish (causal) relations among social phenomena (variables) based upon concomitant variation in the social or spatial occurrence of these phenomena, usually as an extension of the inferential statistics mentioned above.

In the early twentieth century positivism took on a logical deductive form under the influence of the Vienna Circle philosophers. Not that it abandoned its empirical or naturalistic perspective; it was rather that this form of *logical* positivism or logical empiricism sought to develop a *formal* language for the sciences that would allow systematic and precise translation of theoretical statements into verifiable or testable propositions. In other words, the raw data of observation, the sensations, would have to be translated into a common formal or operational language that would allow all science to be unified within a logical mathematical form. It was at this time that positivism as a philosophical system also became separated from social philosophy, separated from any normative visions or declarations about what society ought to be. By the 1930's logical positivism had become the conventional view of science generally, and especially of the social sciences, as they struggled to attain the status of the natural sciences. Thus, also, was positive science permanently alienated from any moral or political concerns, and this as the result of a normative rule of its own making. Any such moral thoughts, or actions flowing there from by scientists, would have to be viewed as taking place within their role as private citizens; true science was no longer to be contaminated by such 'subjective' influences. It was in this 'value free' context that social science was reduced to behavioralism, and theory presented as a form of 'social physics' in the language borrowed from the natural sciences.

At this point mid-twentieth century positivism sought to develop into its ninth form as a ". . . deductive nomological epistemology . . . in which science consists of a corpus of interrelated, true, simple, precise and wide-ranging universal laws that are central to explanation and prediction. . ." (Halfpenny 1982, p.64), and then into its tenth form as a set of 'causal laws' that would explain and predict social phenomena. *Cause,* unfortunately, as it turns out, has proved to be a quite ambiguous term, and much effort has been spent in attempts to define it, and especially to separate it out from 'accidental generalizations' and 'spurious correlations' (Halfpenny 1982, pp. 73-74). One course around this dilemma has been to infer cause through temporal priority: measured variables that precede others in time may be given causal priority in correlation analysis. Another course has been to give theoretical priority based upon previously accepted causal relationships or laws. Halfpenny (1982, pp. 83-86) anticipates my discussion below by suggesting two alternatives to causal explanation: phenomenology and structuralism. In the former, cause is attributed to human intention or purpose, and in the latter to the overall structure of relationships that generate behavior in any socio-economic formation. Needless to say, neither of these alternatives is acceptable to positivists who insist instead on concentrating on ". . . establishing regularities between observables", though the certainty that this would lead to trouble-free, objective science ". . . has faded under the searching analysis to which empiricism has been subject, not least by the logical positivists themselves" (Halfpenny 1982, p. 91).

Ultimately, therefore, positive social science has had to confront the issue of the status of empirical evidence and of theory, or laws, as well as the relationships among them. In addressing this issue one emphasis has given priority to induction as an eleventh form of positivism. Here laws are inferred from empirical evidence, and in the final analysis, if necessary, unencumbered by theory at all. Nor has this approach been trouble free, as a result of which certain assumptions and limiting conditions have had to be granted. For example, it has been necessary to assume that laws are timeless and that there is a uniformity between the past and the future that would make the empirically discovered laws valid in the future; or that strict verifiability would have to be relaxed by formulating laws as probability statements; or in the final analysis by just accepting regularities pragmatically as evidence of underlying order.

The other emphasis gives primacy to deduction in this twelfth form of positivism. Here hypotheses are generated by (deduced from) theory (or thought) and tested rigorously for their empirical validity. Hypotheses that survive the test of verifiability can then be combined into sets of laws governing society. To guard against bias, verified hypotheses are conditionally accepted until further evidence causes them to be discarded. Ultimately, few hypotheses survive the test of falsification and success in this most commonly accepted current form of positive social science has had to depend upon granting some hypotheses and even operational definitions the status of conventions, thus undermining the claim to objective certainty. In spite of Popper's attempts to argue against conventionalism as a basis for building theory through the hypothetical-deductive approach -- by suggesting that corroboration would ultimately fill this gap -- he has not been able to provide a logic that would tie unfalsified hypotheses together to form a coherent whole (Halfpenny 1982, p. 105). Popper (1959) did, however, provide a useful corrective to the overall conception of positive science by suggesting that scientific effort should be directed to falsifying hypotheses rather than confirming them, since the tendency would always be to select confirming evidence from the myriad of tests that could be formulated for any hypothesis. Like most efforts to create an ideal(ist) positive science, Popper (1945) carried this effort to its literal extreme evolving it into his own worldview with general applications to society, as well.

As it turns out even natural scientists do not always proceed strictly according to these positivist prescriptions, as numerous studies in the sociology of science now demonstrate, probably because scientific progress has had more human content than would be admitted by this unending search for objectivity and certainty outside of religion and metaphysics (Knorr-Cetina and Mulkey 1983). Thus, positivist social science in the late twentieth century either drifted towards a gradual acceptance of the idea of conventionalism (based, perhaps, upon the ineluctable inter-subjectivity of scientific communities) as the ultimate source of (un)certainty in science, or simply avoided the philosophical issues of relating theory and evidence by assuming that there is an underlying order that social science will ultimately discover if it is careful and conscientious enough in its empirical work. Rather than deal with the often-troubling relationship between theory and evidence, these realists simply assume that cause and effect exist in society and that this will in time eliminate any untoward scientific conclusions.

Meanwhile, the actual search, however tentative, for a system of logically interrelated propositions or a set of laws governing reality has been manifestly more successful in the natural than the social sciences. The usual response to this observation by positivist social scientists is that social science is in a much more primitive state than natural science, comparable to the time prior even to Copernicus, Newton or Kepler, and that given time social science will also realize accomplishments similar to the natural sciences. Other responses to criticisms of the positivist approach to social science may be related to this main argument. Criticisms about the impossibility of a positivist social science such as the difficulty of carrying on experimental research in large scale societies, or the fact that social phenomena are influenced by culture or the time and place in which they occur, or that the researcher influences the objects of his or her study even to the extent that publication of research results changes the behavior of those under study, or that behavior cannot be understood without the purposes and goals that govern it, or that there are strong social influences and constraints on what social scientists may study such that values are ever present in social research, etc., can all be met by the argument that similar difficulties had to be overcome in the natural sciences and/or that in time all these obstacles will be overcome as a result of the accumulation of experience in doing positive research (Bernstein 1978, pp. 32-42).

At the same time, there is one essential distinction between the natural and social sciences that must be emphasized. The *social* position of the social scientist is qualitatively different because the relationship between natural science and engineering is not the same as that between social science and planning. While there may be social influences on natural science, there is no moral concern about nature, per se, except insofar as it may be thought to be rendered uninhabitable by humans as a result of scientifically inspired technological interventions, but then nature doesn't care about this. The idea of a 'good' or 'evil' nature is obviously not relevant, except as stated above, which, in any case, is an issue in society not in nature. Social science applications, however, always carry moral implications, even though this has often been denied by positive social science as it has evolved in the twentieth century.

Thus, there is a rhetorical dimension to social science that is muted in the natural sciences, where it appears mainly as an attempt to persuade fellow scientists (or grant administrators) about the appropriateness of a given scientific paradigm, and then mainly during times of paradigm crisis (see the discussion of Kuhn below). The social science community constitutes an intellectual (and political) elite whose theoretical pronouncements have rhetorical impact as ". . . an opium for the people, as well as an identity-bestowing myth for its members" (Weigert 1970, p. 112). Weigert believes that when social scientists accept their status as positive scientists, as those who produce knowledge that is ". . . ahistorically lawful, methodologically guaranteed against error, and free of status-group limitations", then their rhetoric is immoral, even though they may on occasion grant that such knowledge is sociologically relative. Weigert (1970 p. 116-7) reviews the various ritualistic and conventionalist uses of tests of validity, reliability, significance, etc., in social science as examples of the "magical rhetoric of methodology". He also characterizes the various machinations that social scientists go through to get published or to gain access to research funds as the "soteriological rhetoric of science". These and the many other criticisms of positivist social science are directed not so much at the idea of such a science, with all the difficulties that might be encountered, as they are at the arrogance and general air of certainty that surrounds positivist epistemology. As Weigert (1970, p. 118) says, if positive (social) scientists ". . . seek certitude, they will not find it within science; this is the proper problem of metaphysics".

The translation of social science knowledge into social policy is particularly vulnerable to this blindness. For the certainty extends not only to the belief that positive science is 'untroubled' if not infallible, but also to the presumption that there are no moral implications to what science pronounces as fact, even if it restricts itself to probability statements about what will happen to 'y' if we do 'x'. The latter, it must be noted, is the framework within which planning theory has evolved. In other words, early scientific planning theory, like the positivist model on which it depended, assumed that if we are aware of our value axioms, if we are logically consistent in following them through, and we base

our planning decisions on an empirical understanding of what consequences will flow from our actions, then we will fulfill the requirements
for making rational decisions, and our planning will be scientific
(Bernstein 1978, p. 48).

The problem with the application of science to planning must then
focus on the issue of certainty. Particularly in social science, as we have
seen above, there are a great many places where uncertainty can arise.
If planning is the application of scientific findings to create a more
desirable future state in society and those findings themselves are
fraught with uncertainty, how can planning be confident that things will
be 'better' as a result of its actions? And this is not even the weakest link
in planning theory, for a much more serious problem has to do with the
way in which planning goals are established in the first place. Positive
social science has little to offer except to assume goals that serve its
own purposes, e.g., the assumption by neo-classical economics that all
individuals are utility - maximizing and informed consumers in the free
market system. In planning theory the conventional response to this
issue is to assume that 'goals are determined democratically in the political sphere'. But critical social science research on the political sphere
does not seem to be very 'positive' that there is much democracy operating in the way in which social values are articulated into planning
goals. Indeed, there is little certainty that the political systems devised
in large scale, urban societies have much to do with what went on in the
ancient agora, which is the inspiration for the idea that goals will be
rationally or at least democratically articulated in the first place. The
question is, would a different kind of social science be more helpful in
this respect, and how could there be a 'different kind' of social science
in any case?

Relativism (and Postmodernism)

All speculation that goes at all deep becomes metaphysics by its
very nature; we knock up against the invisible wall, which bounds
the prism of our knowledge. It is only when a man has been round
that wall on his hands and knees, when he is certain that there is no
way out, that he is driven upon himself for a solution.

'Then for you, Count,' says Theodore, 'the hard and fast structure of the sciences yields nothing more than a set of comparative
myths, some with and some without charm?'

'I would like to pose the problem from another angle. There is a morphology of forms in which our conceptual apparatus works, and there is a censor -- which is our conditioned attitude. He is the person whom I would reject, because he prevents me choosing and arranging knowledge according to my sensibility.'

Lawrence Durrell, *Prospero's Cell*

To reject the relevance of the logical empiricist scheme does not mean to reject the goal of achieving valid general laws; it means that there are other goals as well and that generality is a matter of degree. . . Truth does not have to be timeless. Logical empiricists have a derogatory name for such changing truths (relativism); but such truths are real, while the absolute, fully axiomatized truth is imaginary.

Paul Diesing, *How Does Social Science Work*

The arrogance of positivist epistemology has been under attack almost from the beginning. Even after religious leaders grudgingly accepted the new authority of science, writers and artists were troubled by its inhumanity. Philosophers, too, were critical. Hegel and early Marx renewed interest in the social dialectic, inspired by the writings of Heraclitus, Dimocritus and Epicurus. But perhaps the most forceful critique in the nineteenth century was mounted by Frederich Nietzche. Indeed, he, along with Heidegger, has offered the main inspiration for the late twentieth century philosophical and literary movement called postmodernism, the most energetic and sustained attack on scientific certainty to date. But even prior to this latter movement social philosophers from the Frankfurt School were warning against the excesses of positive science (Horkheimer 1947, Adorno 1984) in a tradition that extends from the pre- and post-World War II period (Fromm 1941, Marcuse 1964) up to the present (Habermas 1971, 1984).

The critique of positive science became much more widespread and popular during the 1960s, inspired in large part by popular movements against the Vietnam War, but also in support of human rights and democracy, movements that climaxed in 1968 in places as distant as China, Czechoslovakia, France, the USA, and elsewhere. A series of books by academics and others became popular reading in the sixties and early seventies, for example, Theodor Roszak's, *The Making of a Counterculture* (1968), E.F.Schumacher's, *Small Is Beautiful* (1973), Herbert Marcuse's, *One Dimensional Man* (1964), Brian Easlea's,

Liberation and the Aims of Science (1973), Jacques Ellul's, *The Technological Society* (1964), etc.

Within the academy there were also a number of developments serving to undermine the certainty of positivist epistemology. Evidence was accumulating from hundreds of field studies in anthropology that culture was a powerful force in conditioning human thought about what exists (ontology) and what one can know about it (epistemology). One academic conflict in this respect pitted a psychologist against an anthropologist, resulting in a federally funded research project to see if culture could influence perception. The study established beyond a doubt that even the perception of geometric shapes was influenced by culture (Segal, et al 1964)

Once it was accepted that other, even less urban cultures were not inferior -- or lower down on the evolutionary scale, as was popularly believed during the 16th to 19th century, thus giving license to the slaughter or enslavement of millions of fellow humans in the Americas and Africa -- anthropologists began to contrast other cultures as successfully functioning alternate systems of thought and behavior, with considerable success in accommodating themselves to their respective environments. Thus, cultural relativity preceded the idea of scientific relativity by several decades at least.

The idea of scientific relativity was introduced, perhaps inadvertently, by Thomas Kuhn in his book, *The Structure of Scientific Revolutions* (1970). Kuhn described the conventional view of science as incremental, linear, and cumulative, as governed by strict epistemological and methodological rules, and as seeking to uncover ahistorical, universal laws governing the relationships and formation of all things in nature. To this he contrasted his own view, developed through historical research, of science as divided into normal and extraordinary periods. Normal periods are characterized by research as a form of puzzle-solving, i.e., routine research where the answers are more or less known in advance, leaving to the scientist the (not insignificant) task of proving how and why this is true. Extraordinary periods are those characterized by crisis and discovery. What is at stake here is what Kuhn called the *paradigm*. A paradigm is a basic set of (especially ontological) presuppositions that constitute the disciplinary matrix within which the relevant scientific community works during periods of normal science. It consists of shared symbolic generalizations, shared models, shared values and shared examples of successful research. It determines the activity of scientists, their methods, their problem field and their standards of solution. The paradigm gives order and meaning to observation. Science, in other words, is more than method, according to Kuhn; empiricism and pragmatism are not sufficient, as random observation is pointless. Also, nature is too complex and varied; something like a map, i.e., a paradigm, is essential to direct all phases of scientific activity. The paradigm, however, is not theory; it is meta-theoretical. Its principles are often unknown or rather assumed by the community of scientists. It is learned, i.e., students of science are socialized, through examples (problem solving), not through explicit discussion. Furthermore, its *presuppositions* cannot be proven either with scientific logic or with scientific methods.

According to Kuhn, normal science activity proceeds through observation and experiment under an accepted paradigm until the articulation of the paradigm is exhausted. In the process, anomalies -- unanticipated experimental outcomes or observations that do not fit into the accepted paradigm -- arise and accumulate until there is a crisis in belief and presupposition, at which time more and more ad hoc explanations are offered, and conflict arises in the scientific community about the accepted standards of explanation. At this time there is a fragmentation of effort into competing groups or schools and a general breakdown in communication. Scientists talk through each other, their arguments become increasingly tautological or circular and there is no agreement on standards of proof. This period of unrest continues until a new, more inclusive paradigm is proposed and ultimately gains the allegiance of a critical mass of the (at first younger) members of the scientific community. What Kuhn emphasizes is that the transition to the new paradigm is likened to a gestalt shift or a sudden flash of insight that changes one's total view of the universe subsumed under the paradigm. While rhetoric or persuasive argumentation intensifies during such periods, the cognitive process whereby this shift occurs is not fully understood according to Kuhn, except that it appears to occur outside the logic of science. The criteria that seem to account for the shift range from the 'elegance' of the new paradigm, to its ability to explain the anomalies of the old paradigm, to its prediction of unsuspected phenomena, and ultimately to a simple matter of faith.

Ironically enough, positive science seems to be little concerned, let alone influenced by Kuhn or others who have subsequently joined this attack on positivist epistemology. Nor, according to Kuhn, do they need to be; normal and revolutionary science may proceed without any philo-sophical awareness by the scientists that such things are happening. Nor does Kuhn see anything to be gained by their becoming more aware. Indeed, as he illustrates historically, scientific textbooks are simply rewritten to blot out the revolutionary periods and make science reap-pear as the linear, cumulative, and incremental process that it was always believed to be within the community of scientists. Another rea-son may be that science does not work according to the strict positivist ideal in any case. The sociology of science has shown that the actual work of scientists is much more relaxed than the positivist paradigm would suggest (Diesing 1981). Hypotheses are much more loosely con-structed and tested than suggested by the logical empiricist model, con-forming more readily to Popper's ideal of piecemeal refutation and cor-roboration.

Outside of the culture of positive science the effect of Kuhn's book has been much more substantial. His concept has been attacked in dozens of locations for its imprecision and incoherence and its 'dis-abling' effects on the whole scientific project (Lakatos and Musgrave 1970, Shapere 1974), while others have seized the opportunity to push the idea of the relativity of scientific knowledge to the extreme (Feyeraband 1975, 1978, 1985). Even before Kuhn, W.V.O. Quine had confronted the issue in his essay, "Two Dogmas of Empiricism" (1953), and subsequently in several other books (Quine 1960, 1981, Quine and Ullian 1970). Christopher Norris (1999) has covered this issue of rela-tivism and the conflict surrounding it in an excellent article entitled, "Truth, Science and the Growth of Knowledge". He carries the discus-sion of relativism from its earliest appearance in Quine through all of the intervening period up to and including its literary and artistic expression in postmodernism, where nothing is certain and all is metaphor (Foucault 1972, Derrida 1981, Morretti 1987). Norris (1999, p.116ff) contrasts this with the work of the realist philosophers who argue that there are regularities in nature quite apart from how they might be described by scientists linguistically or deductively; that there are things that we know now and we did not know in the past; and that science has accumulated a body of knowledge that allows us to better approximate and understand nature. If this does not allow a claim for *Truth*, per se, it does permit a belief in partial truths that can be useful-ly employed in the human project. Perhaps some of the arrogance is missing in this more modest positivist claim; if so, the dialectic corrective of the relativists will not have been in vain.

Meanwhile, relativism has taken on an arrogance of its own in its postmodern form. The notions of ambiguity and uncertainty have become a fetish in many, if not most philosophical, literary, and artistic expressions (Moretti 1987). The simple truth that all representations hide or suppress some meanings while expressing others has been expanded into a philosophy of doubt that can have no other effect than to pre-empt action -- hence the importance of 'silence' in postmodern rhetoric. A noble intent to expose the hidden repression in forms of modern discourse has been carried to extremes that make the critique easily ignored, if not exploited by the true centers of authority in modern society. For example, a recent book on this problem is subtitled "postmodern philosophers' abuse of science", and, indeed, the authors have no difficulty in exposing these abuses (Sokal and Bricmont 1998). In the process, they also provide an excellent summary of how natural science actually works, showing the importance of the middle way between the extreme objectivism of Popper and the Vienna School, on the one hand, and the extreme subjectivism or 'unreasonable scepticism' fostered by the postmodernists, on the other hand (Sokal and Bricmont 1998, Ch. 4).

Indeed, for Sokal and Bricmont (1998, p. 54) ". . . the scientific method is not radically different from the rational attitude in everyday life or in other domains of human knowledge. Historians, detectives and plumbers -- indeed, all human beings -- use the same basic methods of induction, deduction and assessment of evidence as do physicists or biochemists". One should perhaps qualify this by saying *'all human beings influenced by the western tradition dating back to the ancient Greeks'*, for as Hanson and Heath (1998) illustrate so clearly, it is this tradition that differentiates the West from other cultures around the world. It is the consciousness, the self-critique, the idea of open and free discussion among equals free from religious and political interference, the rational search for knowledge for its own sake, on which the scientific tradition, itself, is based. But as Hanson and Heath (1998, p.41) illustrate, that tradition is a great deal more than scientific rationalism, and postmodernism may be nothing more than a reaction to ". . . the Enlightenment's absolute and haughty confidence in the salvation of man through pure reason devoid of custom, tradition, religion and the allowance for the inexplicable . . . "

In other words, scientific rationalism, however more flexible in practice it may actually be than the ideal outlined by the 'hard-line' positivists, is still only a part of the ethos that characterizes the western tradition.This tradition is, in addition, the whole set of institutions that allowed scientific rationalism to arise and flourish in the first place, and to flourish again even after so many centuries of suppression. It is the importance of ". . . (1) seeing the world in more abstract terms; (2) understanding the bleak, tragic nature of human existence; (3) seeking harmony between word and deed; and (4) having no illusions about the role culture plays in human history" (Hanson and Heath 1998, pp. 36-37). It is a no-nonsense 'brutally existentialist' view of the world and its imperfect human inhabitants, undeceived by appearances, sceptical but not ultimately cynical because of an acceptance of the tragedy of human existence. It is a world in which the theater, the library and the agora must complement scientific rationality, if the multidimensional reality of that existence is to be understood. Hence Theodosius' dictum that "all that [theater, library and agora] must be torn down" if the obscurantism of Eastern religion were to assume control of the minds and bodies of the faithful (Koutoulas 1998, Simopoulos 1993, Zographou 1983).

Thus, missing from Sokal and Bricmont's indictment of the postmodern impostures is any appreciation of why these scholars should feel impelled to express their arguments (so foolishly) in natural scientific terms in the first place. Could it be that without such language they would not be taken seriously in academia and the larger society? Is it that positivism has ". . . reigned as implicit official state religion during the 20th century, as Comte had envisioned", and that only ". . . natural scientists, technocrats, and neo-classical economists participate as professions in public decision-making because they have more readily accepted these publicly dominant epistemologies and metaphysical beliefs *and reinforced them through their mode of participation*"? (Norgaard 1994, p. 68-69. My emphasis).

But if social science adopts the ontological and epistemological presuppositions of positive (natural) science, it will treat society as if it were 'natural' in the same sense that nature is 'natural'. That is, it will not be able to ask itself the question, 'should society be organized differently?' Natural science methodologies applied to social reality will thus seek regularities, and explanations of those regularities as if they were 'natural'. The very system of thought precludes questions about the *appropriateness* of those regularities. Social science theory within this framework will not permit questions about whether these regularities are good or bad, just or unjust, etc. This does not mean that social scientists will not raise and examine such questions, but that these questions will likely be distorted or censored as long as natural science is the main inspiration for the research.

Positive social science fits nicely, therefore, with the ways in which (political) power is exercized in modern society. Even though corporate control of research is increasing, particularly in the American university, any attempt to control the free flow of scientific information will sooner or later inhibit the rational process whereby natural science creates new knowledge. The issue here is not whether this process is more subjective than was presented by the ideology of science during the period prior to the 1960's. It has to do with the western tradition of exposing findings to the widespread criticism of other scientists in an open and uninhibited discussion that can test, and then reject or accept these findings. Positive social science carries on this tradition, but it does not question the 'naturalness' of the social order. When other forms of social science and social thought are more problematic to political authority, they run the danger of questioning the legitimacy of the existing social order and, of course, the hierarchies of power and authority associated with that order. Thus, the closer social science -- and the arts and humanities -- approximate the paradigmatic presuppositions of positive (natural) science the more acceptable they will be within and without academia. For natural scientists this is not a question of power but of epistemology. Criteria of success imposed by academic administrators, large numbers of whom are drawn from the natural sciences and/or their attendant professional schools (at least in American Universities), would 'naturally' reflect certain standards, i.e., many publications, early on, and explicit in their use of positive methodologies. Neo-classical economics would have a high status in this academic constellation and the further social scientists distance themselves from this ideal, the lower would be their status, all other things being equal. Academic administration converges nicely with political power here, but for quite different reasons and without the necessity of any unpleasant arm-twisting.

Sokol and Bricmont attack, and rightly so, the misuse and abuse of natural science and mathematics by postmodernists. One would wish that they had extended this critique to *all* uses of natural science and mathematics in the social sciences in particular, but also in philosophy and the humanities, wherever they occur. This might help to liberate these branches of knowledge from the spell of natural science. But this, perhaps, would carry their analyses into dangerous waters, for at some point they would have to confront the reasons for this enchantment. Here they would discover that the use and abuse of natural science concepts is part of a long 20th century tradition, and since postmodernism often tends to border on the absurd, it is not surprising that they should carry this same tradition so far.

In this same framework the efforts by some social scientists to create a 'strong program' of explanation of natural science, i.c.. to explain not only the activities of these scientists in sociological terms, but also the actual content of their theories, may be seen as a desperate effort to liberate social science from the grip of natural science. This they would accomplish by 'proving' that all knowledge is socially relative, and, of course, that social scientists would then be the ultimate arbiters of 'true' knowledge. This pretension is also easily defeated by Sokol and Bricmont, leaving natural science, as does most of their argument, in its supreme (social) position. Thus a companion study should document the abuses of society (and social science) by natural scientists acting in their positions of authority within and outside of academia. But natural scientists are largely unaware and, even more distressingly, uninterested in the social effects of the natural science approach to human affairs, even though there is a long tradition of analysis and documentation of these abuses in literature, philosophy, history and even social science dating back at least to the 19th century, but especially dominant in the turbulent 1960's. Furthermore, there is an apparent contradiction between positive science's claim to the classical tradition in rational thought with free, open inquiry and the empirical testing of ideas, on the one hand, and its disinterest in the cultural roots of this tradition, on the other. How many 20th century scientists have studied the classics? How many are conversant with Greek theater and Greek philosophy? How many are even aware of the indispensable connections between their scientific tradition and the Greek understanding of politics, art, and literature?

In this sense extreme relativism, such as that expressed by postmodernism, may well result from the fact that social reality is drifting further and further away from the conditions that gave rise to the Greek standard. Small-scale society has all but disappeared in the West, and increasingly in the rest of the urbanizing and industrializing world. Democracy has been transmuted into 'representative' democracy, which is increasingly a euphemism for 'representative oligarchy', as one American journalist has characterized it. In academia, C.P. Snow's 'two worlds' are increasingly separated. The natural sciences and their professional schools occupy center stage, while the humanities and arts are viewed as an interesting sideshow, not part of the serious business of mature capitalism. The social sciences confront the dilemma of aligning themselves with one or the other sides of this dichotomy and reap the rewards or punishments of their choices accordingly. In the larger society people are vaguely aware of the classical Greek standard that should govern western society, but their education gives them little intellectual preparation for addressing the human condition in any meaningful way, and the marketplace is an overbearing moral force in any case. What is missing, of course, is that which was indispensable to Greek 'social science', the theater. When Hanson and Heath wish to illustrate the Greek standard they use *Antigone*. "The play is the thing wherein we would catch the conscience of the king", as Shakespeare would observe in the same tradition some 2000 years later. In the banal and commercialized media of today moral and political issues are trivialized beyond recognition. The overpowering force of mature capitalism colonizes mind and body in a mental and military repression that could easily lead to the conclusion that nothing matters and that anything goes.

But this is not true in any sense of the word, and the intellectual resources for explaining the current condition are in force in many domains, for those who wish to find them. Social science and its planning applications are in a particularly favorable position to bring about a synthesis between the 'two worlds' and to re-establish the dialogue that is our heritage from the Greek polis. But it cannot do this by hiding from ambiguity in an oversimplified application of positivist methodology or by glorifying it in a romantic application of postmodern gibberish. The tools already exist within the literature (or literatures) of social science. By looking both to the arts and humanities, on the one hand, and to positive science, on the other, and by exploiting the considerable intellectual resources that have developed over the past century within both these frameworks, social science can seek to heal the schism that has developed between the 'two worlds'.

It is perhaps in this sense that one must judge Kuhn's effort to carry the paradigm concept beyond natural science when he describes revolutionary periods in social history in the same terms as those in the history of science. Thus he suggests that crisis periods in social history are marked by the same tensions. Existing institutions are seen, often by a minority at first, to be unable to solve the problems posed by an environment they have in part created, while at the same time political institutions prohibit the changes recommended by the revolutionaries. This transition period sees a breakdown of major institutions, e.g., the community is weakened by an increase in crime, the family by an increase in divorce, the school by its own set of crises, etc., resulting in a general increase in what sociologists call social pathology: crime, drug addiction, suicide, socially transmitted disease, etc. Ultimately, the crisis weakens the hold of the institutions themselves, people become estranged from political life, and their behavior becomes more and more eccentric.

As the crisis deepens people look to other concrete proposals for the reconstruction of society in a new institutional framework. Here the ordinary forms of conflict resolution fail since there can be no agreement on the institutional framework within which political change is to be achieved and evaluated. Thus parties in the conflict resort to techniques of mass persuasion, including force, and while there may be appeals to higher authority -- metaphysical, religious, or even scientific -- it is the people themselves who ultimately decide whether a change is to be made (often accompanied by great suffering and loss of life, as past revolutions have illustrated). Fortunately the conflict in scientific communities is carried on in symbolic terms, though loss of status or even employment may sometimes be involved. In any case, as Kuhn emphasizes, it is not the logic or method of science that determine the paradigm shift; it is the scientists themselves: "There is no higher authority than the community of scientists". For those scientists and philosophers of science who have attended to Kuhn, it is the latter conclusion that is the most troubling, because of the threat it poses to the certainty of positivism *within the temple of science itself.* It opens the door to the whole question of the sociology of knowledge: of how knowledge is created and accepted socially, of how communication and socialization processes work and, ultimately, of whether and how reality is *socially constructed.*

All of these questions are of utmost importance to social science and its philosophy, insofar as they differ from natural science and its philosophy. The social sciences are in an intermediate position between the natural sciences and larger society in Kuhn's explication above, though actually Kuhn believes that social science is only pre-scientific, since it has few of the characteristics of natural science, as he understands it. Nevertheless, if society is seen by him to contain something like paradigms there is every reason to assume that the social sciences could also be characterized in this way. If so, then social science paradigms will contain some elements characteristically found in both natural science and society. Furthermore, these paradigms must also account for the fact that human societies, themselves, embody something like paradigms, or worldviews, that accompany institutionalized behavior. Thus the ontological presuppositions of social science will be qualitatively different from those of natural sciene: they must account for the fact that societies with more accurate paradigms, i.e., more closely attuned to their own evolving social and physical environment, will be more likely to survive. Kuhn offers the example of the likely deleterious effects of not being able to recognize the difference between a dog and a wolf, but one could also cite the example of Marie Antoinette's inability to recognize the difference between 'bread' and 'cake'!

Meanwhile, if Kuhn suggests that paradigm awareness is not essential for natural science this may also be true to some extent for society. The history of science proceeds without such awareness except somewhat during periods of crisis. Even then the conversion experience of shifting paradigms does not necessitate paradigm awareness, as such, but only content awareness. Also human history has proceeded without worldview (social paradigm) awareness, at least until now. A crisis in institutions may lead to a revolution, but conversion, again, is sufficient to account for the shift; the form of self-reflection necessary for paradigm awareness is simply a rare thing in society.

Ultimately, then the social scientist has a qualitatively different responsibility with respect to paradigm awareness, first, because the object of study -- human society and human beings -- embodies paradigms. Ignorance of the social paradigm or worldview, or what may be called subjective reality, is ignorance of a key aspect of human existence; full understanding and explanation require such knowledge on the part of the social scientist. Second, social science impacts on society in qualitatively different ways from the manner in which natural science impacts on nature; social science enters the dialectic between subjective and objective reality, between thinking and acting, between consciousness and being. Verification in social science is not something happening in the privacy of the laboratory or the office of the scientist, it is social history; it is people acting out paradigm principles, including those propagated by social science. Thus, the concept of paradigm may be a usefully extended into social science, identifying other approaches that might offer solutions to some of the many criticisms of positivism listed above. Positivism, itself, could thus be defined as only one of several paradigms in social science. At this meta-theoretical level there would appear to be at least two other broad areas of theory and research in social science that would qualify as candidates for such a characterization, areas with quite different ontological and epistemological presuppositions: phenomenology and structuralism.

CHAPTER 2

PHENOMENOLOGY AND HERMENEUTICS

> To achieve their exquisitely detailed knowledge of the world around them, human beings living in non-mediated environments had to use all their abilities to observe themselves, the planet, and the things that grow from it. They might not have even considered the planet to be something that was actually outside them since their senses told them that it was also inside them. Their world was organized along flow lines, not in separate boxes.
>
> Knowledge results from personal experience and direct observation -- seeing, hearing, touching, tasting and smelling. There is instinct, for example, gathered by innumerable previous generations and carried forth in the cells. There is intuition, what Eastern religions call 'knowing without seeing'. In addition there are feelings, which may have been informed by previous experience. All of these -- the five senses plus instinct, intuition, feeling and thought -- combine to produce conscious awareness, the ability to perceive and describe the way the world is organized.
>
> Jerry Mander, *Four Arguments for the Elimination of Television*

An important ontological presupposition of phenomenology is that all things have an essence, which can be known. Based upon this, Edmund Husserl (1970), the philosophical father of phenomenology, argued that the human mind was a deeper essence than science, since the latter was a product of that mind. Thus positive science, whose purpose is to discover the essence of nature (and society), can only be a second order essence, derived as it is, from individual and collective thought. The opposite view, that what science seeks to discover is ontologically prior and merely waiting to be discovered, is contested as an idealization, if not outright reification, or the treating of an abstraction or idea as if it had concrete material existence.

What positive science is doing is taking for granted the life-world (Lebenswelt) within which scientists act, and that it is this life-world, which a radically empirical philosophy of science should be explicating. In fact, phenomenology does not take even this life-world for granted, but treats it as an object, in many respects *the* object, subjecting it to the 'bracketing' operation through which its essence can be known. Bracketing refers to the suspension of all beliefs about the object of study, including the belief that it exists at all. Only thus can all subjective biases, paradigm-induced and otherwise, be examined and their effects on the understanding of the object of study be fully appreciated. In this respect, one might suggest that Thomas Kuhn has introduced an important phenomenological aspect of positive science, one that, as pursued in the sociology of science, leads to a better overall understanding of science itself.

Phenomenology holds that what exists is that which is known, not just observed or available to the senses, but also that which is felt and intuited. Like any other scientific perception, these intuitions and feelings should be replicable, thus giving them the same empirical status as positivist sensate observations, whether or not they are reduced to operational and/or measurable terms. It is further postulated by phenomenology that scientific thought is 'inter-subjective', i.e., is generated socially, is dependent upon communication, and is constituted by meanings that are shared across the relevant scientific community. Not only science, but all of human existence is characterized by this inter-subjectivity, which makes it an ontological essence in its own right.

Phenomenological epistemology is tied, as stated above, to a radically empirical suspension of belief. It is directed to an investigation of essences that are revealed by an intense search, which includes not only observation, but thought and reflective abstraction. Objective knowledge is sought, therefore, in full consciousness of the known existential obstacles to such an endeavor. In fact, it is these 'obstacles', insofar as they are constituted by the subjective and inter-subjective nature of the life-world, that represent one major focus of phenomenologically based social science. Nor are they seen necessarily as obstacles to a more 'objective', hence *pure* science, but rather as features of being human and out of which all human projects, including science are created. The essence of social being is thus sought in the dialectical relationship between consciousness and being, between thought and action.

The method whereby phenomenological analysis proceeds is quite the opposite of positivism. Rather than seeking to remain outside, aloof and, all too often, above reality, the phenomenologist seeks complete immersion in the object under investigation. Observation is thus based upon intimate contact, or (what generations of social scientists have mistranslated from the Greek as) empathy, or deep understanding, even identification with the object of study. This empathy will, in time, produce a sense of order in any given situation, an order that is based upon a system of typifications consisting of types of thought and action that are characteristic of a given social group. These insights on typification are then available for confirmation or refutation by other researchers and even one's self as research evolves over time.

Another major ontological presupposition of phenomenology is that all thought and action are directed at something; they are *intentional*. Thus behavior cannot be simply mechanically recorded and analyzed in a search for causation through concomitant variation. All events and objects are to be understood via the intentions of those who produced them; explanation is sought in an understanding of the 'social construction of reality' (Berger and Luckmann 1966). In other words, behavior, including collective behavior, is intended and hence depends upon consciousness. Intended behavior is learned and is consistent with the expectations of the social group within which meanings and intentions are developed for the individual.

In order to give further insight on how and why this is true it will be necessary to further elaborate on the basic concepts of sociological phenomenology as developed by Alfred Schutz (1962a, 1964, 1966). This section draws upon the summary by Helmut R. Wagner found in the Introduction to Alfred Schutz, *On Phenomenology and Social Relations* (1970). Schutz claims that if shared or inter-subjective consciousness is the essence of social life, and consciousness is always directed at something, then the bracketing operation must be directed at knowing this essence; overt action can only be understood within such a context. Furthermore, a conscious or deliberate refusal to act, often unrecorded by any behavioral approach, would constitute a form of action within a phenomenological analysis, explainable by the meaning that such inactivity has for the actor. Such meanings and actions cannot be 'observed' in the positivist sense of the word but only understood by suspending belief in what is obvious. (Positivist observation could be directed at trying to flush out such meanings, of course, if the inactivity were suspected for other reasons as being important, but the researcher would have to engage in a form of phenomenological approach to find out such things in the first place.) Max Weber, who used the term *verstehen* to describe it, also identified this process of seeking to understand and interpret the subjective meaning of conduct by human beings. Thus for Weber, "No causal laws of human conduct can be established; a sociologist deals at best with 'typical chances' that certain factual constellations, accessible to observation, will lead to certain courses of social action (Schutz 1970, p.9). It is important to emphasize here, as both Schutz and Weber did, that such interpretive understanding is not some mystical operation, but something engaged in by everyday people all the time; we are always trying to interpret and understand the subjective meanings and motives of our fellow human beings, and we learn to do this from the earliest moments of our lives. Social scientists are merely asked to refine and systematize this procedure, first by bracketing in order to filter out their own possible subjective meanings, and then by sharing their understandings with other social scientists that engage in the same operation, thereby further controlling their collective understanding.

The phenomenological study of any given aspect of social reality at any given moment must thus account for the subjective reality of that aspect as it is created through the inter-subjective processes of communication, including especially face-to-face communication, the prototypical form whereby humans create and share meanings. It must account for the hierarchical structure of meanings by establishing the systems of *relevance* whereby individuals and groups know things in greater or lesser detail according to their importance to those individuals or groups. The effect of such a hierarchy of meanings is the tendency of all humans to create a system of *typifications* with more or less elaborated and detailed information, ranging from the most intimate and 'atypical' knowledge about a few things and/or people to the most generalized and 'stereotypical' knowledge about things distanced by degrees of 'irrelevance'. A further effect of this is that different people know different things according to their system of relevances; there is, in other words, a *social distribution of knowledge*. Thus, the objective appearance of structure in society is accompanied by an inter-subjective structure of relevances and meanings. The latter can be known to the social scientist, just as it must be known by ordinary people in order to carry on their everyday lives, filled as they are by individual and collective projects and plans.

Yet the scientific approach to phenomena is only one way of transcending the realities of everyday life. It is within the human capacity to create realities and symbol systems to represent them, such that art, science, religion, and even dreams can be known without assuming any metaphysical or mystical powers. Nor is there a requirement that symbols represent reality truthfully. In fact, there are innumerable examples of attempts to disguise and distort reality by *naming* it falsely. Euphemisms, sycophancy, defamation, etc., are cases in point. This purposeful distortion of reality is not just a problem for social science but for everyday people as well. If communication is directed in one way only, as it is in rigidly hierarchical systems, or in societies depending upon the mass media, the ability to distort reality is an important prerequisite for controlling consciousness. Social scientists must be able not only to uncover such deceptions empirically, but should exhibit a moral responsibility to share these insights with the people who suffer from them, hardly possible from within the 'value-free' stance required by the positivist approach. It is in this sense that social science is qualitatively different from natural science. Nature would not be affected at all by revelations about the differences between what is and what is made to appear to be. How social science develops its research, the topics it chooses to study, the way it explains objective reality, and the manner in which its conclusions are communicated are of direct importance to the on-going social construction of reality.

Social scientists 'enter' the aspect of social reality under study as 'strangers'. They must fathom the behavior of the members of that reality as a product of the meanings and goals that direct that behavior. They must understand the manner in which the outcomes of such behavior are anticipated by deliberative planning and projecting as a form of rehearsing such behavior. They must discover how individual consciousness and being are combined into an inter-subjective or shared worldview. They must understand the language or symbol system used to create and sustain this reality and its worldview, and further to probe the background of meanings that are not expressed at all, but merely taken for granted within the life-world of this reality.

When discussing behavior, Schutz (1970, pp. 25-26) identified a dichotomy of motives, consisting of *because* and *in-order-to* motives, to explain human action. The former refer to the background of action, the reasons for acting that are based upon past experiences and influences, often unknown to the actors themselves unless they reflect upon them, but accessible to the researcher in part through the methodology of positivist social science. In-order-to motives, on the other hand, are a product of conscious deliberation, and always result in action that is intended, however skillful actors may be in realizing such action and/or in anticipating its outcome. Schutz (1970 p.22) is careful to define such deliberative action as reasonable rather than rational, as assumed by neo-classical economics, for example. To give an example of because and in-order-to motives one might attempt to explain the presence of students in the university. In-order-to motives are seen as the conscious intention on the part of the students to seek higher education for all the rewards and satisfaction that they anticipate will result from this education. Because motives refer to the factors in their background or their past, factors such as how much higher education is valued culturally, or by their parents individually, the quality of previous education, their parents level of education and/or income, even such things as race, religion or ethnic background, insofar as these things vary throughout the population and correlate with attendance at the university.

It is also possible to see in this context how one person's in-order-to motives may become another's because motives in the reciprocal relationships whereby social reality is constituted. In order for this reciprocity of behavior to operate there must also be a reciprocity of perspectives. Individuals interacting with others must be able to imagine themselves in the other's position with sufficient accuracy to allow cooperative projects to proceed. How is this possible? According to Schutz (1970, p. 35) there are several ways in which this happens: actors may transpose themselves by imagining themselves into the roles of the interacting partners; they may draw upon their experience with similar situations and recall the typifications they have created to understand the motives of the other; or they may simply infer motives from the actions of the other, often again based upon past experience. Each actor has a repertoire of typifications and inferences, which depend upon the social distribution of knowledge related to the system of relevances. Thus some interaction will be highly personal and well informed by repeated exposure to the partner, while other more formal interaction will draw upon shared typifications built up over time in the social group. The structure of society is then a reflection of the social distribution of knowledge along with the concomitant systems of intention and meaning based upon spheres of relevance.

To appreciate how this structuring occurs from a phenomenological standpoint, I will draw upon the application of Schutz' ideas presented in the important study by Peter Berger and Thomas Luckmann, *The Social Construction of Reality* (1966). The authors begin with the postulate, in contrast to positivism, that human existence is characterized by 'world openness'. There are no biological or metaphysical plans, no laws of nature that determine human behavior. This leaves as a major ontological problem for social scientists the question of how to explain the obvious order and organization of society. Such an effort should also, as a by-product, be able to explain why positivist scientists could believe on the contrary that there are such laws and such (pre)determination.

As an introductory answer to such a question Berger and Luckmann suggest the social order is simply there, it pre-exists us. We are born into a world that is already ordered, and, if we don't suspend (bracket) our belief in the naturalness of it, we are inclined to believe that there must be, therefore, some preordained reason for it (God, nature, etc.). As a further postulate, they argue that the inherent instability of the human organism that results from the *lack* of a predetermined order, the fact that behavior is not genetically programmed as in other forms of life, creates an overwhelming *need* for order and for stability. As we shall see, then, both the capacity and the need for order are existent in the biology of the human organism, but the manner and the form that this order takes is not determined biologically but socially. How is this so?

The social order is created by way of a process called institutionalization. Institutions are formed through a progression of stages that includes the following:

Habitualization --> Typification --> Reciprocal Typification --> Institutionalization

Habitualization refers to the human tendency to repeat actions in a similar way once a successful path through a task has been established. Habitualization can range from such simple operations as brushing teeth and using a fork and knife, to more complex operations like driving a car, flying a plane, and to even more complex operations like those found in courtship, diplomatic encounters, or labor negotiations, etc. The sole purpose of such habitualization is to eliminate the intellectual effort required to deliberate and plan such actions so that full attention can be given to the complex and unexpected in any given situation.

All actions that are habitualized become predictable -- to ourselves and to others. Once our actions are predictable, they may become essentialized as 'types' and therefore become part of the stock of knowledge for those who find our behavior relevant to them. The behavior of others can be similarly 'typified' and this system of now 'reciprocal typifications' allows behavior in typical situations to proceed more or less smoothly and predictably. In this way complex institutions can be built up and maintained over time. Insofar as they precede us and we accept the social order that is represented by them, as well as the behavior imposed upon us by them, then the institutional order seems "natural" to us even though it is entirely a *human* creation. This process is so subtle that it is usually not questioned at all, and no further control mechanisms are required to maintain the institutionalized social order. Thus, for example, the television program (game?!), 'Big Brother', may prepare us for the total monitoring of our (even private) behavior that Orwell describes in his book, *1984*. In fact, the appearance of explicit control mechanisms is actually a sign of incomplete institutionalization.

The character of institutionalization becomes more formal and defined as it is passed along to succeeding generations, such that the original spontaneity of the progression of habitualization, typification and reciprocal typification is lost in the myriad of roles and scenarios that mark the orientation of succeeding generations into the already established institutional order. Nevertheless, the institutional order is never a fixed or finalized structure. Each individual who participates in this order stands in a dialectical relationship to it and may choose at any given moment to maintain that order, to doubt it, or to work to change it. This dialectic is working in the same way among all the people who go to make up the social order, thus making the dialectic a generalized characteristic of the entire social world. Berger and Luckmann (1966, p. 61) summarize this dialectic in three moments: *externalization*, whereby actors speak, act and otherwise project themselves into the life world with observable behavior; *objectivation*, whereby these externalizations take on a being apart from their authors, existing in time and space even after the authors leave the scene; and *internalization*, whereby these objectivations are incorporated into consciousness by other actors, particularly during processes of socialization. Various processes of legitimation facilitate the incorporation of objective reality into subjective consciousness. Legitimation gives moral and intellectual justification to the social order, whereby it is explained and justified for its participants. In fact, in its strongest form legitimation will insist that departure from the institutionalized order is a departure from reality itself.

How is legitimation realized? In the first and most subtle instance language itself creates and legitimizes the social order. Thus each language creates its own reality, its own institutional order, simply by naming, classifying and organizing reality for its participants. Beyond this there are proverbs and sayings, theories and ideologies and, ultimately, an entire symbolic universe or social paradigm which structures collective consciousness with most of the same implications that were described by Kuhn for scientific communities, though with nothing like the precision or coherence that characterizes science. Nor is there any guarantee that (inter)subjective consciousness and objective reality will be identical across a population. Indeed, Marxist analysis shows that alienation and false consciousness are common aspects of modern complex societies as much as, though in totally different ways, they may be for pre-modern societies.

Because of these potential gaps between objective and (inter)subjective reality there is always a need for mechanisms of social control beyond the basic instance of institutionalization. This control begins with the initiation of neophytes into the rules and roles that characterize any participation in the social world. If all the world is a stage, as Shakespeare said, then acting upon it requires that we know how and when to enter and leave, what to say and how to act generally, according to who we are once upon that stage, etc. More formally there are the various social rituals of *mystification* and *victimage* used to maintain the social order (Berger and Luckmann 1966, p. 87; Burke 1965, pp. 274-294; Duncan 1969, pp. 258-276). Mystery, according to Burke, arises from difference, and, particularly in the social order, from hierarchical difference. Such mystery can be emphasized and exploited through all manner of dress, habit and speech, in short through the use of symbols of authority designed to separate those in elevated positions from those below. These symbols may range from the medical doctor's white coat and the priest's frock to grand ceremonial performances complete with music and pageantry, all designed to distance and impress those 'below', while imposing authority over them.

While mystification is designed to separate, victimage is designed to incorporate, to incorporate via public demonstrations of sacrifice, actu-

al or metaphorical, in which opponents to the social order are punished
for their transgressions. Such rituals, which may range from a simple
rebuke to elaborate ceremonies of 'crucifixion', must be *public* if they
are to serve their cathartic purpose for all those members of the social
order who might have imagined themselves with the same thoughts and
intentions as the victim. Such guilty thoughts and intentions are thus
'purged' from the onlookers who view the degradation and feel its full
sociodramatic effect. In its newly cleansed state the audience feels united in its support of the (re)established 'order of things'.

Relativity presents an extended example of the need for control. As
the Kuhnian tradition presents this dilemma for science, postmodernism
suggests a similar circumstance for the arts and humanities and, insofar
as literature and art enter the life-world as symbolic representations,
they incorporate all of society in this 'vertigo of uncertainty' (Moretti
1987; Gutenschwager 1996; Lentricchia 1983). Thus confronting other
realities and other symbolic universes poses disquieting questions about
the ultimate legitimacy of one's own institutionalized life world. If the
unrest becomes sufficiently widespread in a society there is always the
danger of fragmentation into chaos at the one extreme or the imposition
of totalitarian control at the other, as such extensive lapse of control
usually devolves into an issue of power.

Meanwhile, at the individual level there are various strategies of
therapy and *nihilation* (Berger and Luckmann 1966, pp. 112-116)
designed to maintain the social order. Therapy is well known by social
workers and psychologists in the modern world and by shamans and
witch doctors in the pre-modern world, and is used to reincorporate
'deviant' individuals into the social order. Therapy is complemented by
nihilation, which is designed to denigrate a competing 'other' reality by
assigning it inferior ontological status, and as something, therefore, 'not
to be taken seriously'. Finally, if power is exercised to maintain order it
must be understood that such power is used first and foremost to *define*
reality and to establish control over all the important socialization
processes. Only as a last resort is physical force used, because it diminishes the effect of the other means of social control. Every effort is made
to establish the legitimacy of the institutional order through control of
consciousness, and it is here that social theory plays such an important
role. The highly abstract symbolism of positivist social science carries
authority because of its association with natural science as the most
important source of knowledge in modern, industrial (and postindustri-

al) society. What appears as empirical validation of *social* scientific theory is to a large extent social validation: "Theories . . .[are] convincing because they *work* [authors' emphasis] -- work, that is, in the sense of having become standard, taken-for-granted knowledge in the society in question" (Berger and Luckmann 1966, pp. 119-120).

If the first two moments of the dialectic are externalization (acting, speaking, etc.) and objectivation (institutionalization and creation of objective reality), then the third moment is internalization (the taking into consciousness of the objective reality). Internalization (Berger and Luckmann 1966, pp. 129 ff) begins at birth and continues throughout life. The early years are marked by *primary* socialization carried out essentially by parents or parent surrogates. Here one's identity is created, as objective reality is incorporated into consciousness. As this process is a part of the dialectic, all individuals respond to, interpret and emphasize different aspects of the outside world as mediated by their socializers, and thus create their own understanding of reality. Language is the chief instrument of the socialization process. By the time a child has learned the mother tongue, a whole world, in fact, *the* world has been created and *the* reality established. Secondary socialization builds upon these foundations, allowing internalization of institutionalized sub-worlds, which prepares individuals for participation in the adult world with all the specialized knowledge necessary to carry out the roles assumed in that world.

It is important to emphasize that the internalization of objective reality is not a simple cognitive process. The factual and conceptual information is also *normatively* and *affectively* charged. In other words, reality is presented as not just a matter of fact, one of many realities, but as the *only* reality, the appropriate and legitimate, hence morally acceptable reality. By the same token, emotional involvement with the significant others who mediate reality, especially during primary socialization, guarantees that there will be a strong affective dimension to internalization as well. For these reasons one changes his or her subjective reality, once established, at great moral and emotional cost; the more profound the change, the greater the cost in this respect.

It is also in this respect that one can speak of the problem of *reification* (of reality). Reification is a technical term that refers to the danger that the entire process described above whereby both objective and subjective reality are created and maintained will seem somehow to be outside of human agency. This explains the common tendency throughout human history for people to believe that some metaphysical force or divine will or, since the rise of positive science, some set of natural laws is responsible for social reality, when, in fact, it is entirely and inexorably a *human* creation. To accept this fact and to address it properly, one must experience a certain *de*-reification of consciousness. This is not to be confused with the *conversion* process described by Kuhn, for example, or as understood by Gestalt psychology. One can shift allegiance from one paradigm to another, from one religion to another or even from one culture to another without experiencing dereification. Only a realization of how reality is *socially* constructed will allow dereification to occur. And only the experience of de-reification in this respect would allow social scientists to comprehend how and why social science can-*not* ultimately be continuous with natural science. Social science is itself a socializing force; it enters the objective reality as a powerful impetus for interpreting that reality in certain specific ways. Once incorporated into the inter-subjective consciousness of the larger society, social theory becomes self-fulfilling; it forces its realization, not because it is 'true' empirically, as that word is defined scientifically, but because people have been persuaded to believe in its truth and to act accordingly. When objective rewards and punishments are projected in the form of social policies and even laws, there is no escaping the force of these reifying agencies of social theory.

If reality is *socially constructed* then the proper metaphor for capturing its essence must be the theater, the text or the narrative, not the mechanism as in positive science. Elements in nature *move*, while human beings *act;* motion is not the same thing as action. This does not mean that there is not a mechanistic dimension to society, especially mass society in which behavior is institutionalized over vast reaches of time and space, nor that nature does not impose limitations on the social order and human behavior, nor even that science and technology are not constantly changing the meanings of those limitations (Wilson, E.O., 2002). At the same time, science itself, whether natural or social, is also socially constructed. Science is a collective enterprise; its work is carried out within communities of fellow scientists with common or shared perspectives (paradigms). Science also exists within a larger society, which rewards or punishes scientists for the things they say or do (Collins 1989). Thus there is a strong rhetorical aspect to science. Within their community scientists attempt to persuade each other that their work is important and useful, apart from its empirical validity.

Fellow scientists are asked to build on each other's knowledge, to respect each other's work so that the rewards may be shared. Scientific rhetoric directed to the larger society is asking that something be done (or not done -- a special form of doing something) in response to the knowledge that is being produced. Often knowledge is produced explicitly for some action that might be useful and/or profitable for those supporting the research. All of this is hidden from both the scientists and their publics within the normative rhetoric of science viewed as a 'search for truth'.

To understand this and any other social situation requires an act of interpretation, interpretation that seeks to understand the various levels of action and thought that compose the particular aspect of reality under study. As most situations contain overt and covert communication, different levels of interpretation or hermeneutics will be required: surface hermeneutics for overt communication and depth hermeneutics for covert communication (Diesing 1991, p.107). The search for communicated meanings is a search for the actions whereby the socially constructed reality is created and maintained. Thus a socially constructed reality is composed of voices, not forces, and these voices must be interpreted, not measured. The organization, the structure of society that is produced by this dialectic of voices, is closer to a work of art than to a mechanism. Nor is interpretation some esoteric, wholly subjective process; it is the essence of human existence, separating human from animal life. Interpretation, while dependent upon cognitive, hence biological capacities, is ultimately a learned skill, and, indeed, a skill that is learned from the first moment of life. Thus we are all interpreting communications from our fellow human beings all the time. We learn to separate truth from deception, at least in our everyday lives, or face the danger of marginalization. Each segment of social reality has its specialized tropes or ways of communicating, and entrance into that segment requires breaking into the codes that allow members of that community to communicate with each other. But just as those codes have been constructed and maintained socially, so they can be learned; 'neophyte' is merely a label attached to those who have not yet learned those codes.

Social research within the phenomenological paradigm is dependent upon learning and extending these human skills of interpretation, hence the term hermeneutics. Interpretation can be extended over space and time, ranging from that required by immediate verbal communication, to that required to understand all forms of symbolic representation, including especially the written word. Hermeneutics requires immersion in the subject (or object) under study, immersion such as that gained by the artist, the playwright or the author. This, of course, differentiates phenomenology from positivism, as the latter seeks causes, while the former seeks reasons (Diesing 1991, pp. 106-145). Nor is the process of interpretation 'subjective' or irrational, as some have suggested. The same principles of rational procedure govern the phenomenological quest for meaning as the positive quest for causation. Hypotheses may be formulated and evidence sought, with evidence modifying the original hypothesis, leading to further search for evidence, etc., in a 'hermeneutic circle' that guides research in the same manner as in positive science.

The same methodology attains in historical research on written texts (Deising 1991, pp. 106-122) or in ethnographic or anthropological research on communities. The search is always for the inter-subjective meanings that govern the thoughts and actions of the members of a given community or society. In this way behavior is 'explained' to the social scientist in much the same way that it is explained to other members of the community or society who share the same language, the same symbols and, ultimately, the same reality. The task of the phenomenologist is to immerse herself or himself in that reality so as to comprehend it, not only as its members do, but also to comprehend the misconceptions and deceptions, and the possible unanticipated outcomes of intentional actions, at both the individual and collective levels. Training in hermeneutics thus allows the phenomenologist to transcend the common-sense reality and to explain it scientifically, not (only) as a set of mathematical equations that express (cor)relations amongst non-reasoning elements, but as a product of the human capacity to reason and act intentionally, however successful those humans may be in achieving the purposes of those intentions.

Finally, the emancipatory potential of science can only be realized phenomenologically. Positive social science, comprehensible only to the chosen few, can only alienate unless it is incorporated into phenomenological explanation, that is, unless thinking and feeling humans can be shown how their individual actions produce (not always intended) collective outcomes, as described in the probabilistic and/or mechanistic terms of positivist science. Positive social science, including, especially, the technocratic rhetoric of that science, is used, often by default, to control and to manipulate fellow human beings. This is simply because manipulation and control are the explicit purposes of positive natural science, which when adopted as the only 'true' science, will impose the same purpose onto the study of society. Habermas (1971) speaks of a separate emancipatory (or critical) science as one which seeks to impart self-knowledge to help individuals understand the 'causes' that determine their consciousness and behavior. While it is true that certain types of science such as psychoanalysis have this as their definitive purpose, any science can accomplish this when in the hands of a scientist who seeks emancipation as an explicit goal. Of course, a 'value-free', amoral positive social science will have difficulty perceiving such a goal *from within that science,* quite apart from what any individual scientist does outside that science as a private individual (citizen). But to exclude one's professional being from such an endeavor is like joining the struggle with not one but 'both hands tied behind the back'.

But why this concern with the emancipatory potential of science? Because, quite simply, to emancipate is to enhance democracy, while to use science for manipulation and control is to suppress democracy. The essence of a humanistic approach to scientific planning is, of course, democracy: the people participating in and deciding on the appropriate programs and plans for their future.

CHAPTER 3

(DIALECTICAL) STRUCTURALISM

Instead of either positivist determinism or a romantic conception of freedom, each must be understood in terms of the other. Failure to do so is costly. Among positivists this ommission materializes subjectivity into a pure in-itself of objective facts; among romantics it idealizes objectivity into for-itself of subjective feelings. In contrast to these views but embracing both, we may understand subjective awareness and objective conditions as two moments of the same historical dialectic. So conceived, freedom is not reduced to naturalistic facts as in positivism, or vaporized into innate mental or spiritual principles as in absolute idealism. Subjectivity is a product as well as an agent of historical processes.

Richard Harvey Brown (1987), p. 62

The relations of the organic individual and its milieu are truly dialectic relations, which cannot be compared to those of a physical system and its entourage or even understood when the organism is reduced to the mirage, which anatomy and the physical sciences give to it.

Merleau-Ponty as quoted in TenHouten et al, (1973),
pp. 148-149

Structuralism adds a new and distinctive layer to the philosophical discourse of social science, new in the sense that a *structure* is not the same as a *mechanism* and hence does not lend itself to causal analysis. Nor would it seem, at first glance, to be related to a phenomenological search for meaning and intention. It constitutes a different *approach* to social scientific explanation (Boudon 1971, p.15), and thus would qualify as a paradigm in its own right. It is important to emphasize here that paradigm, as I understand it and as consistent with at least one of the multiple meanings of the term as introduced by Kuhn, is not the same as a theory. It is a broad meta-theoretical framework within which theories may be formulated and tested. It is, as when applied to positivism and phenomenology, a set of ontological and epistemological presuppositions that would direct the search for certain distinctive aspects of social reality, namely in this case pattern ". . .system, coherence, whole, dependence of the parts on the whole, set of relationships, whole irreducible to the sum of the parts, etc." (Boudon 1971, p. 2). In its deterministic mode it would be used in the same way as mechanism and causal analysis are used under the positivist paradigm. The effort here will be to rescue structuralism from this tendency by using the insights of phenomenology to describe a dialectical structuralism that would not so much benefit the positivist search for certainty as to create a guide for understanding human thought and action.

Structuralism is a concept filled with ambiguity, a fact of great concern for positivist thinking but indispensable for humanism, for it is within this ambiguity that human freedom may be said to exist. One should, of course, attempt to clarify what structuralism (or any other concept) means, but one can never preclude its metaphorical shift to new meanings in different contexts by different authors. For example, structuralism as a term originated in linguistics in the work of Saussure (1959) and his followers. Some would claim that the conceptual framework of structuralism should not be used at all outside of linguistics, at least in the strict scientific sense, as "It fails to produce theory because in none of these areas [of art and literature] is there a 'language' to be found, whether in the sense of a generative grammar or a descriptive combination of elements" (Pettit 1975, p. 62); nor in (Levy-Strauss') structural anthropology are there any hypotheses that can be falsified (Pettit, p.88). Pettit does, however, allow the use of the concept as a metaphor, as something that disrupts our ontology and ". . .challenges the way in which we ordinarily see that which it describes and . . .draws us towards an entirely new perspective on the subject" (Pettit 1975, p. 103). This, in fact, suggests the manner in which all social science theory should be viewed: *as something which allows our perceptions to be (re)organized, hence also our intentions and actions, which would then lead to the fulfillment, modification, or falsification of the theory while*

our collective consciousness absorbs the information of the new per-
spective as part of the on-going social construction of reality. But this
would require a quite different attitude on the part of the scientist vis-à-
vis society, namely a move from *elitist specialization* to *citizenship* that
would involve abandonment of the quest for certainty and security in
science to replace that which was lost in the shift from religion (at least
for the educated), and a move towards the messy reality of the agora,
something which is anathema for most positivist scientists and social
engineers.

Thus, in most social theorizing the question of what happens to
social theory or explanation after it has been formulated, tested empirically and formalized, insofar as this is possible, is left as a residual question. Depending upon how conservative social theorists are, politically,
i.e., to what extent they are (in)sensitive to the ancient Greek belief that
'science without justice and any other virtue is mere cunning', so they
will concern themselves (or not) with what happens to their research
results in the larger social context in which they will be received. Social
theory is a form of communication, not just to fellow social scientists
but also to all humankind. It mediates between the specialized world of
the scientist and the other specialized worlds of everyday people who
compose the world that they and the scientist alike inhabit. All social
theory is metaphorical in the sense that it is always subject to interpretation and application in a process that may always transform it. This is
the sense in which structuralism will be examined.

Piaget's Structuralism

It is probably the case that growing knowledge about the complexity of nature and the actually growing complexity of society associated
with the transformation from a religion-based, small-scale rural society
to a science-based urban, industrial society has encouraged the view
that events and objects exist as parts of totalities of internally related
parts, that these totalities are in some way self-regulating, and that they
appear to be capable of transforming themselves while still preserving
their structures. These, at least, are the axiomatic principles that
describe structures according to Piaget (1968). The idea of totality or
wholeness suggests that there are properties associated with the whole
that are separate from the properties of the individual elements, that the

whole is more than the sum of its parts, and that a structure is *not* a statistical aggregate. While Piaget believes that laws govern the arrangement of structural elements, he believes that these are laws that govern the structuring process itself, laws that constitute the "logical procedures or natural processes by which the whole is formed" (Piaget 1968, p. 9).

Self-regulation, the second characteristic of structures, is a well-known concept, seen in such terms as homeostasis and equilibrium, which are common in both the natural and social sciences. For Piaget the common usages in the natural sciences call for 'operational', usually mathematical formulations. Along side these are time-based regulations such as those found in cybernetic systems involving the 'play of anticipation and correction (feedback)', as well as non-technical regulation such as the rhythms found in or associated with all living beings.

Kenneth Burke, a literary theorist and philosopher (see below), has also identified this type of self-regulation. He sees it as embodied in artistic form, involving such things as crescendo, contrast, reversal, contraction, expansion, magnification, series, and so on (Burke 1968a, p. 46). For Burke these variations are part of the two major divisions of form: 'unity and diversity', the former encouraging cooperation and the group, and the latter, competition and the individual. This division is well known in social science, which must somehow respect the dialectical balance between the individual and the group as it seeks to explain social phenomena. An overemphasis on diversity, in either science or art, may reflect or even encourage a tendency to disintegration in its representations, i.e., its works will 'fall apart' in the absence of any unifying principle, with accompanying effects on its social audiences. Thus some kind of structuralism is necessary to balance the individualism of 'atomistic' positivism, on the one hand, and/or the tendency of phenomenology to suggest that only intention governs the outcome of one's actions, on the other. What is needed is some concept of the whole that will govern the production of social theory, as well as its rhetorical effect on the larger society. 'Mechanism', borrowed from the natural sciences, provides this balance under the positivist paradigm, while 'institutionalization' serves this purpose under the phenomenological paradigm. In the former, self-regulation is perceived as a product of forces or vectors, while in the latter it is mainly human communication in its varied forms, including especially narrative, theater and artistic form more generally, that accounts for self-regulation. More specifically, scientific exposition and technocratic formulations about social reality are complemented by artistic forms that *embody* and condition emotional response, thus completing the task of regulation in what Burke calls 'adult education' or the 'schooling of the masses through sociodramatic techniques' (see below).

Completing Piaget's set of ontological principles is the concept of transformation, which not only provides a dynamic aspect to his structuralism, but also directs attention to the circumstances under which social change is likely to occur. These will be, namely, structural contradictions that become increasingly more difficult to resolve and which lead to a crisis in consciousness that will alter social behavior so as to resolve them (see Chapter 5). Diesing (1991, p. 69) provides an example of this, drawing upon (Marxian) structuralist methodology:

> Capital circulates in a Keynesian fashion in an economy, gradually accumulating in some locations and draining from others; the conflicting interests and varying distribution of power among participants in the circulation process express themselves in politics; the different experiences of participants express themselves in thought and science; the structures of politics and of culture reshape these inputs; and the variable outputs feed back on the circulation of capital and redirects it.

Transformation in this sense does not completely discard what existed before but preserves important aspects of the pre-existing structure. It is ". . .an intelligible change, which does not transform things beyond recognition at one stroke, and which always preserves invariance in certain respects" (Piaget 1968, p. 20).

What distinguishes Piaget's structuralism throughout its application to living structures is his emphasis upon 'construction', or what he also refers to as the 'functional' aspect of structuralism (a quite different meaning from that found in mid-20th century 'structural-functionalism' popular in anthropological and sociological literature at that time). For Piaget structuralism is a "system of transformations" which is "continuous with that of *construction* as continual formation" (Piaget 1968, p. 34, author's emphasis). There are no innate structures, such as those posited by Chomsky (1957) as necessary for language learning in human beings, nor are structures acquired from the outside; all structures are constructed. They are constructed, as Waddington also claims, in a dialectic relationship with an environment such that organisms are selected by, but also select their environment. This has recently been confirmed by research in the Human Genome Project. Life, once thought to be a 'simple' one-way creation from DNA to genes to RNA and to protein and cells, now appears to be a "chaotic network of two-way forces", with environmental factors playing an important role in this process. The interaction between species and environment is so important, or rather, species and environment are so interwoven that it is difficult to even speak of environment as a "non-biological arena" (Shirky 2000).

This issue has also been explored at the socio-biological level as a process of co-evolution (Norgaard 1994). For Norgaard (p. 62), modernism, closely linked to positive social (and natural) science, "destroys cultural and biological systems because of five closely linked metaphysical and epistemological premises . . . which are critically important, for they determine the bounds of acceptable political discourse as well as the process of public fact gathering, decision-making, and implementation". In Figure 3.1, he contrasts these philosophical premises with alternate premises that summarize and extend much of the discussion here about the limitations of the positivist paradigm and the policy implications that derive from its application in social research. On the basis of this framework Norgaard discusses the disastrous effects of the uncritical use of positive science and technology in the 20th century on cultures and environments around the world.

The mechanistic worldview assumes, for example, that pesticides and herbicides will simply reduce the levels of harmful insects and weeds, allowing production to proceed in a new equilibrium. Instead, the combination of these chemicals along with increased use of chemical fertilizers has altered the biosystem in quite unforeseen ways. The effects range from creating resistant breeds of insects to the leaching of nutrients from the soil, and in the long run demanding ever-increasing applications of chemicals to maintain production within a constantly evolving environmental structure. These chemicals enter the environment 'downstream' creating polluted rivers, lakes, and ground water, with pathological effects on humans and animals alike. The economy of agriculture has also changed from extensive to intensive modes, driving out smaller farmers and encouraging large scale agribusiness, and so on.

Figure 3. 1
Dominant and Alternative
[Ontological and Epistemological] Premises

Atomism: Systems consist of unchanging parts and are simply the sum of their parts

Holism: Parts cannot be understood apart from their wholes and wholes are different from the sum of their parts.

Mechanism: Relationships between parts are fixed, systems move smoothly from one equilibrium to another, and changes are reversible.

Systems might be mechanical, but they might also be deterministic yet not predictable or smooth because they are chaotic or simply very discontinuous. Systems can also be evolutionary.

Universalism: Diverse, complex phenomena are the result of underlying universal principles which are few in number and unchanging over time and space.

Contextualism: Phenomena are contingent upon a large number of factors particular to the time and place. Similar phenomena might well occur in different times and places due to widely different factors.

Objectivism: We can stand apart from what we are trying to understand.

Subjectivism: Systems cannot be understood apart from us and our activities, our values, and how we have known and hence acted upon systems in the past.

Monism: Our separate individual ways of understanding complex systems are merging into a coherent whole.

Pluralism: Complex systems can only be known through alternate patterns of thinking which are necessarily simplifications of reality. Different patterns are inherently incongruent.

Source: Richard Norgaard (1994). *Development Betrayed; the End of Progress and a Coevolutionary Revisioning of the Future,* London and New York: Routledge, p. 62

These are well known effects according to Norgaard, as are the disruptive cultural effects of other technologies such as telecommunications, television, information processing, etc., but there is little appreciation of the role played by the paradigmatic presuppositions of positive science and the general unwillingness of (especially corporate based) scientists and engineers to anticipate and reduce the deleterious effects of these technologies. Humans construct and transform the structures that provide the settings for their everyday lives; a proper social science should be able to inform them about the unforeseen, often unintended effects of these 'constructions' and transformations.

It is in this sense that Piaget's emphasis on construction rather than structures, per se, is so important. Piaget traces the construction of psychological and intellectual structures in the twin processes of *assimilation* and *accommodation*. The first refers to the "process whereby an action is actively reproduced and comes to incorporate new objects into itself (for example, thumb sucking as a case of sucking)", and the second to the "process whereby schemes of assimilation themselves become modified in being applied to a diversity of objects" (Piaget 1968, p.63). The structuring of human intelligence out of sensori-motor development as described by Piaget (1968, p. 63) is the same sort of process as the structuring of social institutions out of human behavior, namely:

---

spontaneous movements $\rightarrow$ stabilized selections (reflexes) $\rightarrow$ reflex--complexes $\rightarrow$ acquired habits $\rightarrow$ sensori-motor or practical intelligence $\rightarrow$ representations (thought structures)

---

as compared to:

---

habitualization (routinization) $\rightarrow$ typification $\rightarrow$ reciprocal typification $\rightarrow$ institutionalization (social structures) (see Chapter 2)

As children develop the ability to represent and to think they engage in the use of *reflective abstraction* which allows the extension of thought to new objects, *assimilating* them into new (thought) structures which *accommodate* themselves to existing structures while transforming the latter to incorporate the new meanings, and so on.

> Biologically considered, assimilation is the process whereby the
> organism in each of its interactions with the bodies or energies of
> the environment fits these in some manner to the requirements of its
> own physico-chemical structures while at the same time accommo-
> dating itself to them. Psychologically (behaviorally) considered,
> assimilation is the process whereby a function, once exercised,
> presses toward repetition and in 'reproducing' its own activity pro-
> duces a schema into which the objects propitious to its exercise,
> whether familiar ('recognitory assimilation') or new ('generalizing
> assimilation'), become incorporated. So assimilation -- the process
> or activity common to all forms of life, is the source of that contin-
> ual relating, setting up of correspondences, establishing the func-
> tional connections, and so on, which characterizes the early stages
> of intelligence. And it is assimilation, again, which finally gives rise
> to those general schemata we called structures. (Piaget 1968, p. 71)

By placing emphasis thus on the structuring process, the construction of structures, Piaget not only argues against the idea of 'structure'
as only an heuristic metaphor (which at the same time it certainly is),
but also outlines the epistemological principle, 'reflective abstraction',
whereby all structures can be uncovered. The mind as a structured enti-
ty itself can comprehend other structures found in nature and society. It
can do this by analyzing the processes whereby these structures have
been constructed, even if these processes are unknown or only vaguely
understood by the organisms or humans who create them, hence Levy-
Strauss' analysis of kinship structures or Marx' analysis of the 'deep
structures' of capitalism. Pettit (1975, p. 100) believes that the application of the conceptual framework of structuralism outside of linguistics
will not accomplish science. However, we can see here that the broader
concept of structuralism is a different sort of science, or rather; it constitutes a different paradigmatic framework within science. It does not
search for universal laws within a hypothetico-deductive framework, it
does not seek a causal analysis within a mechanistic framework, it does
not depend upon experimental methodology, etc. But, according to
Piaget at least, what this 'structuring of intelligence' through reflexive
abstraction identifies in its analysis of society (or nature) are 'real structures', like the 'real structures' constructed by the mind. And this is a
social as much as an individual process: there is a ". . .collective intellect [which] is the social equilibrium resulting from the interplay of the
operations that enter into all cooperation", and the mind, like all of

nature and society is "...the as yet unfinished product of continual self-construction" (Piaget 1968, p. 114).

Within the framework of dialectical structuralism the philosophical problem of 'free-will versus determinism' disappears. Individuals are parts of structures (both natural and social) which 'determine' and 'are determined' by them in an on-going process in which ". . .dialectical circles or interactions will always in the end replace linear orders of prior and posterior" (Piaget 1968, p. 124). This may not be science in the positive sense, nor is this to say that structuralism would or should replace positivism. Rather it can complement it, as does phenomenology, creating 'ontological agitation' that, through reflective abstraction, can lead to new insights, which when filtered back into the social construction of reality will change not only our knowledge of it but that reality itself.

Dialectical structuralism undermines not only the deterministic dream of positivist science but also the voluntaristic tendencies often seen in phenomenology. Furthermore, dialectical structuralism brings us closer to the issues raised by Habermas about what is to be done with knowledge, scientific and otherwise. Is it to be 'applied' by engineers of one sort or another to accomplish ends deemed important by the owners of that knowledge, or is it to be used to liberate human beings from their 'reified structures of thought and action' (Habermas 1971), as they seek to improve their lives? This is not an epiphenomenal issue for science as a human endeavor, especially not for social science, which participates in creating its own subject matter. Theodorides (1981, 35-36) describes the way in which this issue was confronted by the Ancient Greeks, keeping in mind that for them philosophy and science were one and the same thing:

> Philosophical theories are not independent creations of the minds of exceptional people, but are determined by the social conditions of each era. Philosophy is politics translated into meanings and thoughts, as poetry is translated into images. The philosopher is formed, more or less self-consciously, within the social struggle. Either philosophers will try to influence that struggle or they will allow others to use them for their own purposes . . . .
>
> In ancient Greece intellectuals were not arm-chair philosophers but important social actors who understood their work as a service to all of society . . . .

Giddens' Structuration Theory

Anthony Giddens (1984) theory of structuration is quite compatible with Piaget's genetic (or dialectical) structuralism, with a similar emphasis on construction, rather than on structures as such. Gidden's effort is confined solely to social science, however, and particularly sociology. He is quite clear about distinguishing social theory from the search for universal laws within a hypothetico-deductive framework such as one would find in positive social science (Giddens 1984, p. xviii). He is also clear about distinguishing between the types of generalizations that might derive from social research within the structuralist framework. One type refers to knowledge that humans have about their daily lives and which social scientists can learn through various hermeneutic techniques. The other refers to knowledge available, in the first instance at least, to social scientists who seek to uncover the unintended consequences of human actions. The first type of knowledge is the concern of phenomenology as described in Chapter 2, while the second is of interest to both positivism and structuralism.

In the case of positivism the knowledge produced, particularly in its mathematical form, is quite mystifying if not alienating to human actors, as is the case of structuralism in its deterministic incarnations. In the case of the latter, Giddens (like Piaget) seeks to overcome this alienation by placing structuration theory in a dialectical framework. He does this by emphasizing that social structures and the humans who create them constitute a *duality*, i.e., a unity with two interlocking aspects, rather than a *dualism* of fundamentally separate entities. The latter concept is tied to the idea of the separation of mind and matter, of the spiritual and the physical, of good and evil, and of the subject and the object. It is a legacy of the Judeo-Christian tradition (quite alien to ancient Greek thought), and has plagued social theorizing almost from the beginning of social science.

Giddens, by emphasizing the duality of social structures, seeks to give equal importance to the agents who create them and the forms that result, to the intended as well as to the unintended consequences of human action. He attends, in some detail, to the question of consciousness, separating discursive from practical consciousness, and these from the unconscious. By discursive consciousness he means those things that people can talk about and can articulate with respect to their everyday activities. Practical consciousness refers to those things that people know implicitly, that they take for granted, and that constitute background assumptions necessary for everyday behavior (Berger and Luckmann 1966, p. 57, 152). Only when these background assumptions are challenged in some way will people articulate them, insofar as they are able to (Giddens 1984, p. 281, Berger and Luckmann 1966, p.155). If the challenge becomes sufficiently threatening and persistent, a crisis in perception or subjective reality could result in a shift in awareness to a different explanation of one's behavior, a different practical consciousness within a different perceptual framework. The world thus would become restructured in consciousness, as often occurs in relation to a restructuring of the objective world without (Berger and Luckmann, p. 158 ff).

Giddens gives special emphasis to the idea of *routinization* or what Berger and Luckmann call *habitualization*, as the ultimate source of institutionalization and hence structuration in society. Routinization gives *ontological security*, which Giddens (1984, p.50) defines as *"autonomy of bodily* control within *predictable routines"* (author's emphasis), and is closely linked to the unconsciousness with its hidden sources of anxiety. Routinization thus not only leads to social structure (via institutionalization), but also encourages psychological well-being by maintaining a structural consistency between subjective and objective reality.

Giddens differentiates between *social integration*, (what Berger and Luckmann called 'reciprocal typification'), as the interaction between actors who are in each other's presence, and *system integration* where such reciprocity is maintained without that presence. Structure is thus given an extension beyond face-to-face contact such that its time-space dimension entails a study of the limits of the institutionalizing practices that compose it. 'Society' thus is fraught with many of the same ambiguities as the term 'region' in geographical thought. Placing boundaries around homogeneous societies and/or regions is much easier than bounding nodal societies and regions. That is, core institutional features in the latter spread their influence outwards in space (and time) towards lesser and lesser intensities, and the boundary is more of a zone than a line. In the same way structures extend routinized practices outward from, usually, urban cores to peripheries of lesser intensity where their dominance is filtered through more traditional forms of institutional behavior. Structures are not only not coterminous with political entities -- though some obviously are -- but they also don't all have the same 'density' over space (and time).

As humans are constrained by the structures they participate in creating and maintaining (or changing), so structures themselves are constrained by the distribution of power and resources within them. Persons with power are able to control the practices of others thus seeking to maintain a structural form amenable to their particular interests. Resources, themselves, can be used to enhance or blunt the effects of power, though we must extend the notion to include not only material and organizational resources but also knowledge. Giddens (1984, p. 261) refers to the 'storage' of resources as ". . .the retention and control of information or knowledge whereby social relations are perpetuated across time-space. Storage presumes *media* of information representation, modes of informational *retrieval* or recall, and as with all power resources, modes of dissemination" (author's emphasis). It is within this nexus that social science could play a crucial role in enhancing democracy, rather than, through political apathy, enhancing the covert systems of domination that storage of resources makes possible. Nor is this simply a matter of writing articles and books within the technical language of their disciplines; social scientists would have to use their knowledge of how reality is socially constructed to enter the flow of communication in ways that would effectively alter the 'storage of resources' so as to bring knowledge to the disadvantaged and to expose the contradictions between intended actions and their unintended consequences throughout the social structure.

Rapid social change increases the likelihood of contradictions, which in turn tends to generate conflict among opposing interests and classes. Because of a global structure that intensifies change as a means to greater profits, the *rate* of change has been increasing continuously over the past 200 years. This change has often had unintended consequences, or at least consequences that are not the prime concern of those with power and resources, causing an inherent instability in all modern social structures. This in turn leads to attempts by the disadvantaged to organize movements that will redress at least some of the extreme inequities caused by this change (Wallerstein 2002).

Giddens (1984, p. 203) rightly observes that social science has given little attention to the question of social movements as organized efforts to change society almost always as an expression of conflict and usually in response to some serious structural contradiction. Much of the language of structuration theory, both in Giddens' book as well as in Berger and Luckmann's earlier version of a 'socially constructed reality', (as well as most of the conventional research in social science) is directed to a static concept of structure, of explaining how the regularities in society have come into being. In the case of social movements, particularly in the early stages, many of the dimensions of structure, e.g., hierarchy, roles, and rules, are either missing or are poorly defined. If social science is to *'enter'* history in an intentional way, there would seem to be much to be learned about how this could be accomplished by studying the reasons why organized efforts to change social structure have succeeded when they have, keeping in mind the dialectical nature of structuration in the first place, i.e., seeking a balance between deterministic and voluntaristic explanations of change (See Chapter 5).

Unfortunately, Giddens' analysis offers little insight into how structuration theory would be helpful in understanding social change. He rightly criticizes the metaphors of change borrowed from biology, showing how evolutionism and adaptation cannot explain human history. Yet when he turns to an examination of change, in his example the formation of the state, his discussion is in terms of variables, e.g., demographic factors, irrigation schemes, warfare, etc., that might 'cause' this new structure to come into being (though he does not, of course, use the term cause). Nowhere do his concepts 'discursive' and 'practical consciousness', or the 'unconscious', appear in his discussion. He rightly observes that for the majority of the cases in which state structures have been formed there were examples available for inspiration and emulation. Berger and Luckmann made the same observation as part of their discussion on how social structure appears in the absence of biological determinants. In other words, the particular problem of how states are formed (out of nothing) is simply not an issue in most cases.

Nevertheless, one would like to have seen some discussion of how consciousness and reflective practices become routinized and integrated, or in Berger and Luckmann's terms, reciprocally typified, in the process of creating new structures in a new institutional order. Such an analysis has been carried out, for example, by Jacques Ellul in his book, *The Technological Society*, where he traces the long progression of minor changes in consciousness and behavior leading to an institutional order where the

> . . .technical means of production and organization . . .in their sheer
> numerical proliferation and velocity, unavoidably surpassed man's rel-
> atively unchanging biological and spiritual capacities to exploit them as
> means to human ends (Ellul 1964, p. xvi).

Another example is David Noble's *America by Design*, which demonstrates how an educational system was designed in the U.S.A. in the late 19th and early 20th century to socialize diverse immigrant groups into appropriate consciousness and behavior so that as individuals they would embody and reinforce the institutional structure of industrial capitalism in their new routinized (habitualized) behavior and thought. Other examples include Stuart Ewen's *Captains of Consciousness*, which analyzes the subsequent (non-accidental) revolution in consciousness and behavior leading to the institutionalization of the consumer society to serve late capitalism's needs, or Hugh D. Duncan's *Culture and Democracy*, which analyzes the role of turn-of-the-century Chicago architecture in establishing a 'scene' upon which this new 'sociodrama' of consumerism could 'play' itself out, and so forth.

In all fairness Giddens (1984, p. 327 ff) does invoke the concepts of structuration theory in discussing the levels of analysis that would be necessary to carry out proper research within the framework of a 'dialectical structuralism'. He does this by identifying four levels of social research:

1. Hermeneutic elucidation of frames of meaning
2. Investigation of context and form of practical consciousness (the unconscious)
3. Identification of bounds of knowledgeability
4. Specification of institutional orders

Hermeneutic elucidation refers to the interpretive understanding of the subjective reality of the group, community, or society under study, formulated in social science terms and not necessarily comprehensible to the subjects under study. *Practical consciousness* refers to that which the subjects, themselves, know and can report to the investigator, e.g., as would informants in participant-observation research, and which would be comprehensible to them even when expressed in the 'meta-language' of social science. *The bounds of knowledgeability* refer to the "unintended consequences and unacknowledged conditions of action", which, along with the *institutional order* itself, is often the object of positivist social science research. Here the information that might be gained in the first two levels of research is often taken for granted by researchers who are (likely to be) members of the same culture as the subjects under study.

Within this context Giddens locates the distinctions between qualitative research (Levels 1&2) and quantitative research (Levels 3&4), demonstrating that they are complementary rather than conflictual. Quantitative research must depend upon the sorts of insights that pertain to the 'social construction of reality', even, if only when, as mentioned above, the cultural context under study is not exotic to the researcher. At the same time it is usually necessary to explore the broader implications and extent of cultural phenomena by quantitative researchers who seek to place their findings in a larger context.

What happens to social science generalizations once formulated distinguishes it from natural science. Natural science has a technological relationship with nature; it seeks to control and manipulate it (usually for social ends). Positivist social science seeks the same relationship with society, seeking to 'control and manipulate it' (again for social ends). However, as Giddens (1984, p.334 ff) points out, the relationship between social science and society is simply not the same as that between natural science and nature, such that attempts to compare the two always claim social science to be inferior in its accomplishments. But as Giddens points out, social science knowledge is constantly being filtered into society, altering the very subject matter under study. Thus social science is in a *dialectical* relationship with society, something which cannot be claimed about natural science and nature (except, insofar as natural science is changing nature, though in a somewhat different time frame). Social science, itself, is a ". . . *practical intervention* in society, a political phenomenon in the broad sense of that term" (Giddens, p. 340, author's emphasis). Common sense people, including specialized professionals, read social science treatises and alter their behavior accordingly, sometimes in the process encouraging additional research to clarify issues raised by the initial research (Giddens 1984, p.351). In this context, there is a remarkable lack of attention by social science to the ways in which its knowledge is incorporated into the social world, to the kinds of actors that become informed by that knowledge as well as to the use to which they put it, to the forms that scientific communication should take in a democratic society, and so forth. If social science is a 'practical intervention', then it coincides with planning in both practice (and intention), which gives added importance to the question of what kind of science (scientific) planning imagines itself to be.

Burke's Sociodramatic Structuralism

A purely humanistic and quite different perspective on the question of social structure may be seen in the work of Kenneth Burke (1959, 1965, 1968a, 1968b, 1969a, 1969b, 1973), a literary theorist, whose interests also extend to music criticism, literary criticism, philosophy, and by extension, especially through the work of Hugh D. Duncan (1962, 1968, 1969), to social theory as well. Burke began writing in the 1920's, and his work includes more than a dozen books and hundreds of articles, reviews, stories and poems. There have been over 150 articles and reviews and a number of books devoted to Burke, including an excellent anthology edited by William H Rueckert (1969), in addition to the theoretical works by Duncan cited above. Almost every student of literature in the U.S.A. since the 1930's will have been exposed to at least some of Burke's writing, and most of the small number of humanistic sociologists will also have read about him through the efforts of Duncan. In spite of this Burke is not well known outside the U.S. for a variety of reasons, some of them related to criticism of him in the U.S. as well. This has primarily to do with the fact that Burke is too sociological for the literary theorists and too literary for the sociologists, a problem not uncommon for those who choose to work across disciplines, especially bridging the humanities and the 'sciences'.

Burke has a rather flamboyant style, skipping from metaphor to metaphor in a seemingly haphazard fashion. He makes generous use of italics and quotation marks in an attempt to shift meanings back and forth as a way of emphasizing the elasticity of language and meaning, and hence, potentially at least, of behavior as well. In his early writings there seemed to be no system to his remarks. Gradually, however, there evolved a more or less coherent approach to the study of society and of the human behavior that constructs it. He became less interested in analyzing or theorizing about the formal aspects of literature, and of art more generally, for their own sake, though his respect for the technical aspects of artistic creation is substantial, as his own creativity in poetry and fiction would testify. Rather over time he became more interested in humans as symbol-using beings and in the social order as a primarily language-based phenomenon. Thus for him literature, as all art, contains a rhetorical dimension which he believes plays an indispensable role in creating and maintaining (or changing) the structure of society.

One of the most serious problems with using language as a theoretical basis for social structure from the standpoint of science is that it is filled with ambiguity, as Burke would declare many decades before postmodernism appeared on the scene (as it were). But whereas postmodernism merely celebrates ambiguity, Burke was intent on mining it in a search for resources that could be used to soften the conflict that automatically arises because of it. In other words, social reality is created through the use of symbols, primarily language, and, as we saw in the discussion of phenomenology, those symbols are charged not only with meaning but with emotion and moral value as well. Here Burke explores the exhortatory negative, a thing *not* being what it is supposed to be, as an exclusively human meaning deriving from the manner in which social reality - as opposed to nature - is created or constructed in the first place. Things 'not being what they are supposed to be' creates (individual and) collective emotional, as well as moral tension, leading to conflict, as the collectivity seeks to (re)establish the 'proper' order. When one collectivity's 'no' is another's 'yes', conflict is bound to ensue, and that conflict may range from verbal disagreements to 'holy wars', depending upon how 'sacred' are the symbols being violated. It is in this sense that Burke sought to *humanize* conflict by showing its linguistic origins. Not that he would suggest that there were some more substantial reality behind the ordering symbols. Rather, as the phenomenologists would also argue, reality with all its 'vested interests' is created through the symbols, which are constitutive of that reality.

Burke's effort is to explore the dramatistic forms whereby reality is created and maintained, especially when contradictions are encountered. He would classify speech according to its 'attitude' towards its object and its 'history', or social context. He would say that ". . .approximately the epic, tragedy, and comedy gravitate towards the positive side [in their attitude], whereas elegy, satire and burlesque stress the negative", while adding two other modes, the grotesque which "focuses in mysticism", and the didactic which "today is usually called propaganda" (Burke 1959, p. 57). These collective poetic categories Burke (1959, p. 99) calls "major psychological devices whereby the mind equips itself to name and confront its situation". Insofar as it is possible, power (hegemony) will be used in society to control these devices, leaning in favor of the positive devices of tragedy, comedy and epic, with elegy, satire and burlesque left as residual categories tolerated as an escape valve for the draining of negative emotions.

Artists are in charge of a good many of the technical aspects of these forms, and have a certain 'liberty' to experiment so long as their devices are not too critical (revolutionary). For example, when social realism in the already turbulent 1930's in the United States threatened to undermine the already somewhat tenuous legitimacy of capitalism, the FBI (Federal Bureau of Investigation) stepped in to support the apolitical abstract expressionist artists with funding, gallery exposures, and so forth (Shapiro and Shapiro 1977), while denying the same exposure to the social realists. The Hollywood Ten expulsions in the 1950's is another example of political control over art, as was the McCarthy witch-hunt in general, insofar as it affected artists and actors.

Conflict is not just between opposing symbol systems and their socially (linguistically) constructed realities, however. An equally common conflict is between a symbol system and its own corresponding social structure. Here Burke (1959, p. 225) coined the phrase 'bureaucratization of the imaginative' as a way of expressing the tendency for all 'good ideas', often utopian in the first instance, to 'harden' as they are "embodied in the realities of a social texture, in all the complexity of language and habits, in the property relationships, the methods of government, production and distribution, and in the development of rituals that reinforce the same emphasis", in short during their routinization and institutionalization. Here even positivist social science may constitute a negation of the existing social order as it exposes the unintended consequences of collective human, 'bureaucratized', action, especially if the research findings work their alienating effects on the larger society (as they disclose contradictions).

In anticipation of postmodern discourse several decades later - *Attitudes Toward History* was first published in 1937 - Burke refers to Andre Gide as saying somewhere that he ". . .distrusts the carrying out of one possibility because it necessarily restricts other possibilities". But people do not change allegiance easily for ". . .obedience to the reigning symbols of authority is natural and wholesome. The need to reject them is painful and bewildering" (Burke 1959, p. 220). Furthermore, those in hegemonic positions will seek to control the rhetoric or the poetic devices presented to the people by controlling the 'priests', not only in the pulpit but in the schools, the mass media and the arts generally, ultimately calling for 'bridging devices' that will either seek to legitimize the (contradictory) status quo or seek, metaphorically at least, to find a way to transcend that reality towards something better in the future (including the after life!). Burke's linguistic solution to such impasses is to formulate a "perspective by incongruity" by "bureaucratizing the mass production of perspectives", i.e., by "democratizing them", thus making ". . . a resource once confined to a choice few of our most 'royal' thinkers" available to all, in spite of any ensuing "deterioration in quality" that this would entail. To be gained by this "democratization of incongruity" would be a "corresponding improvement in the quality of popular sophistication" (Burke 1959, p. 229).

Today even more than in the 1930's human kind suffers from rapid change linked to an 'over-production' of scientific information and a corresponding (technological) compression of space and time (Harvey 1989). The resulting 'under-consumption' of this knowledge and its social meaning has led to an increase in 'incongruities'. One challenge for social science in this context would be to make people at home rather than 'bewildered' by the 'complexities of relativism', and this to be accomplished by increasing and improving our 'perspectives by incongruity'. Burke (1959, p.229 ff) discusses the various ways in which this has been accomplished historically, that is by "stretching" meanings across oppositions, by the "stealing back and forth of symbols of authority", by "symbolic mergers", etc. One may thus use the same hegemonic symbols for different purposes. He points to John Dewey's theoretical distinction between "education as a function of society" and "society as a function of education", the former referring to circumstances where society is running smoothly with little alienation and few contradictions between the symbolic universe and every day life, and the latter when the opposite seems to hold true and where education must play a role in "constructing a better world" (Burke 1959, p.331).

Burke wishes to confront 'incongruity', the disjuncture between intention and outcome, in a comic frame of mind: humans are mistaken not (necessarily) sinful (or as the Ancient Greeks said *'ουδείς εκών κακός'* - nobody willingly does evil). They, or rather we, as he refers to all humans, including himself, are to be laughed at, not crucified. Within this comic frame we can observe ourselves 'while acting'. This should lead to 'maximum consciousness', not 'passiveness'. "One would 'transcend' himself by noting his own foibles. He would provide a rationale for locating the irrational and non-rational" (Burke 1959, p.171). By avoiding the tragic frame we can avoid the burden of guilt that might inhibit our own self-consciousness and allow those who are different from us to live, both metaphorically and literally.

> The progress of human enlightenment can go no further than in picturing people not as *vicious*, but as *mistaken*. When you add that people are *necessarily* mistaken, that *all* people are exposed to situations in which they must act as fools, that *every* insight contains its own special kind of blindness, you complete the comic circle, returning again to the lesson of humility that underlies great tragedy. The audience from its vantage point, sees the operation of errors that the characters of the play cannot see; thus seeing from two angles at once, it is chastened by dramatic irony; it is admonished to remember that when intelligence means *wisdom* (in contrast with the modern tendency to look upon intelligence as merely a coefficient of power, for heightening our ability to get things, be they good things or bad), it requires fear, resignation, the sense of limits, as an important ingredient (Burke 1959, pp. 41-42, author's emphasis).

As Frank Lentricchia (1982, p.129) notes in connection with the same quotation, "what the comedic historian [social scientist] knows, what he [or she] takes to be the single truth of. . . history. . . [is that] there is no truth but only fools of truth".

In his *Grammar of Motives* (1969a) and *Rhetoric of Motives* (1969b), written in the late 1940's, Burke anticipates both the subsequent development of scientific structuralism *and* its post-structuralist critique. His structuralism is based on *theater* as the master metaphor or framework (or phenomenological essence) for his analysis of history, theater both as a living process and as a commentary on that process. He analyzes history as text, as any sort of text: "metaphysical structures, . . . legal judgments,. . . poetry and fiction,. . . political and scientific works, . . . news,. . . and bits of gossip offered at random" (Burke 1969a, p.xv). Then he 'deconstructs' the text by way of his dramatist pentad: *act, scene, agent, agency and purpose.* The *act* "names what took place in thought or deed"; *scene* "the background of the act, the situation in which it occurred" (in positivism, the environment, mechanism or system; in Schutz' phenomenological framework, the 'because-motives'); *agent*, the "person or kind of person who performed the act"; *agency,* "the means or instruments used; and the *purpose*, (in Schutz' framework, the 'in-order-to-motives'; and in hermeneutics, the 'intention').

Following Lentricchia's excellent summary of Burke's theory (1982, p. 133 ff), we note his reference to Burke's use of 'positive' and 'dialectical' terms, the "former being terms that do not require an opposite to define, the latter being terms that do require an opposite" (Lentricchia 1983, p.133; quoting Burke 1973, p. 109 n), which would be roughly equivalent to the distinction between natural science and its positivist extensions into social science, on the one hand, and the humanities and their humanistic extensions into social science, on the other. As Lentricchia says (1983, p.134):

> The further Burke can manage to move his key terms, and the temporarily frozen model they imply, toward the dialectical or differential status, the closer he engages the inherent synchrony of his grammatical project with a fluid diachrony of historical process.

In other words, Burke addresses the inherent static quality of most social science formulations, including those of phenomenological social science and scientific structuralism. The transformative quality of dialectical terms disrupts not only the mechanisms and systems of positive science but also the idea of 'institutions' based in habitualization and institutionalization. Thus, these terms ". . . preserv[e] forces of change internal to the totality (that untotalize, unsynchronize it)" (Lentricchia 1983, p. 134).

While institutionalization, whether in Berger and Luckmann's "social construction of reality' or Gidden's 'structuration theory', portrays a human process, the human agents are left more or less passive in this process. What Burke's dramatism does is to *activate* the human agent, particularly in the adult world, since rhetoric, and the ability to exploit the dialectical resources of language, is available to all of us and is inherent in every speech act. Burke's outline of these resources and their capacity for persuasion in *the Rhetoric of Motives* emphasizes the extent to which "Man, *qua* man, is a symbol user. In this respect, every aspect of his 'reality' is likely to be seen through a 'fog of symbols'" (Burke 1969b, p.136). But, most importantly, these linguistic symbols are available to all who use a language, and may be used to support the existing social order or to change it (or to bring doubt to bear upon its legitimacy). This gives dynamism to Burke's structuralism (as well as to the social structures he examines), a dynamism that leads both to the structuring but also to the potential for re-structuring the social order (as well as to the theories that seek to explain it).

To better appreciate the relationship of Burke's literary theory to social science, it will be necessary to review briefly its application in the work of Hugh D. Duncan. Duncan gives sociological form to Burke's categories. For example, the dramatist pentad is defined by Duncan (1968, p.19) as:

> ... the scene as a social stage; the act as the basic social contexts of action we find in social institutions, such as the family, government, economics, defense, education, entertainment, sociability, health, religion, art and science; the actor as the various social roles enacted in these basic social institutions; agency as the medium in which communication takes place; and the purpose as the struggle to achieve the consensus necessary to integration in social action.

For Duncan, social integration (structure) is achieved through naming (Duncan 1968, p. 21). Names are 'goads' to action; by naming we define rhetorically and socially (as well as scientifically) what is appropriate, 'good', or proper, on the one hand, and what is improper or 'evil', on the other. Through this symbolization, this naming, we organize and structure the behavior of our fellow humans and ourselves in our social settings. "The sociological function of the dramatic structure of action is, therefore, an act of organization" (Duncan 1968, p. 22). The act of organization requires not only an intellectual understanding but also, mainly, an emotional and moral identification with the principles of social order embodied in the symbols. We identify with heroes in their struggle against villains who are the personification of these principles of good and evil.

In the great drama of the Cold (and frequently 'Hot') War that occupied the mind of the world for most of the 20th century, democratic heroes (rarely named capitalist for obvious symbolic reasons) struggled against communist 'villains', who had to be purged (sacrificed) from the world stage so that people could be 'free'. This struggle took place in the cinema, on television, in the newspapers and in all the bits and pieces of casual conversation whereby the social order is maintained. Not surprisingly, the Cold War was indispensable to the United States, the military-industrial complex being the cornerstone of its economy.

Dwight D. Eisenhower warned about the dangers of this dependence as early as the 1960's, and the incestuous relationship between the Pentagon, the Congress and the military industry has been well-known ever since (The Iron Triangle). The military and all its related expenses regularly account for more than 50% of the U.S. national budget. This information is hidden by the inclusion of the Social Security budget in the spending totals given to the public, when in fact Social Security is a totally separate account with its own income and expenditures. The military-industrial complex absorbs nearly $500 billion annually; could this be possible without an enemy, a sociodramatic villain? Indeed, the eclipse of the Cold War at the end of the 1980's found the U.S. scrambling to find new villains on the domestic and international scene, villains who could serve the symbolic purpose of justifying the continuation of 'military welfare', with the colossal waste of human and natural resources that this entails.

In the other great drama of the 20th century, consumerism, the struggle was carried out by symbolic heroes, the consumer goods, themselves aided by 'great consumers', the 'rich and the famous', against the great abstract villains of under-consumption and the thousand forms of dirt, ugliness and psychological impotence that must be vanquished for the consumer-hero to live the good life. (Ewen 1976). Duncan's first research (1965) was on the architectural 'stage' upon which this great drama first unfolded in Chicago at the turn of the last century. Chicago in 1900 and throughout most of the 20th century was the home of the distinctive American architectural style. Louis Sullivan, in particular, helped create a 'home' for consumerism in the famous Merchandise Mart and the first great department stores that were to revolutionize shopping, first in the U.S. and subsequently throughout the world. Since 60% of the Chicago population did not speak in English in 1900, the shift from a thrifty, conservative mentality to a wasteful consumerist mentality had to be staged and played out visually. Here architecture played a major role, as did the pictorial sections of the newspapers, to be joined subsequently by the mail order catalogues shipped from Chicago to homes throughout the country. With the advent of radio and television, advertising combined the talents of artists, psychologists and merchandisers to produce the greatest selling drama ever known to humankind - with no end in sight! (McChesney and Foster 2003).

Thus, the organization of today's global system is pure (economic) theater, just as the feudal order of the middle ages was pure (religious) theater. Third World extensions of this modern theater confront audiences who attend to the television and movie fictions, but who could care less about the clumsy acting and trite emotions that are portrayed. They are consuming images of the 'good life', embodied in the automobiles, the houses, the clothing, and, unfortunately, the values of the heroes and heroines who clutter their screens.

It is inconceivable that globalization could proceed without this sociodrama, without the values and rhetoric embodied in this theater. Capitalism could never have survived the 20th century without confronting its endemic contradiction of overproduction — under-consumption in this symbol-driven manner. Sociodrama is a ". . .drama of order, . . . a drama of legitimation, the attempt to legitimize authority by persuading those involved that such order is 'necessary' to the survival of the community" (Duncan 1968, p.49). Nor is this sociodrama an epiphenomenonon on a material base (scene); it is constitutive of that base and its forms are the means by which that base is constructed. In short, the instrumental and the symbolic are merely conceptually different aspects of a single reality, a reality constructed simultaneously through instrumental, emotional and ethical means. It is a reality constructed by *actors*, pursuing intentions or *purposes*, through *actions*, and using various means (*agencies*), against a backdrop (*scene*), which, collectively, these actions, themselves, compose. Any scientific attempt to short circuit this dialectical process will necessarily lead to distortions. Any search for certainty in the form of 'natural laws' or 'human nature', or 'economic forces', or 'divine will', may apparently relieve the psychological tension of this dialectic, but will not make it disappear; it is inherent in the human condition.

Does this leave Burke with a 'master paradigm', or perspective, that would avoid all ideological or 'bureaucratizing' effects? I think not, for he includes himself in his 'comic' attitude toward history, seeking through his exegesis to illustrate how any perspective runs the danger of overemphasizing one or another dimension or 'ratio of dimensions'. In so doing, he describes not only the everyday human being, but the theorist (and philosopher) as well. In fact, much of the second section of his *Grammar of Motives* (1969b, pp127-320) is taken up with an exploration of various philosophical schools and their tendencies to focus upon one or two aspects of the pentad with a resulting abbreviation of the dialectic and a corresponding set of over-emphases or misrepresentations of the nature of human existence.

Burke's humanism contrasts with the determinisms inherent in nearly all social theorizing, but is not at the same time a surrender to 'free will' or to idealism, because ". . . it is seen as having a constraining context, which is precisely what humanism can never admit about itself" (Lentricchia 1983, p. 134). Furthermore, by identifying the tendency to determinism in all theoretical or 'systematic' thinking, Burke also points to and seeks to undermine the 'will to power' inherent in such intellectual activity. He identifies philosophical schools according to their use of 'ancestral terms' that would give a 'paternal' sanction to one particular emphasis, but terms that, in their isolation or overemphasis, would tend to distort reality away from its true dialectical nature. Thus for Burke, an emphasis on scene would correspond to the terminology found in *materialism*; an emphasis on agent would correspond to *idealism*; an emphasis on agency to *pragmatism*; an emphasis on purpose to *mysticism*; and an emphasis on act to *realism*. While the intention of these emphases is theoretical and philosophical, their effect is rhetorical; they are asking us to think and act in certain ways. While they seek eternal truth, they are in fact historical (social); they are born in history ". . . for the purpose of generating the history [society] . . . [their authors] want" (Lentricchia 1983, p.12).

Deconstruction, and postmodernism generally, have sought to 'unmask' the epistemic and cognitive deceptions inherent in these theories and philosophies, and in every use of symbols to represent or explain reality, or, indeed in the futility of ever attempting a 'true' representation of anything. But they ignore the rhetorical or political use of symbols, whose use does not depend upon epistemic accuracy, real or illusory, but upon the ability to exhort, to move to action, with all the socio-political consequences that result (Lentricchia 1983, pp. 50-51). Furthermore, the postmodern emphasis on ambiguity and uncertainty to the point of paralysis (silence) is itself a master metaphor, and, as an extension of the nihilism inherent in modernism, its rhetoric is a plea for *in*action and hence acceptance of the status quo.

Science and Society

Burke explodes the myth of 'disinterest' in modernism and post-modernism alike by demonstrating that artistic expression is not a thing apart from the world but a (potentially) disruptive voice aimed at undermining any one rigid scheme of living, any one paradigm. Thus, you can theorize about the autonomous nature of art (and science), but such ". . . theorizing is itself a form of action. . . So the question that Burke asks us is not what social structure might become if autonomous art [and science] were to prevail (he does not believe in any such thing) but what social structure is implied by a certain type of modernist theorizing about art [and science] " (Lentricchia 1983, p. 89).

Burke and Lentricchia's critical attitude parallels that of the Frankfurt School, which has sought to develop a critical social theory and philosophy. Their effort has been to return science theory and understanding to its original (ancient Greek) purpose, which was to inspire and inform life, and to improve human existence. This would require that we confront the fact that a science separated (in its value-free attitude) from society is a "subtle form of ideology" and that when joined with technology has become a ". . . powerful and invidious tool for manipulation, repression, and domination, rather than the way to enlightenment and freedom" (Bernstein 1978, p. 176). In the same passage, Bernstein points out that the reaction to this 'ominous state of affairs' ranges from 'pessimistic despair' on the one hand, to 'romantic protest', on the other. The need is for a social theory that will not separate theory and practice, not categorize and separate science, art and politics and the various subdivisions that characterize the modern pursuit of knowledge. It would be a theory that would not allow social scientists to separate their theoretical work from their work as 'citizens', however the latter is defined.

Unfortunately, the early Frankfurt School theorists directed their critical intent over time more and more to ideology rather than to political economy, and it wasn't until the postwar period that Jurgen Habermas (1970, 1971, 1984) turned back to their original Marxist intent. Returning to the ancient Greek idea of *politeia* he challenged the epistemological foundations of the distinction between descriptive and prescriptive theory, as well as between theory and praxis. In other words, social reality is *socially* constructed and is always subject to symbolically legitimizing social processes, including those deriving from social theory, which impose a self-fulfilling definition of that reality unless unmasked within the skeptical framework of critical theory. Positivism and empiricism pre-empt this critical intent because of their ideological predispositions about the nature of the relationship between theory and practice: either they are functionally separated and the value free theorist has no traffic with the political activist, or the latter is a deterministic extension of the former, and political action is reduced to social engineering.

Thus, it is true that adequate knowledge must be produced within a community of scholars as Kuhn described, and must be subject to all the empirical tests and critical discussion that one expects within the scientific endeavor. Nevertheless, one must still address the question of what happens to that knowledge in the larger society. If one rejects the social engineering approach, to say nothing of its aloof alternative found in the 'ivory tower' mentality, then one must still search for a way to use scientific knowledge, socially. Habermas (1984) proposed that such knowledge be used for the purpose of enlightenment, which he defined as a communicative act that extends this knowledge into the social world to incorporate those affected by it. The purpose is to set into motion a process of reflection and self-understanding that would "dissolve the reified power relations and resistances" that inhibit freedom in thought and action. His critical knowledge sought 'authentic insights' in anticipation of the collective praxis that would follow.

Enlightenment broadens the responsibility of the critical theorist to include those beyond the community of scholars. The critical intent of theorizing requires that the scientist seek out those to whom the theory applies in an effort to free them from a 'naturalistic' or fatalistic attitude about the social reality that they inhabit. The 'natural' or common sense view is a reified perception of reality, one that forgets the human authorship, not only of the social world itself, but of the explanations of that world that constitute common sense. Enlightenment is, therefore, a political act, seeking as it does to uncover the power relations and the reified symbolic explanations that legitimize that power and, hence, largely determine behavior in society. It is also a moral act, as it seeks to raise consciousness about the appropriateness and the worth of a society so constructed.

Proceeding from theory to practice poses a complex communications problem for those inspired by Hambermas' writing at that time. Change, if necessary, usually confronts social and psychological obstacles. People prefer the familiar. Furthermore, information about the effects, especially the unintended effects of one's actions are often difficult to establish, and the complexity of social (and natural) systems further confuses the efforts. How, therefore, should planning interventions, as an extension of social science, proceed. First, as I have tried to demonstrate, we must have an adequate social science, one that is sensitive to all the mechanistic and humanistic dimensions of social reality. We must be well informed about the technical aspects of the problems that we are trying to solve, knowing all of their abstract and theoretical dimensions, and be able to judge the, sometimes conflicting, theorems being formulated.

Second, we must identify the audience to be enlightened about the problems, particularly those least able to defend themselves against the effects of any planning intervention (or lack of intervention). We must organize the information *so as to be understood by those audiences.* This usually entails a good deal of 'translation' of technical information into terms that are closer to the experience of the audience and understandable by them. We must also give special attention to the 'reified power relations and resistances' that are likely to be encountered.

Finally, we must develop, *with those affected,* a political (and technical) strategy to solve the problems. This assumes that any change will meet resistance, especially from those who benefit from the status quo. It also assumes that there will be political and economic risks for those involved in the struggle for change. The scientific planner should not impose a strategy, technocratic or otherwise; those affected must join in making 'prudent' judgments about what they are willing and able to do.

The next three chapters will serve to illustrate how research could be carried out under the three paradigms that have been discussed above, as well as the kinds of analysis and results that might be expected from each. This will then lead to a discussion of how scientific planners could proceed in their professional work within a more holistic definition of their responsibilities.

PART TWO

RESEARCH UNDER THREE PARADIGMS

CHAPTER 4

POSITIVIST RESEARCH
ON THE USE OF TIME *

Among the criteria for evaluating cities and regions and the plans for changing them, economic benefits and costs have long enjoyed premier status in industrial societies. Critics of economic rationalism have not been able to offer alternative quantitative criteria that would extend the narrow definition of benefit and cost to include the social or human dimension. Yet this dimension appears to be growing in importance as the deleterious human and social effects of technological growth are better understood in the western world (Ellul 1964, Marcuse 1964, and Habermas 1970).

The time budget-activity systems approach may in part broaden the perspective on planning problems by researching urban and regional patterns in terms of the time used and 'traded-off' to create them. Thus, added to the understanding of individual and system opportunities and stresses based on financial resources is an understanding based on time resources. Furthermore, the relationship between these two resource bases can be explored and the extent to which one is exploited to maximize the other assessed. The time budget perspective does not escape the bias inherent in quantification, of course, but it does permit system-

---

* Reprinted with permission in part from Gerald Gutenschwager (1973) "The Time Budget - Activity Systems Perspective in Urban Research and Planning". *Journal of American Institute of Planning*, Vol.39, No.6 (November), pp.378-387, and from Gerald Gutenschwager and Mary Gutenschwager (1978), "Research on the Use of Time", *Review of Sociological Research*, Athens Centre of Social Research, Vol.33-34, pp.335-348 (in Greek).

atic attention to otherwise somewhat neglected aspects of the urban scene.

The Time Budget Perspective

The time budget is ostensibly a behavioral approach to social and planning research: the intentions and evaluations of activities are difficult though not impossible to ascertain. The time budget statement is an average or typical account of aggregated individual activity systems. It is, at first, a record of all activities (except private ones) that transpire during a 24-hour period for a set of randomly selected individuals. The input for the 'budget' or system is time, which is constant at 1440 minutes, and the output is the use of time in various activities. The 24-hour input is universal for all members of the population and the output choice of activities represents a combination of preferences and constraints within the population. Sorting out the two - preferences and constraints - is, of course, the essence of the analytical effort, since public policy must be informed about this distinction.

The population to be studied is sampled randomly, and if location and movement are important analytical considerations the sample must be randomized both geographically and demographically, the effect of which is to restrict somewhat the degree (and economy) with which the sample can be clustered. Generally, a large sample is required because of the degree of variation in time use across certain characteristics such as sex, employment status, stage in the life cycle, etc., and the immediate stratifications that such variation entails. Thus, the number of observations for any given analytical cell diminishes rapidly when further cross-classifications are carried out in search of 'explanation' for less commonly understood variation in activity patterns.

Usually, all days of the week are sampled, as equally as possible, although distinctions may be made between weekdays and weekends during the analysis, if this is deemed important. Since seasonal variation is more difficult to work with, the (same) sample is usually restricted to a 'typical' time of year for the range of climatic and other seasonal variation of the particular location. Thus summer in temperate climates, for example, is treated as a special condition requiring a separate sample if there is interest in the activity patterns and time use during that season.

The survey technique, itself, while fraught with methodological complexities, is conceptually very simple. The respondents merely record all their activities and the time spent in them for the 24-hour period from midnight to midnight for the day preceding the actual interview. The interviewer transfers this record onto a pre-structured form designed to facilitate coding. This is followed by transferring the coded information into the computer, where it is available for analysis. The day of respondent recording itself is generally preceded by a visit from the interviewer who explains the technique and leaves instructions and a simplified form for the respondent's use on the following day. This latter convention on the prior visit by the interviewer varies somewhat, although there seems to be an increase in the number of activities recorded by the respondents if they have been contacted in advance. This, of course, has to be balanced against the possible bias arising from this contact.

Time use analysis treats individual and averaged budgets as *activity systems*, i.e., as coherent *patterns* of time and space use. Classification of time users by stage in the life cycle, sex, socio-occupational class, employment status, location of residence, etc., permits averages to be expressed for each of these types. Activities are analyzed by amount of time devoted to them, by sequences, by location, by frequency, by others present, etc. While the time use inventory is purely descriptive in itself, its cross-classification with other variables permits more analytical behavioral understanding and potentially suggestive inferences about causation. Different types or classes of people thus show different patterns expressed as proportions, sequences, locations, etc., of activity, which in sum constitute the total behavioral system. What is unique is that individuals are treated as totalities as far as their activities for the sampled time span are concerned, their behavioral integrity is preserved and the entire system of pattern and activities is analyzed and not just isolated parts. This does not mean necessarily that the patterns or systems are fully explained as intended or understood by the individuals who create them, but at least the totality is there for examination.

The Time Budget Perspective in Relation to Other Urban and Regional Research Efforts

The time budget perspective, it would appear, is complementary to other urban research frameworks. Recurrent inventories of time use patterns may be the only way, ultimately, to assess the effects of public policy on behavioral patterns in time and space. Many policies, particularly those involving extended or large-scale capital investments (such as transportation networks) may take many years to reach fruition. The effects on the population may take even longer to be discerned. This is surely one of the reasons that the Hungarian National Statistic Service instituted a time budget survey *as a part of its dicennial census of population*; that is, a sample of the population completed a time budget schedule along with the census form, itself, every ten years. Thus, the Hungarian census surveyed not only the 'residue of past activities' in the form of traditional census data but collected a dynamic and detailed record of current activities in the form of typical and representative time budgets from the total population, as well. Not only can the general long-term trends in the national activity patterns be assessed in this way, but also specific populations directly affected by public policies can be singled out for special analyses. The results can provide a necessary and useful sociological balance to the usual economic biases of national and regional accounting systems (Meier 1962, p.54).

A special case for time budget analysis is that found in the social change dimensions of urbanization. The highly industrialized countries, which are for the most part fully urbanized, find such change problematic as a change in degree, e.g. increasing stress from the need to maximize activities in relation to time, etc., while currently urbanizing countries must understand and accommodate the dramatic changes in lifestyle that accompany rural-urban migration, particularly since it is now becoming clear that different cultures respond in different ways to this transition. This is also a matter of present urbanization taking place at a faster pace and under much more severe constraints, as well as a question of preserving traditions that are essential to social cohesion in the wake of often dehumanizing industrialization. The 'Chicago School' research and the subsequent literature is full of hypotheses about the changes in activity patterns that modernization, urbanization and industrialization are likely to bring: increased leisure, increased use of the mass media, a knowledge explosion and concomitant increases in time devoted to educational activities, increasing travel times and traffic congestion costs, increase in voluntary associations and secondary contracts, weakening kinship relations, lessening of place-bound (neighbourhood) interaction, heterogeneity of contacts, etc. Almost every one of these hypotheses is open to examination and (at least) further interpretation under more recent conditions of urbanization.

The time budget can be used not only to examine the above hypotheses but may be instrumental in improving understanding of changes that have not otherwise been so comprehensively studied cross-culturally, such as changing roles in the family, effects of increasing hours of employment and/or time spent away from the home, *unexpected decreases* in time availability after 'labor-saving' technological change, etc.

There are several ways in which the time budget approach can be used to examine these issues of modernization either cross- or intra-culturally. Perhaps the most common is to classify an urban population (sample) synchronically by scaling into more or less modern groups and to make time use and activity pattern comparisons between them (see below - Athens study). Another is the diachronic or longitudinal study of the same urban population (as described above). A third possibility, a variation of the synchronic method, would be to compare the time and activity patterns of urban population *by size of place*, i.e., along the hierarchy of towns and cities within the same socio-cultural system. In this way trends in pattern change, which vary by size of place, could be extrapolated for those urban populations in the future, assuming that those trends were sufficiently linear and/or regular. One obvious tie-in for this approach would be with the central place theory used by geographers to explain the urban (central place) hierarchy. General urban policy and planning implications would also seem to be considerable, as, for example, in transportation scheduling and planning, planning for recreation and leisure activities, and even general land use planning as it relates to shifts in activity patterns as size of place increases.

Time Budget Research and Public Policy

The ultimate value of the time budget perspective to urban and regional planning research is its applicability to public policy, hence, the question of how and in what ways it can be organized to provide evaluation of these policies. There are two issues here, requiring a distinction that is sometimes overlooked in applied social science research. One is the ability of the time budget perspective to predict the outcome of various policy decisions and/or trends resulting from past decisions on the activity patterns of the urban society. The other has to do with *evaluation* or *judgement* about which patterns are better or more compatible with the values of that society, a judgement that enters at every stage of the research effort. The ultimate judgement about better or worse is made by the people, of course, but public policy narrows the options in degree almost in proportion to the size of the capital investment that accompanies the policy. Thus, for example, the preference for the automobile today is in part the outcome of a long history of public policy decisions favoring its use, a history which is not totally unrelated to systemic pressure by the petroleum and rubber industries and the subsequent gigantic automobile industry itself (though the automobile was and is obviously preferred for other reasons as well). Thus it is that so-called 'pure social science prediction' is, itself, biased by normative decisions from the past, which merely emphasizes further the need for being explicit about the criteria and techniques used for evaluating patterns and policy recommendations growing out of current research.

In relating time budget research to public policy, at least three approaches seem possible: (1) direct search of sampled population for attitudes about their past, present and potential future patterns of activity choice and time use, as well as how they would relate these patterns to public policy, if possible; (2) analysis of trends in activity and time choice and their locational implications based upon either (a) longitudinal studies of the same population, (b) synchronous studies of different 'types', e.g. modern-traditional, etc., in the same population, or (c) comparative studies of different populations, e.g., those living in different size cities, or in more versus less industrialized cities of the same size, etc.; (3) empirical tests, to the extent possible, of theoretical and normative statements in the academic literature, such as Meier's argument (above), or those by deGrazia (1962) and Linder (1970) that technological development has *not* produced more leisure but has in fact restricted and regimented populations as claimed by recent social critics, etc. By following some or all of these three strategies, the descriptive and analytical results of time budget research can more readily and explicitly contribute to meaningful policy decisions affecting the urban scene.

In addition, time budget research can also contribute to social theory as in the cross-cultural studies of Szalai (1966a, 1966b, 1966c, 1972, UNESCO 1966) and others in the multinational project, to quality of life or social indicator research usually carried on at the national level (Patrushcv,1970) and to the understanding of micro environments such as buildings or urban spaces. Though time budget work has been largely descriptive, the potential for policy applications at the regional level would seem to be considerable as more and more experience accumulates at this scale.

Time Budget Research in Athens

As part of an Athens (Greece) Plan Section research effort, I carried out a pilot time budget investigation in the Athens Metropolitan Area (Gutenschwager 1969, pp.163-189). The effort in that study was to relate time use patterns to the modernization of the individual Greek. A modernity scale, based upon awareness[1], was developed for the Athenian pilot sample and was used to classify individual time budgets. The differences between modern and traditional men and women were about as one might expect: more modern Greek men were seen to spend less time in work-related and sleep activities and more time in family care, especially child care, and educational activities than their more traditional counterparts. For more modern women, the opposite was in

---

1. The scale defined awareness of self, other and society in more rational or functional, rather than tradition-bound, terms as the measure of modern; for example, recognizing one's opportunities and planning for the future rather than accepting one's 'station in life' would constitute a modern awareness of self; recognizing the various functional roles in the urban society and when and how to use them rather than seeking functional and professional help exclusively from friends and relatives would constitute a modern awareness of others; and recognizing the demands, problems and potential of the national and even international system as a totality beyond the self and family rather than treating one's own interests as the ultimate would constitute a modern awareness of society.

part true: they spent more time in work, and less time in family care, especially housework, than their traditional counterparts, although, like more modern men they spent more time in education and less time in sleep than more traditional women.

Location of activities also showed this contrasting pattern for modernizing versus traditional men and women: more modern men spent more time at home, while the more modern women spent less time at home than the more traditional. As to contacts, modern men spent less time alone and more time with their families than traditional males, while modern women spent more time alone and less time with their families than traditional women. For both modern men and women impersonal contacts accounted for more time use than with traditional men and women.

The sample for this study was small, but the time budget results were predictable enough to encourage confidence in the findings and to inspire further research into time use and activity patterns in Greece, one of the few so-called developing countries where the technique had been applied.

In Athens in 1972-1973 the Athens Plan Section of the Ministry of Public Works organized a time budget research project. Some 1733 completed interviews were obtained from the 2000 plus sample and these constitute the basis for the portion of the results reported below. The 13% refusal rate was rather high but not unusual in a study of this nature where several hours of respondents' time on two different interview occasions were demanded, along with the more or less continuous effort required to record activities during the intervening 24-hour period.

Method of Analysis

One common means of discussing the use of time by a population is to examine the average time spent in various activities. When computed over a fairly homogeneous population these averages may be expected to reflect more or less typical actors from that population. Even where the averages are drawn from more heterogeneous populations they summarize tendencies; and when informed by more detailed analysis of the variations around this mean, may be safely used to represent those populations.

Experience with time budget studies, as well as common sense, indicates that time use is extremely sensitive to certain variables. Two of the most important in this respect are gender and employment status, and most of the averages presented below refer to populations that have been filtered by these two variables. A third significant variable is age: one would expect that average time spent in various activities would vary according to age, as, indeed, was shown to be the case. This variable is complicated by the presence of children in the household, however, and a third concept, stage in the life cycle, is a more appropriate summary of the two combined. Four stages are defined:

1. 18 - 24
2. 25 - 39
3. Any age with children under age 18 present in the household.
4. 40 - 65

The first stage represents youth, the second early maturity, the third parenthood, and the fourth late maturity. In spite of the importance of this life-cycle variable it was examined separately and then dropped because the sample itself would have to have been at least three to four times larger in order to support a division into so many classes with numbers remaining for variation in relation to other factors.

In essence, therefore, three basic and more or less homogeneous population groups were used to examine other variables thought to be significant in terms of time use. These three groups were:

1. Employed Males
2. Employed Females
3. Unemployed Females

In 1973 employed males represented nearly 90% of the male population, the remainder being mostly students and retired persons. There were also some students among the unemployed females, but the majority were housewives. Other variables examined were income, education, occupation, the presence of 'modern' conveniences (television, automobile), and location in the city. Finally, some international comparisons were made. Eight major activities are presented in the tabulations, with eleven subcategories as follows:

1. Work
2. Travel
   a. To Work
   b. To Shop
   c. All Other
3. Shopping
4. Active Leisure
   a. Education
   b. Recreation
5. Passive Leisure
   a. Personal Communications
   b. Mass Media
   c. Other Entertainment
6. Eating
7. Home and Family
   a. Housework
   b. Child and Adult Care
   c. Personal Services
8. Sleep and Rest

These activities were organized to range from the most public: Work, Travel, Shopping, to the most private: Personal Services and Sleep. Contrasting the first four major activity types with the last four may provide a rough comparison between public versus private activities. The so-called discretionary activities fall in the center of the list and are included in the two categories Active and Passive Leisure. The two are distinguished from each other by the nature of participation on the part of the individual. In active leisure the individual must play an active role, either intellectually or physically, in order for the activity to occur. Theoretically, some learning or re-creating is taking place.

In passive leisure the individual is required simply to attend to what is going on. Though some learning and re-creating may occur, this is not the main purpose of the activity, which purpose may be thought of as ranging from simply allowing time to pass to actually seeking escape from the present time (with its attendant problems and anxieties). This is not to imply that passive leisure is not an important activity. For example, personal communications are essential for sorting out and interpreting the 'impersonal' communications found in the mass media. Moral judgement is developed during the personal communications and the moral integrity of a culture depends upon them.

The averages shown in the tables that follow include Sunday activities, which amount to about one-seventh of the total. The effect of this inclusion is to deflate work hours slightly as well as possibly shopping and other weekday activities and to inflate slightly Sunday activities such as those in leisure, sleep, etc.

A Sample of Results from the Research

General Characteristics of the Population

Briefly, the Athens Metropolitan population in 1972-3 was characteristically urban, without, however, the level of material wealth found in Western Europe at that time. Families were small (average size of household 3.5 persons). Dwelling units were also small (average size 2.8 rooms), 50% of which were owner-occupied. This means that the Athens population had not yet reached the international standard in developed countries at that time of one room per person. For the most part Athenians were satisfied with the conditions of their lives, except for their displeasure with the physical environment, particularly the absence of greenery. Socially and economically, the household heads were mostly lower middle to middle class, the three largest categories being skilled workers (18.5%), clerks (24.8%) and small businessmen, tradesmen and cottage industrials (19.6%). The small numbers of unskilled (5.6%) and executive and professional (5.9%) indicates how few Athenians were to be found in the upper or lower class extremes. More than three-quarters of the household heads were employed, though a goodly number were retired (12.7%). Nearly 50% of the household heads had only an elementary school education at that time, with 15% having less and 23% having completed high school and 12% university. At the same time the general level of education had been increasing steadily and it has always been apparent in Greece that education is a highly valued form of investment. As far as communications behavior was concerned, newspapers were clearly preferred at that time, with about three-quarters of the population using them as their main source of news. The radio was used mainly for music listening and television and the cinema for entertainment.

Variations in Time Use - Comparisons Between Males and Females

In a gross comparison of males and females (Table 4.1) it can be seen that men were much more likely to be found in public activities than women, on the average more than nine hours a day versus a little more than four for women. The main trade-off here was between work on the one hand and home & family activities on the other. The combined totals for these two types of activities were 7.8 hours for men and 7.9 hours for women. Men traveled twice as much as women, mainly in the 'journey-to-work'. Shopping was more a female than a male activity, while the active and passive leisure total hours were about the same, accounting for about 4.5 hours or a little less than twenty per cent of the total time budget.

The largest average number of hours worked was by men with children under the age of 18 present in the household. Generally, where children were present, employed men worked more hours and spent more time in home and family activities. As their age increased these men spent more time in work and in sleep and rest, and somewhat more in eating. They spent less time in travel, in leisure activities and in personal care. Mass media activities, primarily television viewing, were quite constant across age groups, slightly more, in fact, among the youngest groups.

TABLE 4.1
Average Time Spent in Primary Activities
(Hours and Tenths)

Primary Activity	Males (N=797)		Females (N=902)		Total (N=1699)	
Work	6.4		1.9		4.0	
Travel	1.5		0.8		1.1	
to work		0.9		0.2		0.5
to shop		0.1		0.2		0.2
other		0.5		0.4		0.4
Shopping	0.2		0.4		0.3	
Active Leisure	1.0		1.1		1.1	
education		0.6		0.3		0.5
recreation		0.4		0.8		0.6
Passive Leisure	3.4		3.4		3.4	
personal comm.		1.0		1.4		1.2
mass media		1.8		1.8		1.8
other entertain.		0.6		0.2		1.2
Eating	1.2		1.3		1.2	
Home & Family	1.4		6.0		3.9	
housework		0.3		4.3		2.4
child, adult care		0.3		1.0		0.7
personal services		0.8		0.7		0.7
Sleep & Rest	8.8		9.1		9.0	
TOTAL	24.0		24.0		24.0	

For employed women, the presence of children in the household decreased the average hours spent at work compared to other age groups, except the youngest. In fact, the combined demands of housework and child care, plus work, on employed women with children were so great as to decrease average time spent in nearly every other activity when compared to all other employed women. Generally, in Athens, when there were older women present in the household, the younger women spent little time in doing housework. Unemployed women spent more time in shopping and personal communication and less time with the mass media, compared to unemployed males.

The Effects of Income on Time Use (See tables 4.2 - 4.4)

Income had a definite effect upon time use for both men and women. Low-income males, for example, worked more hours on the average and spent less time in active and passive leisure as a result. As income increased, time spent in sleep and rest decreased for employed men and this 'extra' time also appeared to be devoted to leisure activities, as well as to a lesser extent, to travel. Time spent in education increased with income for employed males. Time spent with the mass media appeared to peak with middle-income males.

TABLE 4.2
Average Time Spent in Primary Activities
(Hours and Tenths)
Employed Males by Income Class

Primary Activity	Income Class							
	Low (N=206)		**Middle** (N=303)		**Upper** (N=93)		**Total** (N=687)*	
Work	7.5		7.1		6.8		7.3	
Travel	1.5		1.5		1.7		1.5	
to work		1.1		1.0		1.1		1.0
to shop		0.1		0.1		0.1		0.1
other		0.4		0.4		0.5		0.4
Shopping	0.2		0.2		0.2		0.2	
Active Leisure	0.4		0.6		0.7		0.6	
education		0.2		0.2		0.4		0.2
recreation		0.2		0.4		0.3		0.3
Passive Leisure	2.9		3.5		3.5		3.2	
personal comm.		0.9		1.0		1.1		1.0
mass media		1.5		2.0		1.7		1.7
other entertain.		0.6		0.5		0.7		0.5
Eating	1.2		1.2		1.2		1.2	
Home & Family	1.3		1.4		1.4		1.4	
housework		0.3		0.2		0.3		0.3
child, adult care		0.3		0.3		0.3		0.3
personal services		0.8		0.8		0.8		0.8
Sleep & Rest	8.9		8.6		8.4		8.6	
TOTAL	24.0		24.0		24.0		24.0	

* TOTAL includes 85 cases where no income was reported.

For employed females an increase in income meant less time spent in work, but more time spent in travel. Employed upper income women spent more time in shopping and active leisure but not necessarily more in passive leisure. They also spent more time in child care and sleep and rest. For unemployed women increased income resulted in more time spent in travel, in shopping and in personal services. However, increased income resulted in less time spent in sleep and rest for unemployed women, with low income women spending seven-tenths of an hour more on average than high income unemployed women.

TABLE 4.3
Average Time Spent in Primary Activities
(Hours and Tenths)
Employed Females by Income Class

Primary Activity	Income Class							
	Low (N=82)		**Middle** (N=90)		**Upper** (N=38)		**Total** (N=247)*	
Work	6.7		6.1		5.2		6.2	
Travel	1.2		1.2		1.4		1.2	
to work		0.7		0.8		0.9		0.8
to shop		0.2		0.1		0.1		0.1
other		0.3		0.3		0.5		0.3
Shopping	0.2		0.2		0.3		0.2	
Active Leisure	0.2		0.5		0.7		0.4	
education		0.1		0.1		0.1		0.1
recreation		0.2		0.4		0.6		0.3
Passive Leisure	2.4		2.8		2.5		2.5	
personal comm.		1.0		0.9		0.9		0.9
mass media		1.2		1.6		1.3		1.4
other entertain.		0.1		0.4		0.4		0.3
Eating	1.0		1.1		1.0		1.1	
Home & Family	3.4		3.8		3.8		3.7	
housework		2.4		2.4		2.4		2.5
child, adult care		0.2		0.4		0.6		0.4
personal services		0.8		0.9		0.7		0.9
Sleep & Rest	<u>8.8</u>		<u>8.2</u>		<u>9.1</u>		<u>8.6</u>	
TOTAL	24.0		24.0		24.0		24.0	

* TOTAL includes 37 cases where no income was reported.

TABLE 4.4
Average Time Spent in Primary Activities
(Hours and tenths)
Unemployed Females by Income Class

Primary Activity	Income Class							
	Low (N=254)		Middle (N=221)		Upper (N=61)		Total (N=655)*	
Work	0.2		0.3		0.3		0.3	
Travel	0.5		0.7		0.9		0.6	
to work		0.0		0.0		0.0		0.0
to shop		0.2		0.2		0.3		0.2
other		0.4		0.5		0.6		0.4
Shopping	0.4		0.5		0.6		0.5	
Active Leisure	1.1		1.4		1.0		1.3	
education		0.2		0.4		0.6		0.4
recreation		0.9		1.0		0.4		0.9
Passive Leisure	3.7		3.7		3.6		3.7	
personal comm.		1.6		1.5		1.5		1.6
mass media		1.9		2.0		1.7		1.9
other entertain.		0.2		0.1		0.4		0.2
Eating	1.4		1.4		1.5		1.4	
Home & Family	7.0		6.8		7.2		6.9	
housework		0.3		4.8		4.9		5.0
child, adult care		1.2		1.3		1.3		1.2
personal services		0.5		0.7		0.9		0.6
Sleep & Rest	9.6		9.3		8.9		9.4	
TOTAL	24.0		24.0		24.0		24.0	

* TOTAL includes 119 cases where no income was reported.

For unemployed women (Table 4.4) increased income resulted in increased time spent in travel, shopping and personal services, as one might expect. Unlike with employed women, however, time spent in sleep and rest for unemployed women decreased as income increased, though the low income women slept and rested what would seem to be an inordinate 9.6 hours on the average.

International Comparisons of Time Use (See Tables 4.5 - 4.9)

Eight countries were chosen for comparison from among the dozen or so involved in the multinational Time Budget Study carried out in Europe in 1965-66. These countries were Belgium, Bulgaria, Federal Republic of Germany, France, Hungary, U.S.A., USSR and Yugoslavia. In a broad comparison of the total numbers of these countries it was found that the gross similarities and dissimilarities provided a social 'map' not unlike the geographical map of Europe. In this sense Greece fell quite naturally into the southeast quadrant of the European social geography and was the most truly representative of its type.

Greek men spent more time in work than all other countries except Bulgaria and Hungary (Table 4.5), and employed Greek women the same, if the USSR were added to the other two eastern bloc countries.

TABLE 4.5
Average Time Spent in Primary Activities
(Hours and tenths)
Multinational Comparisons

Average Time Spent in Work

Country	Employed Males	Employed Females	Unemployed Females	Total
Greece	7.3	6.2	0.3	4.0
Belgium	7.1	5.7	0.3	2.6
Bulgaria	7.6	6.7	0.3	5.6
F.R.G.	7.1	5.0	0.4	2.0
France	6.9	5.7	0.1	2.6
Hungary	7.8	6.7	0.6	4.3
U.S.A.	6.9	5.2	0.1	2.4
U.S.S.R.	6.9	6.3	0.1	5.1
Yugoslavia	7.1	5.8	0.2	2.6

TABLE 4.6
Average Time Spent in Primary Activities
(Hours and tenths)
Multinational Comparisons

Average Time Spent in Daily Travel

Country	Employed Males	Employed Females	Unemployed Females	Total
Greece	1.5	1.2	0.6	1.1
Belgium	1.0	1.0	0.6	0.8
Bulgaria	1.4	1.3	0.8	1.2
F.R.G.	0.8	0.6	0.2	0.3
France	1.1	0.9	0.7	0.7
Hungary	1.4	1.2	0.7	1.0
U.S.A.	1.5	1.2	0.9	1.1
U.S.S.R.	1.5	1.4	1.2	1.5
Yugoslavia	1.5	1.2	0.9	1.1

Daily travel time in the Greek sample was also very high (Table 4.6), and once again it was the eastern European countries that equalled or exceeded it. The one exception to this was the U.S.A., which had almost exactly the same daily travel time patterns as Greece, though probably the distances covered were not the same. One would have expected Greek travel time to have been higher than the average since the work day was divided into two segments at that time, requiring four journey-to-work trips for much of the labor force, and in this sense it is surprising that Greece was not the highest in this category since it was the only Mediterranean country in the sample group.

TABLE 4.7
Average Time Spent in Primary Activities
(Hours and tenths)
Multinational Comparisons

Average Time Spent in Shopping

Country	Employed Males	Employed Females	Unemployed Females	Total
Greece	0.2	0.2	0.5	0.3
Belgium	0.1	0.3	0.6	0.5
Bulgaria	0.3	0.3	0.7	0.4
F.R.G.	0.1	0.4	0.7	0.6
France	0.2	0.4	0.7	0.6
Hungary	0.1	0.4	0.6	0.5
U.S.A.	0.4	0.5	0.7	0.6
U.S.S.R.	0.2	0.5	0.6	0.5
Yugoslavia	0.3	0.4	0.8	0.6

Shopping was largely a female activity in Greece as in most of the other countries (Table 4.7). However, Greek women, whether employed or not, spent less time than their counterparts in other countries and the total Athenian sample spent as little as half as much time in shopping as other countries in Europe. One explanation for this pattern might be that Greece was less a consumer society than the others at that time, which was hardly the case, or, otherwise, that shopping was somehow better organized in Athens than in the other cities included in the multinational study, i.e., that the stores were closer to the dwelling units requiring less time to get there and back.

The Greek sample spent a large amount of time in education at that time, exceeded only by the USSR in this activity (Table 4.8). The time spent was particularly high among unemployed women and men, which accounted for the half-hour daily average in the total sample, exceeded only by the USSR. The effects of the Soviet emphasis on continuing education were already clearly seen for the employed men and women in their sample, while the high totals in the Greek sample represented young unemployed men and women, many of whom attended private college preparatory schools, and for whose families education was seen as a means to social mobility.

TABLE 4.8
Average Time Spent in Primary Activities
(Hours and tenths)
Multinational Comparisons

Average Time Spent in Education

Country	Employed Males	Employed Females	Unemployed Females	Total
Greece	0.2	0.1	0.4	0.5
Belgium	0.1	0.1	0.3	0.2
Bulgaria	0.2	0.1	0.4	0.2
F.R.G.	0.1	0.0	0.0	0.0
France	0.1	0.1	0.3	0.2
Hungary	0.4	0.2	0.1	0.2
U.S.A.	0.2	0.1	0.2	0.1
U.S.S.R.	0.7	0.5	1.8	0.5
Yugoslavia	0.3	0.2	0.2	0.2

In 1973 Greece was low in time spent in active recreation, similar to most Eastern European countries. The Federal Republic of Germany was the highest in all categories, which was probably related to the relatively lower amounts of time West Germans spent in work and travel. On the other hand, Greeks spent up to one whole hour more than half the other countries and up to three-quarters of an hour more than the remainder in personal communications (Table 4.9). This is a purely cultural phenomenon and since no other Mediterranean culture was represented in the list, Greece seemed like an extraordinary country in this respect.

TABLE 4.9
Average Time Spent in Primary Activities
(Hours and tenths)
Multinational Comparisons

Average Time Spent in Personal Communications

Country	Employed Males	Employed Females	Unemployed Females	Total
Greece	1.0	0.9	1.6	1.2
Belgium	0.3	0.2	0.2	0.2
Bulgaria	0.1	0.1	0.2	0.1
F.R.G.	0.2	0.2	0.4	0.3
France	0.3	0.2	0.3	0.3
Hungary	0.2	0.2	0.3	0.2
U.S.A.	0.2	0.3	0.5	0.4
U.S.S.R.	0.2	0.1	0.3	0.2
Yugoslavia	0.4	0.3	0.6	0.5

Time spent in personal communications may have resulted from less time spent with the mass media, as Greeks spent the least amount of time on average in this latter activity, which may also have reflected a north-south trade-off between these two activities. Greeks also spent surprisingly little time in eating, thus destroying, as it were, one of the expected stereotypes of its southern location. It was not the lowest, however, and, if it were not for the exceptionally high amounts of time spent in Germany, France and Belgium, it would have been average to high compared with the other countries on the list.

Activities in Time and Space (Figures 4.1-- 4.4)

In addition to the average time spent in various activities, the time budget study in Athens in 1972-3 examined the evolution of activities over the course of the average day. This daily rhythm of activities expressed the way in which the population scheduled its activities throughout the day, demonstrating the dynamic use of time in this respect. Different sub-groups were constrained differently in their scheduling of activities and this showed up clearly in the diagrams.

Figure 4.1 shows most clearly the total average schedule of the Athens population. The vertical axis represents the total time available to the sample population during the hour shown along the horizontal axis. In the case of Figure 4.1, where the total sample is shown this would mean that 1699 person-hours are represented by each hour space along the horizontal axis. The activities themselves are shown as a percentage of this total, so that in every case the top of the diagram is the 100 percent line irrespective of the size of the sample sub-group being portrayed. Thus, in Figure 4.1 during the hour from midnight to 1:00 a.m., about 86% of the person hours available are being used in the activity sleep. Two other activities, passive leisure (7.5%), and work (3.5%) accounted for most of the remainder of the person-hours of activity available at that time.

Figure 4.1 shows clearly the characteristic schedule of the Mediterranean society found in Athens at that time. There was a double surge of activity peaking at about noon and 8:00 p.m., and broken by a rest period that reached a maximum between 3:00 p.m. and 4:00 p.m., at least for the fall-winter period during which the survey was carried out. All other diagrams showed the same double peaking, some anticipating the mid-day break more than others. Work and household activities were the dominant morning activities, while passive leisure was the dominant late afternoon and evening activity. Sleep, of course, dominated activities from midnight to about 7:00 a.m., by which time at least half of the population was up and about.

Figure 4.2 not only examines the sub-groups of activities more closely, but also displays each major activity on its own horizontal axis, eliminating the distributions that might result from cumulating the percentages as in Figure 4.1. Thus, for example, home and family activities clearly had a higher peak in the morning and were in any case dominated by housework as the main activity in this category.

Child and adult care, on the other hand, was more important in late afternoon and evening between 5:00 p.m. and 8:00 p.m., while personal services were more common early in the morning up until 9:00 a.m., and peaked again in the evening between 5:00 p.m. and 7:00 p.m.

Shopping peaked in the morning between 10:00 a.m. and 11:00 a.m., with a much smaller peak in the evening between 6:00 p.m. and 7:00 p.m. Travel, on the other hand, peaked before and after the shopping peaks, dominated in the morning and midday hours by the journey-to-work.

Figures 4.3 and 4.4 portray the location by kilometer grid-square of the two major activities of work and travel. The density patterns were a product of the number of persons present in the grid-square multiplied by the number of hours spent there in the activity being portrayed. Because the range of densities resulting was very large, the classification was developed from a logarithmic scale. Thus, the densities shown at the denser end of the scale were disproportionately greater than those at the sparser end. The person-hours were totalled over the entire average day for the sample.

Work locations (Figure 4.3) were highly concentrated in the Athens case, though there was a secondary concentration in the Piraeus center and a goodly number of minor concentrations throughout the metropolitan area. The densities in the Athens center would have been accounted for by the heavy concentration of commercial, financial and government activities, while other concentrations reflected the localities of industrial activities, on the one hand, and a myriad of smaller retail and cottage industry locations, on the other.

Figure 4.4 shows the density of person-hours in travel according to the grid-square location of the destination of that travel. Time spent in travel was, as expected, much less than time spent in work. Thus, the overall density was much lower than in Figure 4.3. The pattern of densities was, however, quite similar owing to the fact that the journey-to-work was the most important type of travel. Thus, the heaviest concentration of destinations by person-hours was found in and around the Athens core, with a secondary concentration in Piraeus. Time spent in travel to destinations in the rest of the metropolitan area was quite insignificant except for scattered locations.

The above, briefly, are some of the results of the analysis of time use in the Athens population in 1973. Similar studies should take place on a regular basis, as is already the case in some European countries, in order to trace changes in time use that might suggest changes in urban policy and planning that could resolve problems that arise. Differences in time use between males and females, employed and unemployed, etc., could suggest planning decisions related to work place, shopping, leisure time, and so forth, and all of those in relation to location of places of residence. Similar decisions could result from indications of shifting patterns of time spent in journey-to-work, as one of the most important activities in the metropolitan area. Finally, all Athenians are aware of the serious problems of their city and the need for a comprehensive socio-economic program to relieve these problems. Time budget research could contribute significantly to such an effort.

Figure 4.1: Cumulative Per Cent of Person-Hours in Eight Major Activity Types. Total Sample (N=1699)

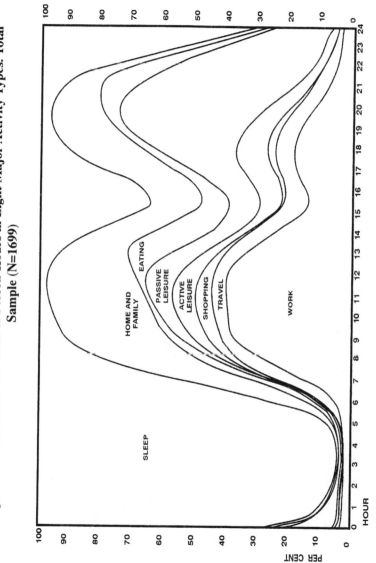

Figure 4.2: Cumulative Per Cent of Person-Hours in Various Activities.
Total Sample (N=1699)

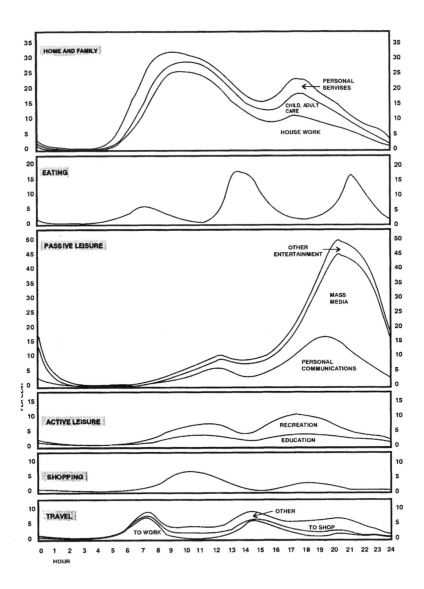

Figure 4.3: Density of Cumulative Person-Hours in Work.

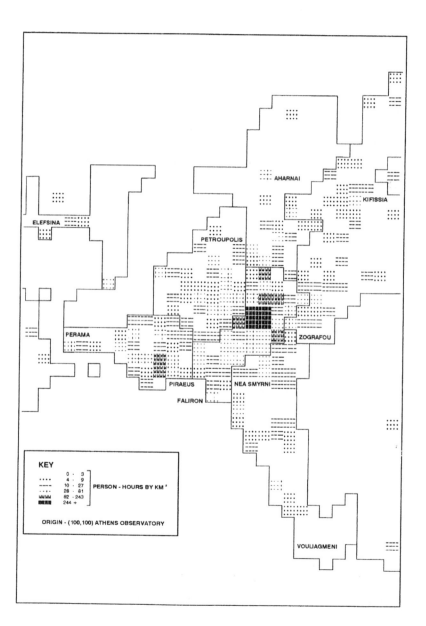

Figure 4.4: Density of Cumulative Per Cents of Person-Hours in Travel.

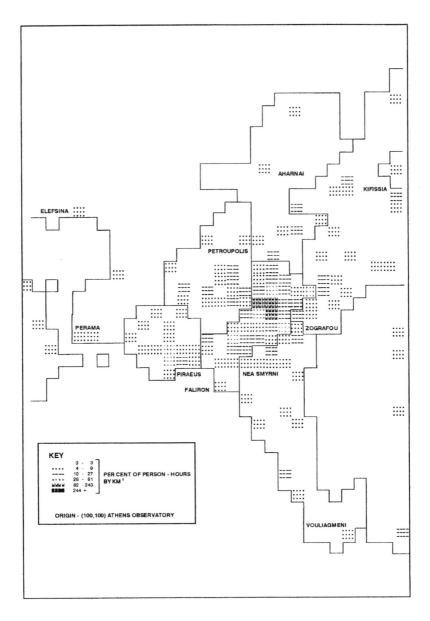

CHAPTER 5

THE PHENOMENOLOGY OF SOCIAL CHANGE *

Social change is one of the most challenging and perplexing problems of concern to social science. Understanding it demands periodic revision of analysis and interpretation to accommodate unpredicted, often unsignaled alteration in society, and caution against the deception of past experience, which is the only basis one has for speculation about change. Conceptualizing methods, bound to static situations and constant interactions, rarely transcend a 'comparative statics' approach in their formulations.

While the problems of dealing with social change arise from the complexities of society itself, it may well be that these problems are compounded by a mechanistic view of the social order which depends to a large extent upon the simple causal link and the concept of mechanical equilibrium. The effort of this chapter will be to examine an alternative to this view, namely a multidimensional, phenomenological perspective on the over-all process of social change.

The Social Order: Three Modes of Reality

In the application of phenomenological thought to social theory by Berger and Luckmann, as described in Chapter 2 above, reality is

* Reprinted with permission from Gerald Gutenschwager (1970) "Social Reality and Social Change", *Social Research,* Vol. 37, No 1 (Spring), pp 48-70.

derived from the unique socio-linguistic origin of common-sense knowledge in human groups. These authors trace in detail the social-psychological processes whereby common-sense knowledge is acquired and social reality defined for the typical members of society. These processes summarized as 'externalization, objectivation, and internalization', account for the fact that humans, their social and natural world, and their understanding of that world are different though dialectically related, each participating in the creation of the other. 'Society is a human product. Society is an objective reality. Man is a social product'; and as Berger and Luckmann (1966, p.61) further point out ". . . an analysis of the social world that leaves out any one of these three [dialectical] moments will be distortive".

Here we are, if, fact, concerned with developing a model of social reality and social change that will include all of these moments[1]. Thus, three modes or aspects of reality will be referred to. One of these will be called the *environmental* or *physical* aspect, including both the natural and social surroundings. This might be characterized as the mode of 'manifest reality', constituted by the total set of phenomena available to the objective sense perception of common-sense humans, as well as of social scientists. It consists not only of natural phenomena and events, but also recordable and observable social phenomena and occurrences. It is the truly statistical aspect of the social order, and its manifest availability makes it susceptible to all the various mechanistic and mathematically systematic formulations that have proven so successful in the natural sciences. It is the aspect demonstrating ". . . the possibility that the indeterminacy seemingly inherent in situations involving human motivations, volitions, etc., *may* disappear as the events are taken on a larger scale" (Rapoport 1957, p.56, author's emphasis). It is here that Boulding would see ". . .mechanical elements, independent of the image, of great importance in any social system and which we neglect . . . at our peril" (Boulding 1964, p. 10). It also includes humans as biological and physiological beings, subject to needs and restricted in their physical capacities by their own mortal condition and the environment around them.[2]

---

1. See Figure 5.1, p. 115.
2. The environmental aspect includes what Berger and Luckmann refer to as 'objective reality', but is also used here in a somewhat broader and more general sense to include the natural order as well.

While it is true that the *environmental* aspect, the manifest reality, is available to our sense perceptions, its vast temporal and spatial complexities make it quite impossible to be fully grasped in an objective manner. Even science, the most systematic human effort to understand the environment objectively, is admittedly limited in this respect. Common-sense humans, therefore, understandably utilize highly subjective images of this reality to help in finding their way around. The image constitutes a second *meaningful* or *spiritual* mode of appearance of the social order, which could be labeled as the 'subjective reality'. It is the naive picture carried by non-scientific humans, their interpretation of the vast and only partially known world around them. It is the philosophical vision, the religious faith, the ethical system, the complex of attitude, stereotype, and common sense construct that constitute the spiritual paraphernalia of the beings in the social order. It is an aspect from which social scientists, themselves, are not free[3], and, as in the manifest reality, there is a considerable variation in complexity within the meaningful aspect, with images ranging hierarchically from the smallest bias to a scope of '. . . great complexity and many dimensions'.

Intervening between the subjective and manifest reality is the level or mode of human *intention* and *intentional action*. It is the link between what is imagined as real and what is manifestly real. It is both the main locus and main obstacle to the understanding of social change. It is here that the distinct human sciences demand radically different scientific formulations if they are to study society adequately. To agree with Bertalanffy (1962, p. 14), however, that ". . . a great deal of . . . human behavior is beyond the principles of utility, homeostasis (equilibrium) and stimulus-response, and that it is just this which is characteristic of human and cultural activities", is not to agree that the 'dynamic open system' accounts fully for the intentional, goal-oriented activity of humans.

Human activity is intentional within a certain frame of reference:

---

3. [T]he student of man as man is compelled to interpret the facts which he discovers. This interpretation . . . will ultimately have to reach a supra-empirical level, and thus always requires a hermeneutic horizon. Consequently, the empirical scientist will either have to make use of someone else's philosophical vision that is known to him or propose his own philosophical interpretation of his findings (Strasser 1963, p.292).

> I anticipate of necessity what I will perceive, experience or
> discover. By anticipation I assign to that which I expect a
> place within the framework of my conceptual systems
> (Strasser 1963, p. 255).

Humans pre-interpret the outcome of their actions, the anticipated results, while their means of arriving at them are largely pre-interpreted for them. These constitute for Alfred Schutz (1962b, pp. 69-70) the (a) "in-order-to motive", that is, the "state of affairs, the end which the action has been undertaken to bring about", and the (b) "because-motive", which relates to past experience or the project of action itself. Thus both the anticipated outcome and the means to arrive at the outcome have reference to individuals' subjective reality, and, to the extent to which individuals in society typify the social group of which they are members, their actions are motivated within the meaningful aspect of that group.

We see here, in other words, the chief reason why mechanistic models are insufficient for penetrating and accounting fully for social reality. The human grasp of the realm of manifest reality is extremely limited, on the one hand, and highly distorted by their own image of it, on the other. Their actions are motivated and carried out in reference not to the manifest reality but rather to their own - and typically their social or reference group's - subjective reality. Not only are their means chosen and the action carried out, but also the results are anticipated and, once achieved, evaluated in reference to that subjective reality.

Individuals are not born with a subjective reality, of course, and its development constitutes the socialization process for them as members of a social group (Berger and Luckmann 1966, pp. 129 ff.). The nature of that process in any particular group creates an attitude toward future change and flexibility in the subjective reality. Social environments within which an 'open mind' is encouraged, and rewards and punishments organized accordingly, will tend to produce individuals with a less rigidly structured subjective reality. The long-run implications for change are obvious in such circumstances, and this does much to explain the difference between modern open and traditional closed societies (Berger and Luckmann 1966, pp. 116-128).

Images are extremely resistant to change, since they constitute both the individual's and the group's basic orientation to life.

> There is an . . . insertion between man and his environment
> of a pseudo-environment. To that pseudo-environment his
> behavior is a response. But because it is behavior, the con-
> sequences, if they are acts, operate not in the pseudo-envi-
> ronment where the behavior is stimulated but in the real
> environment where action eventuates. If the behavior is not
> a practical act, but what we call roughly thought and emo-
> tion, it may be a long time before there is any noticeable
> break in the texture of the fictitious world. But when the
> stimulus of the pseudo-fact results in action on things or
> people, contradiction soon develops. Then comes the sense
> of butting one's head against a stone wall, of learning by
> experience, and witnessing Herbert Spencer's tragedy of
> the murder of a Beautiful Theory by a Gang of Brutal
> Facts, the discomfort, in short, of a maladjustment
> (Lippmann 1922, p. 15).

In this sense there must obviously be some degree of consistency
between a society's subjective and manifest reality or serious maladjustment will cause a breakdown or revision in the existing order.
Nevertheless, if it is true, a Lippmann points out,

> . . . that under certain circumstances men respond as pow-
> erfully to fictions as they do to realities, and that in many
> cases they help to create the very fictions to which they
> respond. . . (Lippmann 1922, p.14),

then the " triangular relationship between the scene of action, the human
picture of that scene, and the human response to that picture working
itself out upon the scene of action" (Lippmann 1922, pp. 16-17) is the
nexus within which social science must work and the origins of social
change be sought.

A Model for the Study of Change

Alfred Schutz was another phenomenologically oriented social theorist who worked with a multi-aspect view of society in an effort to develop a rigorous scientific model of the social order. Although it is not possible to discuss here the full development of his thinking, a number of the
relevant principles may be presented. (Schutz 1962a, Natanson 1963).

Since there is in the essence of an individual's thoughts and actions a certain similarity with the thoughts and actions of other individuals within his or her group (as well as a certain uniqueness), and since these similarities are even stronger when a particular situation or set if situations is defined, it is possible for the social scientist (while it is necessary for common-sense humans) to typify the actions and thoughts of the social subject. This is possible because it is in the inherent nature of social relations that humans will know their counterparts in a fragmented yet typical way, according to the environmental conditions defining the encounters among them. (Simmel 1959, pp. 337-356, Natanson 1963, pp.73-92). In other words, given a particular situation, the commonsense human is able to predict with some confidence the actions, indeed, to some extent the thoughts of his fellow humans. This is true because every situation in its typical aspects has been partially lived and pre-interpreted by other persons in the same group. These kinds of information are transmitted to each member of the social group in the process of socialization, and adulthood finds most of the typical thoughts and actions taken for granted.

This typicality, however, also constitutes the basic datum for social scientists. Their constructs, based upon the taken-for-granted constructs of the individuals within the group, permit reliable, albeit limited predictive ability. Thus the model of the social world constructed by Schutz consists of, first, a circumscribed and well-defined situation, an environment which constitutes a section of the manifest reality, second, a typical actor or actors with their subjectively defined modes of perceiving the manifest reality, and, third, a set of typical "because" and "in-order-to-motives," i.e., situational objectives and courses of action appropriate to those actors which together constitute the third or intentional aspect of social reality. This descriptive model may be transformed into an analytical model by altering the environmental constraints, i.e., by changing some of the conditions in the section of manifest reality. The analysis would consist of a prediction of how these typical individuals would be likely to meet the varying conditions of a changed environment.

How would such and analysis proceed? One must recall that the actions and interactions of the actors in the model are outlined by the social scientists themselves. They reflect, however, their understanding of that which is typical and shared in the subjective reality of the members of the social group under study. They constitute, as it were, second-level abstractions, based on the everyday constructs that are a necessary component of the commonsense individuals' interpretive understanding of their fellow humans within the particular context of their mutual interaction. Social scientists, in manipulating the manifest reality, the environmental conditions, do not manipulate the subjective reality of the actors in the model. They merely interpret the changing environmental conditions *as they would be interpreted by the actors themselves*, and "move" the actors as they themselves would act, given their typical interpretation of the manifest reality.

Social scientists thus re-enact the thought processes of typical common-sense humans who are faced with information from the environment. Common-sense humans rehearse in imagination the typical circumstances similar to those that are being communicated to them. They search for their own past solutions or reactions to such circumstances, extract that which is typical, and apply to the situation, in turn, as many of the typical past solutions as they can recall. When and only when they have decided upon that typical course of action that they think will best satisfy the present circumstances, will they actually move into overt action.

Thus the overt action of common-sense humans depends largely upon what they have experienced typically in the past. Knowing this social scientists can reconstruct with some reliability that which is typical of the members of a social group and can use this understanding to predict how the members of that group will react to changing environmental conditions. Furthermore, social scientists may estimate which changes in the environment would probably transcend the past experiences of the typical members of the group, and in so doing produce a crisis in their subjective reality necessitating a search for new images. The magnitude of the crisis would indicate the degree to which the subjective reality would have to change, but would not always indicate the direction of change. Small-scale changes in the subjective reality would be easier to predict in this sense, although, in any case, changes of this nature would not be strictly covered within the analytical model itself. An effort will be made to discuss such changes in the following section of this chapter. Meanwhile, there is one further refinement that could be added to the Schutz model; this has to do with the manner of manipulating the environmental conditions.

Rather than altering arbitrarily the conditions of the manifest reality, one would do well to consider possible functional or evolutionary change, such as long run statistical trends, apparent in the environmental aspect. For it is here that the analytical manipulation of the section of manifest reality could be meaningful in the study of change. In other words, one could impute changes in the environmental mode, as they seem functionally necessary or statistically inevitable. The typicalness of response by the actors would then make it possible to predict their actions and the course of events as they might be expected to proceed within a functioning and evolving social situation.

Perhaps an example would serve to illustrate the way in which such a model would work. In a book written some years ago, Anatol Rapoport (1960) discussed the conditions surrounding conflict on the international level. He demonstrated quite clearly how the force of events, i.e., military preparations, diplomatic exchanges, etc., within the environmental aspect might lead sooner or later, perhaps inevitably, to the realization of conflict on a large scale, *given the propensity of the leaders of the opposing countries to view the situation as one of conflict in the first place.* In other words, past experience has shown that when two countries are engaged in a situation of opposing interests to the point where anxiety about national security becomes an issue, war preparations ensue such that the actions of one country have a reciprocal impact and generate similar actions on the part of the other. This cumulative reciprocal relationship can be plotted as a set of per capita arms expenditure curves leading to full-scale preparations, such that ultimately almost any minor incident is sufficient to precipitate open conflict between the opposing forces. Rapoport then drew a parallel with the arms race between the United States and the Soviet Union in which he gave considerable weight, in the form of an analysis of the mathematical probabilities of war, to the argument that the arms race could well have led to ultimate mutual annihilation.[4]

---

4. That the arms race, itself, led to the ultimate economic collapse of the Soviet Union whose smaller GNP could not sustain the ever increasing military expenditures, is, perhaps, fortunate for the history of war (though not for socialism), but this does not alter the basic argument of Rapoport, nor the possibility that a future situation could arise where the economic potential of the opposing forces would be more equal and the outcome more catastrophic.

Rapoport (1960) went on to discuss Game Theory in its use as a basis for American foreign policy. Game Theory is a mathematical method designed to account for the intentionality and rationality of human action. Given a situation that assumes competition, together with the logical premises of Game Theory, then the 'what-to-do-in-case-of' strategy principle provides a solution, a choice for the best course of action *in such a situation of competition*. Rapoport's main criticism, however, was in the use of Game Theory, or its premises, as the basis for American Foreign policy. He demonstrated how a different view of the United States-Soviet Union relationship, i.e., one which sought "areas of validity" or agreement between the two value systems or what we have labeled subjective realities, could be exploited in an ultimate compromise between the two countries.

In terms of the model one can see that a certain typical subjective reality has governed the relationship between countries with opposing interests in situations that their political and military leaders have interpreted as competitive. This attitude has produced typical courses of action and interaction, which have often led to war. The formalization of this attitude in Game Theory and a careful analysis of the logic of that theory led Rapoport to question neither the statistical trends that interested him and Lewis F. Richardson in their study of conflict, nor the inherent logic of Game Theory itself, but the very subjective reality that produced those trends in the first place. His plea was reasoned scientific statement to the heads of state to view the situation in a different light, to change their subjective reality, for should these typical images continue to influence the actions of the heads of state, the forecast for the future would be open warfare.

Thus, given the pertinent conditions of the manifest reality in the form of a gradual trend to full armament, and given the typical subjective reality which has marked participation in such trends in the past, namely, a competitive view requiring 'strategies', the intentional acts of the typical actors, as well as the probable outcome of the situation itself, can be foreseen. Meanwhile it is not inconceivable that the force of Rapoport's argument could in the long run, especially should a sufficient number of other scholars take up the cause, produce a change in the subjective reality of some heads of state. In such a case the model could be re-examined under new typicalities for changing outcomes that might be generated. At any rate when new information is available to typical actors, and should they be willing and able to give it their attention, as, for example, when events encourage them to do so, they would begin a re-examination of the manifest reality. And it is in this condition of a changing manifest reality that new or tentatively altered images are sought, and that social change characteristically arises.

Social Change in the Larger Context

We have been examining a model of social reality with regard to its applicability in specific cases. One of the assumptions implicit in the Schutz model is that change itself, as far as the social order is concerned, is at first largely unintentional and thus probably incremental. This, we have shown, results from the fact that common-sense humans act in a typical pre-interpreted ways even though the environmental conditions may be changing. Their actions, based in their subjective reality, tend to exert some force to bring the manifest reality into line with their view of it. But since they have knowledge of and control only a small portion of the larger environment, the possibilities of unintended change are always present, and this is the maladjustment about which Lippmann speaks.

The discussion up to now has prepared the ground for filling out the multi-aspect model of the social order. The Schutz model, it will be recalled, was sufficient to predict relatively small changes that might not necessarily produce a significant change in the typical subjective reality of the actors themselves. As the Richardson and Rapoport mathematical examples demonstrate, this might be sufficient to account for long run, perhaps repetitive trends of cumulative social change. Meanwhile, Rapoport's main argument, indeed, the publication of his book, is a demonstration of how change not accounted for in the Schutz model might be provoked in the typical subjective reality of the important actors on the international political scene. Rapoport is offering a new image, which, however, is, communicated as a physical or environmental 'event' - the manifest appearance of his book, his reasoning. Since the political and military leaders may be exposed to, perceive, and be influenced by this information, a series of such manifest events, i.e., more publications, demonstrations, arguments, ever more destructive armaments, etc., might produce a change in the *meaningful* aspects which would gradually be translated into modified intentions and actions that could ultimately result in an altered manifest reality.

Generalizing on the specific case, we may describe the over-all process of change. The three interrelated modes of social reality are referred to as the *meaningful* aspect, the *intentional* aspect and the *environmental* aspect. The *meaningful* aspect is defined as the code of ethics, the vision, the organizing concept, the set of images of self, society and nature, and may be thought of as the level of 'actionless' meaning. The *intentional* aspect, which derives from the *meaningful* aspect, is the human implementation of values and images, and their translation into typical courses of action, and may be thought of as the level of rehearsal, deliberation and plan. The *environmental* aspect, which derives from the *intentional* aspect, is the field or ground of facts and events, both social and natural, resulting in large part from the encounter of the intentional actions of humans with each other and with the structured order of nature and society. The *environmental* aspect may be thought of as the level of 'meaningless' action (See Figure 5.1).

The manner of influence is not causal nor is there an absolute correspondence among the three aspects implied. In each case the succeeding aspect grows out of the preceding one in a process of selection, interpretation and experimentation that is more or less typical for any social group in a given context at a particular time. Thus, it is not possible to say that variable A which is a value in the *meaningful* aspect will cause or even necessarily co-vary with variable A' which is a typical intention related to A but within the *intentional* aspect, although there will undoubtedly be some correspondence. In other words, the *meaningful* aspect becomes the *intentional* through human deliberation and through orientation to action. Since this process is only humanly rational and not scientifically so, it will be oriented not to the sum total of possibilities in the environment, but to the interpretation of those possibilities based upon past experience and resting in the *meaningful* aspect.

Just as meaning becomes intention through a human process of rehearsal and plan, so intention becomes action (or a decision not to act) in a process of interaction with the environment. The *environmental* aspect expresses the intentional act of an individual or group in relation to the intentional acts of others on the same scene, as well as in relation to the structure or order of nature that is pertinent within that context. The feedback through observation of the environment, which is channeled through the *meaningful* aspect results in a constant reassessment of intention even while the action, itself, is in progress (Miller, Galanter and Pribram 1960). Thus the intention governs the action, yet never fully realizes itself. It "...carries along its horizon of empty anticipations" (Schutz 1962b, p.72). So likewise does selective perception and retention of the environment produce the meaningful aspect. Experience tells us what to perceive and how to perceive it. In the process this perception becomes incorporated in our experience and helps to determine what we will perceive in the future. Thus while what is in the environment will condition perception, it will not dictate by itself what will be selected and how it will be interpreted.

We have outlined a cycle which is a continuous process engaged in by the members of a social group, a process which in its shared typicality is common to all those members. This process is more or less integrated, depending primarily upon the scope of the environmental aspect. In closed traditional societies the social and natural environments incorporated in the three modes of social reality are strictly limited, in the first place by the small numbers of human actors and social situations that could be encountered, and secondly by the very restricted proportion of nature which is brought under the control of intentional human action itself (and not left to chance or the will of the gods). In modern open societies the numbers of fellow humans and their actions that have to be contended with, both directly and indirectly, are so great that adjustment in the three modes is almost a continuous process for those who wish to participate in the larger society. In addition, control of the natural environment is extensive and relegated to highly specialized actors whose actions are beyond the understanding, let alone interpretation, of most of the commonsense fellow humans in the same society. The result is a greater distance between the three aspects of any social group, and a greater likelihood that changes in its environment will go unnoticed and uninterpreted for longer stretches of time. The greater complexity of the *environmental* aspect demands more complex, hierarchical organization of the images in the *meaningful* aspect and hence more highly differentiated intentions and plans.

It is for these reasons that social change is seen most often as arising in the *environmental* aspect. Changes in the meaningful and intentional aspects lag behind. Over-all change evolves in a process whereby specific successful solutions to minor problems, though largely typical, gradually create behavioral trends, which themselves encourage slightly more innovative behavior. This behavior may gradually become inconsistent with the higher levels of the subjective reality or *meaningful* aspect. In this case personal maladjustment and efforts at reducing the inconsistencies gradually alter the images, especially at the lowest levels. An example of this process can be seen in Gunnar Myrdal's observations on the Welfare State:

> No development has been more unplanned than the gradual emergence and the increasing importance of planning in all the Western countries. Ideas and ideologies, theories and propaganda, political programs and political action directed consciously towards promoting planning, have played an altogether insignificant role...While admittedly the state and citizen, step by step, have been taking over more and more responsibility for the direction and control of economic life, they have been led by events, not by conscious choice (Myrdal, 1960, p.19).

This should not, however, be interpreted to mean that events cause change or that they are somehow removed from the human actors who produce these events, but rather, that the accumulation of events which constitutes social, as distinguished from individual, change, is a product of subjective reinterpretation of the manifest reality by successive numbers of individuals whose actions are changing in response to these new images, and who may or may not be intending social change as such. Opinion leaders interested in change may play a critical role in this process by emphasizing and communicating their changed world-view, thus acting as catalysts among an expanding group of changing individuals, although social change does not depend necessarily upon any formal process of persuasion. Likewise, key decision-makers -- those with power to influence the actions of others in a society or social group -- have more than normal influence over events relating to change. Thus, in the Rapoport example cited above, political and military leaders could alter the cumulative trend toward war by decisions that would minimize competitiveness, i.e., by decisions *not* to increase arms supplies, etc. But social change may also occur in spite of or in opposition to such decisions, as the large-scale opposition to the Vietnam War illustrated.

The problem of studying change within a social group is then one of identifying changes, often in the form of emerging trends (which may themselves arise from contact with other social groups), within the *environmental* aspect of the group. At the same time, the *meaningful* aspect must be surveyed for the stock of values and images that would probably be drawn upon by that group to meet the changing conditions of the environment or that would imply similar change in the future. This analysis could be continued through a series of future states resulting from successive interactions of meaning, intention, and action, to attempt to foresee when and if changes in the environment might reach crisis proportion, i.e., when major alterations in images might be necessary and likely. Finally, the range of such innovations in meaning available to the group either from its own "deviants," e.g., scientists, poets, messianic leaders, etc., or from outside the group, e.g., the larger, international stock of scientific or spiritual images, must be surveyed for those that might, on the one hand, be more compatible with the existing subjective reality, and on the other hand, be likely to solve the crisis or series of crises that could be anticipated. Thus the cycle could be entered again to see where the intended actions would lead in efforts to produce a new *environmental* aspect. The actual search for appropriate new images would likewise have to allow for the characteristic ways in which people change their values and opinions. This would involve consideration of the nature of the communication processes of the group, the types of influence of opinion leaders, the level of sophistication of images with which the members of the group could deal, and so forth (Rogers 1962).

Thus social change arises out of the nexus of a changing environment and a continuous re-interpretation of that environment by the human actors whose combined actions produce the environmental changes in the first place. Efforts at re-orientation generally proceed from the lower to the higher orders within the *meaningful aspect*. Accurate information about the environment aids that search, which emphasizes the importance of effective communication. Meanwhile, the potential open-mindedness of modern societies, coupled with an ever more elaborated and sophisticated stock of images, decreases the need for and likelihood of abrupt, large scale changes in the *meaningful* and hence *intentional* aspect, in part because of the built-in flexibility of choice afforded by a wider range of past experiences. Hence, lower order or non-revolutionary change is for the most part continuous though gradual, marked along the way by successive minor shifts in direction and timing that can be fully appreciated only from a perspective on society that accounts for human involvement in that process.

Figure 5.1: The Dialectic of Social Change

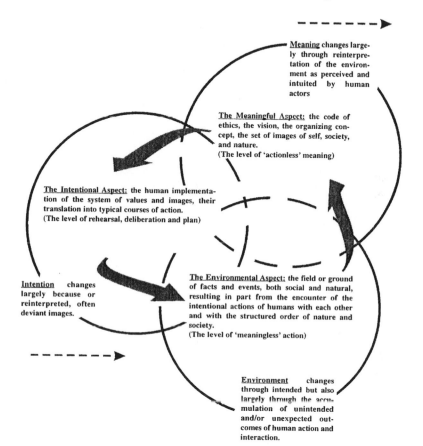

Meaning changes large-
ly through reinterpre-
tation of the environ-
ment as perceived and
intuited by human
actors

The Meaningful Aspect: the code of
ethics, the vision, the organizing concept, the set of images of self, society,
and nature.
(The level of 'actionless' meaning)

The Intentional Aspect: the human implementation of the system of values and images, their
translation into typical courses of action.
(The level of rehearsal, deliberation and plan)

Intention   changes
largely because or
reinterpreted, often
deviant images.

The Environmental Aspect: the field or ground
of facts and events, both social and natural,
resulting in part from the encounter of the
intentional actions of humans with each other
and with the structured order of nature and
society.
(The level of 'meaningless' action)

Environment   changes
through intended but also
largely through the accu-
mulation of unintended
and/or unexpected out-
comes of human action and
interaction.

CHAPTER 6

THE SOCIAL STRUCTURE OF HEALTH AND DISEASE *

Inasmuch as a scientific approach to disease is less than 150 years old, the idea that the fatefulness of disease could be moderated by human action is quite recent in human history and probably not shared by all the world's population even today. The idea that human behavior could actually create disease, as well as be instrumental in promoting its spread, is even more novel. Yet William McNeill's (1976) account of the history of infectious disease and its importance to the success of European imperialism over the past four to five hundred years clearly shows the extent to which such an idea should be closely examined.

The stimulus for imperialism, apart from the technological advances in navigation and armaments that made it possible, was the development of industrial capitalism in Western Europe. The success of this unplanned but highly successful economic system produced a parallel explosion in knowledge, including scientific knowledge about nature. At some point scientific inquiry was turned to the biological processes that attended disease. Following the discoveries of Pasteur and Koch, and particularly in the 20th century, science has been very successful in controlling infectious disease.

Unfortunately, modern medicine, inspired by these early successes and by the developing positivist paradigm of natural science, now often acts as an impediment to the further understanding of human health and disease (Navarro 1980). It fails to take account of the intimate relationship between poverty and disease (Hall, E. 1979), and to

---

* Reprinted with permission from Gerald Gutenschwager (1984) "The Social Stucture of Health and Disease", in *Greek Review of Social Research,* Vol. 53, pp 24-49 (in Greek).

be concerned about devising health care strategies that will prevent disease at its source, i.e., the social or man-made environment that gives rise to it. It is true that complex forms of modern society tend to obscure the manner in which health and disease are social problems. Certain types of ill health such as occupational disease are easily recognized as human products, and certain segments of the medical community are more sensitive than others to the social implications of ill health. Nevertheless, the prevailing attitude, and certainly medical training, tend to perceive health as a problem more or less exclusively within the realm of natural science. There is considerable resistance to any broadening of the scope of health care beyond the now conventional pharmacological and surgical intervention, particularly within the medical profession. This is true in spite of the fact that a social perspective on medicine has been a serious concern since the early nineteenth century and has probably been as important as the germ theory in conquering the infectious diseases that have preoccupied medical workers since that time (McKeown 1976).

Sanitary engineering and improvements in nutrition and family planning were, according to McKeown (1976), the important factors accounting for the long-term decline in mortality from infectious diseases. These improvements can be traced to gradual adjustments by the new capitalist social order, some a product of its success such as the increase in food production, and some a victory over its neglect, such as the successful political struggle for the reform of sanitary conditions (Ringen 1979). Many solutions predated the microbiological discoveries of Pasteur and Koch, as well as the subsequent experimental work that established the basic principles of the germ theory of disease. This in no way diminishes the continuing importance of the germ theory nor its applications to disease control before and after the discovery of antibiotics. Rather, it is to emphasize that social medicine did not await such precise laboratory understanding in order to accomplish significant improvement in the state of the health of the populations served by its understandings and reforms.

Social Theory and Disease

Historical work in social medicine (as well as conventional knowledge in evolution theory and genetics) demonstrates that traditional or slowly changing societies are marked by a gradual adaptation to their environments. They also adapt to their own behavior as a social structure often as determinant as the physical environment in which they find themselves. Selectivity thus operates both in the relationship between human organisms and their physical environment, and in the relationship between these organisms and their social environment. The sickle cell as a defense against malaria would be an example of the former, while the evolution of the equilibrium between human host and microbiological parasite under the conditions of commerce as described by McNeill would be an example of the latter[1]. Thus all societies may create and institutionalize social practices that constitute a maladaptation between selected individuals and their physical environments with the resulting potential loss of those types of individuals from the population. In this way modern societies sacrifice a portion of their populations to heart disease, cancer, accidents, etc., largely because of the social structures that characterize them.

The assumption that the health of a population results from the intersection between society and nature suggests a particular perspective on the problem of health. Human populations do not only adapt to natural environments in active and passive ways, but also have the possibility of creating and changing those environments, with or without information concerning the health implications of those changes. Whether or how a population uses information about health problems, deriving from its own behavior, which has created or modified its environment, is related to how that population is structured socially. This depends in particular on whether it is a population with a consciousness of its own power to change that environment if it wishes. This in turn is related to

---

1. McNeill (1976, p.7) further states that: ". . . the slow processes of evolution apply to human societies and their symbolic systems as much as to human bodies, so that when logic cannot decide, survival eventually will. Terms that direct attention to the critically useful facets of a situation clearly do have enormous survival value for human beings. It is this aspect of our capacity to communicate with one another that has allowed Homo Sapiens to become such a dominant species." It is for this reason that it is so important to broaden the analysis of health and disease to include the social as well as biomedical perspective.

the way in which knowledge is structured in a society, with the question of who controls it, who may have access to it and who may 'understand' it. In short, however dramatic the contribution of either medicine or laboratory science to the understanding of human health, if there are no *institutional* means for translating this knowledge into social behavior which alters the conditions leading to ill health, the health problems will remain. Furthermore, so long as the medical profession has a vested interest in a biomechanistic definition of human phenomena related to health, it will be bound to emphasize therapeutic and preventive measures within such a framework. It will also be at a loss to confront problems for which there are no such techniques. To the extent that disease problems surpass this framework, health is not only a medical problem, but is also a problem of social theory and related social action.

There are two separate but related problems confronting an attempt to define disease as a social problem. One is sociological, having to do with understanding a social formation or the way in which a society is ordered, resources allocated, production and consumption organized, behavior institutionalized, etc. The other is epistemological, having to do with how knowledge about the social formation and about disease as a social problem is to be gained.

To illustrate, modern medicine generally perceives mortality and morbidity in a natural science framework. Causal explanations by and large end at the level of the organism with epidemiology suggesting strategies for experimental research that will ultimately pin down the 'true' causes of disease. The idea that societies will actually *produce* different disease patterns is only of preliminary interest at best to this perspective. Thus to explain disease as a social problem one must first outline a theoretical framework within which this effort may take place. Involved would be the question of whether society is to be perceived as a black box, where only inferences about variables may establish cause and effect relationships, or whether conscious human participation in disease causation may be addressed as an issue in its own right, quite apart from the bio-medical evolution of any disease process.

The contention here is that disease processes may be seen to originate in human behavior, and that a non-mechanistic socio-theoretical framework is required to explain the origins of that behavior and the resulting patterns of disease. Thus, an attempt will be made to illustrate how the structure of organization of modern capitalist society leads to the predominance of certain forms of ill health, just as former social formations created their own characteristic diseases. The argument will take the form of an application of dialectic structuralism to the problem of health and disease. This will require first the establishment of a theoretical-historical framework and subsequently application of this framework to modern capitalist society in relation to the problem of health. The first effort will be to review briefly the history of social formations leading to modern industrial capitalism and to recall some of the health patterns peculiar to each of those formations, and then to concentrate more specifically on the patterns of illness related to capitalist society today (Navarro, 1978).

Institutionalization of Disease Risk Behavior

A basic argument advanced here is that society creates health problems by institutionalizing certain forms of disease-risk behavior. Institutionalization refers to the human origins of the established order in any social setting. It is an order that is constructed or abstracted as a logical extension of the habitualization of successful behavior (See Chapter 2). Over time, habitual behavior becomes institutionalized first by generally succeeding in its purposes and second by being passed along through succeeding generations in the process of socialization. Socialization refers to the process of establishing appropriate behavior among the young through the use of rewards and punishment on the one hand, and the use of a canopy of symbols to explain that behavior, on the other. These symbols are embodied in language and serve to legitimize a particular social world. They establish a 'symbolic universe' in which it is proper and appropriate that the world be organized in *this* way, that behavior be in *this* form rather than in some other. Societies of great complexity can thus be organized and controlled by controlling the symbols that define and legitimize the reality of that society. Disease-risk behavior can therefore be institutionalized far beyond the reach of any well-meaning medical profession or enlightened citizenry. The individual may have a marginal, though not unimportant freedom within the institutionalized world, but it is a freedom that depends upon the rare ability to grasp the manner in which social reality is constructed, rare because institutionalizing processes are not likely to be also self-critical. To alter them often requires confrontation with no less than one's own identity.

The seriousness of this confrontation with social identity can be

appreciated by understanding the manner in which it is tied to the material base of society, for a social order does not arise out of thin air. As noted
above, it arises gradually and continuously out of the successes and failures of the human endeavor to survive. One must, however, expand the
references to the historical evolution of a set of practices and priorities
that govern the basic ways of producing and consuming goods and services and the social relations involved; in short, the extraction of things
from nature and their transformation into usable entities. This is the material base from which the institutionalized interdependencies of the social
order are inescapably derived. Since material production must be perpetuated if a society is to survive, one can begin to grasp the urge to determinism that is inherent in all socialization and institutionalization. But, in
order to turn these basic sociological principles into a useful historical
analysis, one must answer the question as to why a particular social structure and its corresponding definition of reality are found in a particular
time and place. The abstract concepts that explain social reality must be
given concrete form; they must be placed in a historical context.

The History of Western Social Formations

As Western society has developed its institutionalized world, it has
produced a modern technological order that has grown out of the past in
a history characterized by a gradual progression from small scale agrar-
ian to a mass industrial society. What marks this progression since the
earliest recorded history is a continuous elaboration in the production of
surplus. Hunting and gathering societies were known to have little surplus and, therefore, little ability to increase production and accumulation. Population densities were limited, and mortality and morbidity
patterns were characterized by gradual adaptations to environmental
factors, including serious nutritional deficiencies (Boyden 1970).
Historically, infectious diseases may have wiped out entire hunting and
gathering settlements, but rarely found the population density thresh-
olds necessary to form chronic patterns (McNeil 1976, p.53).

The first real surpluses were created in the agricultural societies
formed along the great flood plains of the Nile, the Tigrus and the
Euphrates, the Indus and the Yangtze Rivers, starting from 7,000 to 5,000
B.C. Here fifty or more agricultural workers were needed to produce the
surplus necessary to support a single person, but this was sufficient to cre-

ate a class of people who exercised control over the production process and over the lives of those engaged in production. This control was ultimately formalized as the slave society, which also was marked by advances in technology and by elaborations in social organization.

Subsequent developments in production resulted in important changes in social form. The specialization of tasks in society created a gradual division of labor, which over time increased the interdependencies among the various members and classes of society. This division of labor and these interdependencies were in turn reflected in an increasing need for exchange and ultimately in the development of the market. The market, and commerce in general, facilitated communication and exchange, including the exchange of disease pools[2]. Because of the concentrations of population and their increased contacts, infectious diseases reached epidemic proportions, first in the Mediterranean and later in other parts of the urban world. Thus, as specialized goods were first bartered and subsequently impersonalized as commodities to be bought and sold, so also was disease brought to a new level of exchange. The evolving division of labor and the resulting formalization of exchange through the use of money were to have profound effects upon subsequent human history, even while disease was preying upon these urbanizing and developing populations.

Once goods and services were transformed into commodities, whose sole function was to be exchanged for other commodities and whose exchange value was then abstracted as money, the nature of human society was transformed. A new class of merchants set as its sole objective the accumulation of profit or surplus with little concern for the nature of the commodities that were being exchanged (Kay 1975). Mercantilism in turn encouraged improvements in the technology and efficiency of production, which in time created a class of industrial producers who were solely concerned with the production system.

The production system, as the term implies, is more complex than

---

2. According to McNeill (1976, p.55), "Person to person 'civilized' types of infectious diseases could not have established themselves much before 3000 B.C. When they did get going, however, different infections established themselves among different civilized communities in Eurasia. Proof of this fact is that when communications between previously isolated civilized communities became regular and organized, just before and after the Christian era, devastating infections soon spread from one civilization to another. . ."

exchange. It includes, in addition to the technology of production, the industrial labor force itself (including the workers' skills, education, welfare etc.), all of which have an ultimate bearing upon production. Thus, while the spirit of accumulation marked the birth of industrialism, it was tempered, in part, by broader concerns. In the first place the industrial accumulation was derived from the more formal and complex relationship between owners and workers. Surplus was gained not from buying cheap and selling dear but from selling the product for more than it cost to make it. If this production surplus or profit were too great it would threaten the welfare of the workers and be reflected in lower productivity, besides threatening the ability of the workers to buy the commodities that were produced.

Thus, in time the industrial bourgeoisie developed some concern about the health of its population since it became fairly obvious that the production of surplus and the long run success of accumulation would depend on that population. This may in part explain the successes of Chadwick and other reformers in bringing about the sanitary reforms in nineteenth century Europe, with the attendant first real success in dealing with disease as a social problem among concentrated urban populations. While it is probably true that diseases were evolving and adapting along with their human hosts, it was industrial capitalism that brought the first concentrated effort to deal with disease on a societal level[3]. At the same time industrialism also benefitted from and encouraged and supported science, which in turn produced the first real understanding of disease mechanisms in the human body.

---

3. As Knut Ringen (1979, p.14) points out, this concern by the industrial bourgeoisie for the health of its workers was as much political as medical. "The health conditions were leading to a radicalization of the working class, he [Chadwick] said, for the epidemic diseases were weeding out those older members of the working class who had a 'responsible' view of the relationship between capital and labor, and the unions were being taken over by ' . . . a population that is young, ignorant, credulous, irritably passionate and dangerous'. . . Chadwick . . . felt strongly that sanitary reform was one means to stabilize a potentially revolutionary working class." In addition, however, it was clear that the urbanization attendant upon the growth of the industrial capitalism both encouraged the conditions for epidemic diseases and increased the social overhead costs for dealing with their effects, to say nothing of the fact that in a city, after all, the wealthy may be as susceptible as the poor to vector borne disease.

Figure 6.1: The Social Structure of Health and Disease

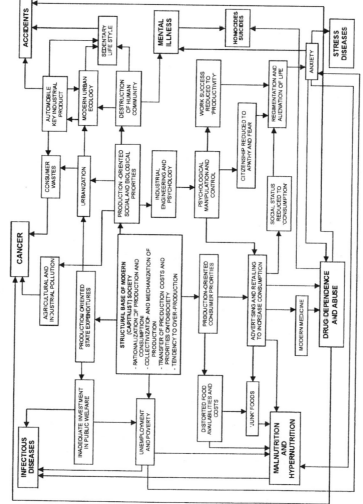

Disease Risk under Modern Capitalism

Today we find ourselves with a set of modern priorities, which represent the cumulative 'wisdom' of this long historical progression. These priorities are summarized in the center box of the diagram.

STRUCTURAL BASE OF MODERN (CAPITALIST) SOCIETY
- RATIONALIZATION OF PRODUCTION AND CONSUMPTION - COLLECTIVIZATION AND MECHANI-ZATION OF PRODUCTION - TRANSFER OF PRODUCTION COSTS AND PRIORITIES ONTO SOCIETY - TENDENCY TO OVER-PRODUCTION

Their wisdom focuses upon a narrowly defined rational order of social and economic life in which domination plays a key ideological and instrumental role (Leiss 1974). The human and biological implications of this rational order are only dimly perceived by the theorists who provide the key symbols that legitimize modern society.

Jacques Ellul (1964) characterizes this technological society as one

PRODUCTION-ORIENTED SOCIAL AND BIOLOGICAL PRIORITIES

given to over-standardization, rationalization, resolving in advance, reliance on method (not individuals), and the machine as the ideal or prototypical form. Political-economic theory has been replaced by methods and techniques such as econometrics, accounting, input/output, modelling,

INDUSTRIAL ENGINEERING AND PSYCHOLOGY

etc., and society has been reduced to an aggregate of probabilities and utilities. Individual behavior is anticipated (and manipulated) through opinion polls and various psychological techniques.

Anxiety and Stress

These polls and techniques are all pervasive in modern capitalist society and they influence a good deal of behavior that places individuals at risk for disease. In other words, alcoholism, smoking, drug abuse, improper diet, lack of exercise, stress, even accidents are not simply chance occurrences. It is clear that a great deal of money is being spent to encourage people to smoke, to drink, to eat junk food,

PSYCHOLOGICAL MANIPULATION AND CONTROL

to drive big, fast cars, and so forth. There are people who work very hard to encourage others (and often themselves) to engage in this kind of behavior. The advertising industry, for example, is a multi-million dollar industry composed of businessmen, social scientists, and artists. The businessmen are pragmatic, hardheaded and sophisticated account- ants. They watch the weekly effects of their investments and do not make random decisions about advertising and marketing (Ewen 1976). Psychologists are also very important in the consumer society. They know the structure of stimulus-response and reward and punishment, and they use the accumulated experimental and theoretical knowledge of psychology in an effort to persuade people to engage in what often amounts to disease risk behavior (McChesney and Foster 2003).

Finally, there are the commercial artists, the people who are the technicians of the aesthetic, and more significantly from the standpoint of per- suasion, the dramatic; those who under-

PRODUCTION-ORIENTED CONSUMER PRIORITIES

stand, in other words, the importance of 'sociodramatic form' (Duncan 1962). This form depends upon the natural cycle of introduction, ten- sion, climax, and relax, a form that we find throughout nature and in the art of all societies. As an application in advertising, for example, we have 'the lady next door' who discovers dirt on her husband's shirt. The laundry soap is presented, the shirt goes in the washing machine, and voilà, the shirt is clean. Or a more subtle kind of sociodramatic form: a large billboard which may be seen in many black neighborhoods in the U.S.A., a billboard all in black with a beautiful, reclining black woman and a black man leaning over her. This sign is advertising Black Velvet whiskey, and the slogan underneath says, "Try Black Velvet on your neighbor!" One possible extension of these techniques of persuasion was described in a book called *Subliminal Seduction* (Key 1974), which outlined the extremes to which advertising persuasion might be carried. In short, consumerism constitutes one form of institutionalized behav- ior, which places people at risk for disease and health.

Consumerism is, however, but a recent aberration in human society, effective in persuading individuals who have been separated from their traditional reference groups. The basic material and ideological forces designed to isolate individ-

ADVERTISING AND RETAILING TO INCREASE CONSUMPTION

uals, to destroy the primary group and the human community, have been at work for centuries. It was the gradual metamorphosis of the products of labor in the marketplace and ultimately of labor itself into *commodities* that marked the transformation to a modern capitalist society. Bookchin (1974) describes this transformation to

> a society that dissolves the natural basis of civic life by transmuting the fraternal relations of the medieval commune into harsh commodity relations . . . with the enormous physic a well as economic changes that were to be introduced by the capitalist mode of production. The commodity, like a mysterious external force, now seems to rise above men and determine their destiny according to a suprahuman autonomous law. With the increasingly problematic abstractions of labor from its concrete forms, all relations, objects and responsibilities acquire a monetary equivalent. Natural life shrinks from the community to the individual; the city becomes a mere aggregate of isolated human monads - a grey featureless mass, the raw materials of bureaucratic mobilization and manipulation . . . With the emergence of a highly monetized economy, human beings become interchangeable with the very wares that are the result of their human powers. They too become commodities, the passive objects - whether as workers or spectators - of economic laws.

> **DESTRUCTION OF HUMAN COMMUNITY**

While these material forces were at work, the philosophers were preparing the ideological base for the new social order. Macpherson (1962) analyzes seventeenth century English thought from Hobbes to Locke in which the basic philosophy of 'possessive individualism' was first carefully laid out. These philosophers cleverly sought what amounts to a metaphysical basis for individualism and for the class order evolving in capitalist society at that time, Ironically, they sought this basis in physical nature, drawing upon their interpretation of the 'laws of nature' as a basis for the 'nature' of society. Accumulation and accumulative behavior were thus claimed by Locke to be rational and natural within the " . . . condition of human life [which] necessarily introduces private possession of land and materials to work on" (Macpherson 1962, p. 236). Furthermore, the class order that was derived from this accumulative behavior, where advantages of any kind were turned to the expropriation of others' labor, was considered to be equally natural. Thus, society as it appeared to these philosophers, with its basic division into property owners and propertyless workers, was well within the appropriate order of things and derivable, according to their logic, from natural law.

More recently, Social Darwinism (Hofstadter 1959) has provided the ideological basis for an alienated class society. This vulgar interpretation of biological law has rationalized much of the twentieth century exploitation that characterizes the capitalist social order.

> **UNEMPLOYMENT AND POVERTY**

Individuals find their place in society according to their 'natural' abilities. If the material conditions of the more advantaged are superior it is because they are endowed with superior abilities. Life is a struggle for the upper hand, each individual pitted against every other in order to survive (Goulet 1971).

Insofar as these principles order the behavior of individuals, separating and alienating them from one another, it is not surprising to find that stress diseases, mental illness, and drug dependence and abuse are among today's most common dis-

> **WORK SUCCESS REDUCED TO 'PRODUCTIVITY'**

eases. The main source of stress can be found in the workplace. Work has been reduced to a set of mechanical operations, which, as Ellul (1964) says, imply an absence rather than a presence. Here the clock is the most important invention. Once time has been quantified, workers can be ordered and controlled; they become extensions, indeed, are organized as models of the machines that determine their work and lives. But control does not end here. Entire professional disciplines -- industrial engineering and industrial psychology - devote themselves to the development of techniques for the manipulation and control of the work process. Incentive systems are invented to pit workers against each other in competition for prizes, all the while increasing production. Lie detectors, wiretapping, and psychological testing are used to

> discover and weed out employees with potential personal and family problems, undesirable personal characteristics like aggressiveness or inquisitiveness, and union sympathies (Dollars and Sense 1979).

These techniques are part of a long tradition to create a "flexible labor force . . . manipulated as required by the opportunities for investment and profit" (Eyer and Stirling 1977). This labor force began to move from the small-scale communities in the countryside to the market and subsequently industrial towns

> **URBANIZATION**

in England and northwest Europe as early as the fifteenth and sixteenth centuries. Rural-to-urban migration and the breakdown of the small scale community has characterized capitalist development since that time, and can be seen today in continuing south-to-north worker migrations in Europe and North America. These migrants, isolated from their communities, are isolated even further by language and cultural barriers and by the advancing specialization in the work process itself. Capitalism and industrial engineering add further impetus to the competitive, aggressive and hence fragmenting and diminished existence of the working class, which finds itself increasingly under the impact of physiological and psychological arousal without any means of resolving this tension.

Even as consumers of the products of their labor, these twentieth century populations were unable to experience the relaxation of this tension. They were coaxed

> **SOCIAL STATUS REDUCED TO 'CONSUMPTION'**

and goaded to an endless striving for the 'good life', toward ever higher standards of material well being. Retailing and merchandising were revolutionized in the United States (as well as in Europe) with an emphasis on packaging and impulse buying. Complemented by an ever more sophisticated advertising technology and an elaborate credit system, the modern production system has created a consumer to suit its own needs. This is a consumer whose emotional needs can only (yet never) be satisfied through con-

> **CITIZENSHIP REDUCED TO APATHY AND FEAR**

sumer goods, a consumer isolated from all social interaction by an ever more pervasive mass media that commercializes and trivializes all feeling and thought. This cultural domination is amplified worldwide through commercialization of the broadcast media (Schiller

> **REGIMENTATION AND ALIEN-ATION OF LIFE**

1976). The metropolitan centers provide 'entertainment' and the advertising messages that surround it. The content of both generates anxiety, relating either to sexual inadequacies and fantasies or to the romanticization of power and violence. Political

> **ANXIETY**

affairs are reported as mindless events, and in-depth reports provide 'all sides' and no bases for judgement about why things occur.

Drug Dependence and Abuse

The overall effect of these cultural forces is reflected in the alienating and mindless producer, consumer and political roles that reduce the average citizen to apathy and fear. The anxiety that derives from this feeling of powerlessness is reflected in increasing rates of alcoholism and drug abuse, including especially smoking. Respiratory diseases, particularly lung cancer, heart disease, stroke and cirrhosis of the liver are directly related to these dependencies and are among the leading causes of death in industrial countries.

The tobacco industry, which in the United States alone sold over $17 billion worth of tobacco products in 1978, spends millions of dollars on advertising each year and hundreds of thousands on direct political lobbying. Nicotine, a physically addictive drug, works directly on the central nervous system. As Gwenda Blair (1979, p.33) says,

> Cigarettes provide the ideal solution to the tedium of routine lower-level jobs. At about ten minutes apiece (plus occasional coffee breaks to give the day a few high points), smokes not only help pace out a day - on the production line, in the typing pool, behind a lunch line - but they give you a steady flow of small rewards to keep on trucking. No wonder, according to the U.S. Department of Agriculture, cigarettes are the first luxury item poor people buy.

The alcohol industry, too, works hard to promote dependency. Most of the examples from Key's book *Subliminal Seduction* were taken from the alcohol industry. At one point Anheuser-Busch, one

DRUG DEPENDENCE AND ABUSE

of the largest brewers in the world, briefly introduced Chelsea, a new soft drink for children, which foams like beer when poured. Its 0.4% alcohol placed it just outside the limits of alcoholic beverages, but the intent was clearly to capture future addicts early in their lives.

The number of women alcoholics is also increasing in the United States, where they constitute half of the estimated 10 million addicts. With women, alcoholism is often combined with abuse of prescription drugs, particular-

MODERN MEDICINE

ly psychotropic drugs, anti-depressants, and amphetamines, indicating an uncritical participation by the medical profession in fostering these dependencies (St. Louis Post-Dispatch 1977, Waldon 1977). Use of marijuana, cocaine, and heroin is also widespread among Americans, particularly within the military. The latter is not surprising, given the role of the military and paramilitary in promoting the $500 billion global narcotics industry (McCoy 1972, Fraser and Restrepo-Estrada 1998, p.24).

Mental Illness, Homicides and Suicides

   Mental illness is a complementary, sometimes corollary, response to anxiety. Advancing rates of suicide, mental hospitalization and even

> **MENTAL ILLNESS**

homicide are indications that this is also a growing problem. Dr. Harvey Brenner has shown that the state of the economy has had a great deal to do with the mental health of the population of the United States over the past cen-

> **HOMICIDES - SUICIDES**

tury (Brenner 1973). This is particularly true for the poor, who are, of course, most likely to suffer un- or under-employment even when the economy is doing well.

Stress Diseases

   Finally, for those who do not react to anxiety with drug abuse or mental illness, there is a host of stress related physical pathologies rang-

> **STRESS DISEASES**

ing from coronary heart disease to ulcers and possibly cancer. As Eyer and Stirling (1977) have demonstrated, it is primarily the young (ages 15-30) and the poor who suffer the greatest stress and corresponding elevations in death rates because of the unstable economic conditions in the capitalist world. It is they who are poorly or inappropriately trained for the increasing number of white collar or service jobs, and who are unprepared for the growing uncertainty in their sector of the job market.

> In response to this worsening of conditions, there has been a decline of marriage, increased marital breakdown, and a dramatic fall in the birth rate, accompanied by a rise of illegitimacy. These changes are themselves further sources of stress (Eyer and Sterling 1977, p.31).

Accidents

Drug abuse has the further misfortune of correlating highly with motor vehicle accidents. This is true, of course, because of the supreme importance of the automobile in the capitalist world. In 1973 there were 3.5 million workers in the automobile industry worldwide and together they produced upwards of 40 million cars in that year (Bloomfield 1978). General Motors at one time had an annual budget ·exceeded by only a half-a-dozen countries in the world. The automobile has completely transformed the western city and is increasingly altering cities all over the world in the same way. Eighty percent of Americans depend upon the automobile for their journey to work. The automobile determines urban residential patterns and even commercial and industrial patterns.

MODERN URBAN ECOLOGY

AUTOMOBILE KEY INDUSTRIAL PRODUCT

This 20th century transformation of the city would not have occurred without a significant intervention by the state at all levels. The automobile runs on channels - public streets and highways - that are provided by the state. This substantial investment is hidden from the car buyer though it is collected ultimately through a series of taxes. As a means of public conveyance the automobile is the least efficient in terms of person-costs per distance travelled. Furthermore, hundreds of thousands of individuals are killed and injured every year because of automobiles, and nearly everywhere where pollution is a problem, the automobile is a serious contributor.

ACCIDENTS

The tremendous costs of pollution and accidents are borne by the people of capitalist societies so that this critical industry can survive; and the cost is borne willingly and eagerly because the automobile adds yet another attractive means of escape from the alienated life of these societies. As a final irony, the automobile contributes to an increasingly sedentary lifestyle, which is more and more recognized as a contributor to heart disease and stroke.

SEDENTARY LIFE STYLE

Cancer

As societies develop and industrialize, the state at all levels more and more mediates this process. Under socialism this role was formal-

| PRODUCTION-ORIENTED STATE EXPENDITURES |

ized and the attendant responsibilities were clearly recognized, but under capitalism this has occurred in a much more haphazard way. Nevertheless, the state in capitalist societies regulates the economic process and therefore participates in the distribution of the benefits and costs of this process as much as in socialist countries. The philosophy of liberalism and neoclassic economic theory tend to obfus-

| CONSUMER WASTES |

cate this role by referring to it as 'government intervention', but monopoly business knows well its importance. The provision of streets and highways mentioned above is one example of this. Equally important is the management and regulation of the production process in relation to the overall social welfare of society. In the industrialized and industrializing countries, the contradictions between production and welfare are seen in the health costs of pollution and occupational hazards. It is widely agreed for example, that pollution of various kinds accounts for the majority of cancer deaths. In 1977, the World Health Organization estimated that each year 4.5 million people were dying of cancer worldwide and that six million were developing the disease. For Europe where the data are quite reliable, it was estimated that 14 million died during the 1970's.

One of the leading causes of this large number of cancer deaths may be the increasing use of nuclear energy. A 1978 study by Ernest Sternglass of the University of Pittsburgh Medical School showed that increases in cancer rates were greater in the less urbanized and otherwise less polluted states, which, however, had greater development of nuclear power (*Mother Jones* 1978). Nuclear power is deadly in all

| AGRICULTURAL AND INDUSTRIAL POLLUTION |

stages of its development and use (Caldicott 1979). Mining emits a radioactive gas called radon, which is inhaled by the miners, and mining produces huge piles of waste, which again produce radon. But the enrichment and fuel fabrication process are the most dangerous, for here the deadly plutonium is produced. Plutonium also enters the lungs of its victims. With a half-life of 24,000 years it can produce cancer over and over again for countless generations. Breeder reactors continuously increase the amount of plutonium, and at this time there are no known means of permanently storing or disposing of if. Even the waste from the enrichment process contains dangerous radioactive elements such as radioactive iodine, strontium 90, cesium and other highly toxic radionuclides, all of which are cancer-causing agents.

For industrial workers, radioactive materials are but one category of hazards in their work environment. In 1978 alone, 100,000 American workers died from job-related injuries and illnesses (Shirk 1978). The National Cancer Institute and the National Institute of Environmental Sciences reported at the time that between 20 and 38 per cent of cancer deaths, or 80,000 per year, resulted from exposure to carcinogens used in industry. Asbestos was then one of the most important carcinogens, affecting over four million American workers, but there are over 2,000 other known or suspected can-

> CANCER

cer-causing agents as well. Of these, the U.S. Occupational Safety and Health Agency had regulated only 20; clearly in he United States at least, there has been no intention to resolve the production-welfare contradiction in favor of the latter.

In the developing capitalist countries the situation is even worse, for there are virtually no regulations at all. The history of occupational and environmental pollution is short, of course, so that the long run effects will take years to appear; but whereas political reformists have some margin for success in the political institutions of the metropolitan centers, in the countries of the periphery there is virtually no opportunity at all. Many of these countries are under dictatorships or threatened by them, and in any case their parliaments are often sold out to the multinational corporations. Thus, the future effects of pollution should be even more disastrous for these countries, adding to the existing burden on their inadequate welfare systems.

Infectious Diseases

In the tropical countries, in particular, the inadequacies of welfare investment are reflected in elevated mortality and morbidity rates from infectious diseases. Except for a variety of newly discovered viral diseases and several resistant strains of older infec-

> INADEQUATE INVESTMENT
> IN PUBLIC WELFARE

tions, the technology for controlling these diseases is well known. It is a technology related to immunization, nutrition and sanitary reform, and wherever these diseases are serious problems, it is the lack of this kind of investment that is important (Kane 1976).

There is good reason to believe that for developing countries, the lack of investment in public health is a direct result of imperialism, both for today and in the past (Doyal and Pannell 1976, Turshen 1977). Since the same diseases were conquered in the past in Europe and North America as a result of the improvement in the living conditions, then it must be lack of such improvements in the third world countries that accounts for their persistent importance.

| INFECTIOUS DISEASES |

Furthermore, it was mainly in those countries that had broken with the world capitalist system - Cuba, Vietnam, China - that mortality rates from infectious diseases had decreased substantially. Ironically, most third world countries have actually contributed, through their exploited labor, to the improvement of health in the imperial centers. While slavery was the most blatant example of this, the process of using third world labor for first world accumulation continues even today. A good example of this exploitation is found in the Sahel, a region along the southern edge of the Sahara in western Africa. There, periodic famines claim the lives of hundreds of thousands even while the region is exporting barley, beans, peanuts, cotton, fresh vegetables, and beef (Lappe and Collins 1977). During a drought, relief food may be coming into the Sahel on the same planes that are carrying these commercial crops out!

Malnutrition and Hypernutrition

Malnutrition and infectious diseases are closely linked, particularly in relation to infant mortality, which generally accounts for as many as half of the deaths in the third world countries. Multinational companies such as Nestle, Abott, American Home Products, Bristol-Meyers and Cow and Gate have contributed to the infant mortality rate in a particularly insidious manner. In pushing baby formula they encouraged third world mothers to accept an expensive substitute for their own milk. The special prerequisites of pure water, sterilization procedures, and exact measurements can hardly be met among these populations, many of whom are illiterate. The cost encour-

| DISTORTED FOOD AVAILABILITIES AND COSTS |

ages the mothers to dilute the formula and this, in combination with the unsanitary conditions, has resulted in a three-fold increase in infant mortality and morbidity among these 'bottle babies'. Infant malnutrition is observed after eight months instead of two years as in the past, with resulting chronic diarrhoea and other symptoms.

Thus, the multinational companies use cheap labor and unscrupulously market their goods in the third world countries, following policies that they have developed on their own poor and uneducated populations through these practices. By directing needed public investment from disease prevention they contribute more than anything else to the pattern of infectious and nutrition-related diseases throughout the world.

Since the nutrition-robbed products of the food industry are equally available throughout the world, there is a growing suspicion that various forms of hyper-- and malnutrition--related diseases plague the populations of industrial countries as well. Nutrition is likely to be one of the key variables in a prevention-oriented medical care system. That is, with the environmental dangers of pollution, stress, infection, etc., it may become increasingly necessary to defend oneself through carefully planned nutrition. Often, this may mean nothing more than returning to more traditional foods, such as the high fiber foods that were common before hyper-refining became | **'JUNK' FOODS** | necessary to protect the long shelf life of the products of the monopoly food industry. But it would also probably entail more careful long-term research on the effects of specific nutrients on aspects of human chemistry, physiology and disease pathology (Williams, R. 1971).

Meanwhile, epidemiological evidence from a host of sources implicates nutrition as a key health variable. One unusual source was a study of U.S. Navy pilots held prisoner in North Vietnam whose health was compared with a carefully selected group of non-prisoner fliers, alike in all other respects. The prisoners, who followed an austere diet and exercise program | **MALNUTRITION AND HYPERNUTRITION** | with little or no alcohol or tobacco, were significantly healthier than their 'free' controls in half a dozen areas: glandular problems, heart disease, genito-urinary disease, bone and joint difficulties, and others, including headaches (*St. Louis Post-Dispatch* 1977).

A longer-term study of mortality among Seventh Day Adventists in California showed similar results (Phillips 1975). The Adventists are vegetarians and use no alcohol or tobacco. They also have a strongly supportive socio-religious context in which these practices are encouraged and supported. In a study of 50,000 Adventists aged 35-and-over, compared to the entire California populations of the same age who died during the years 1958-65, it was found that the Adventists had mortality rates ranging from only 5 percent of the California total for mouth, throat and larynx cancer to 72 percent in the case of breast cancer. The Adventists death rate for all causes in the 35-and-over age group was 59 percent of that for the total California population with the result that Adventist men had six years more life expectancy at age 35 and women three more years than the California men and women respectively.

But Adventist behavior is abnormal in North American society, as must be the behavior of anyone seeking a healthier diet and lifestyle. More common are those who live as modern capitalism socializes them to live: in a polluted environment; under stress from traffic, work and debt; seeking escape through drugs, fantasy or consumerism; eating the junk food that is readily and cheaply available; and hoping that the probabilities that combine these risks into disease will be true for others but not for oneself.

Conclusion

In this context disease-risk behavior is no longer an abnormality. Abnormal is the person who seeks to avoid paying the heavy price for membership in modern capitalist society. Yet now humankind has the social and intellectual capacity to create a social order free of many of these risks, a capacity which it has used over the past hundred years to free itself from so many of those infectious disease risks that plagued earlier generations. A simple germ theory of disease and a mechanistic social science do not constitute the theoretical nor ideological canopy under which such a social order could be created, however. We must now begin to understand how society is like a complex tapestry, structured through our own intentions and behavior, and to examine consciously the priorities and effects inherent in that behavior.

What this implies is that health is no less a political-economic problem today than it was in Chadwick's time. The refusal of most health related professionals to see this connection and to concern themselves with understanding the disease implications of modern capitalism is one of the greatest obstacles to improved health today. While this is ironically true even for the inhabitants of advanced capitalist societies, it is grotesquely true for the less developed countries, which supply the cheap raw materials and labor to keep the advanced capitalist economies going. There the conditions of exploitation and super-exploitation (Gunder-Frank 1981) maintain pre-industrial patterns of poverty, malnutrition and disease while introducing the new forms of illness described above. It is painfully clear that only a transformation in the perception of health as a social problem in the broadest sense will allow this problem to be comprehended and solved in terms appropriate to its scale and origin.

PART THREE

PLANNING THEORY AND SOCIAL
REALITY AT THE TURN OF THE CENTURY

CHAPTER 7

SOCIAL STRUCTURES AT THE TURN OF THE CENTURY

To turn economistic, technocratic planning into a more humanistic endeavor would require attention to the ways in which society is structured at every level, from the individual to the collective. It would require treating individuals as human beings with consciousness and intention, and society as a product of that consciousness and intention, however misinformed and misdirected they may be on occasion. In fact, one major challenge for a humanistic planning would be to find ways to confront misinformation and dispel it so as to better inform collective intention and action. This would require research and understanding about the existing state of society, the forces working to structure it in various ways, forces that are often unknown or only partially understood by the people who compose, indeed create it, as well as about the existing state of social theory that seeks to explain these forces at both the individual and social level.

Informing collective intention and action is not, however, a simple technical procedure. It requires public discourse, a dialectic that can express complex technical information in humanistic terms. This requires translation, a process that is well known to artists, writers and dramatists, but suppressed in the technocratic world of positive science and bureaucratic planning. This chapter will attempt to open the path to such a discourse by looking briefly at the structures and forces that appear to characterize contemporary society at the turn of the century.

Objective Reality at the Turn of the Century

The 20th century began and ended with capitalism as the dominant force on the world scene. Its purposes, its forces, have influenced, and in most cases determined the social structures in developed and under-developed countries alike. At the beginning of the century its major forces - industrialization, urbanization and mass society generally - were the focus of concern by artists and social theorists. Gustav Le Bon's book *La Foule*, (1897) (The Crowd, or The Mob), among oth-ers, inspired much concern about the loss of tradition and of culture generally, that the evolution to mature capitalism seemed to entail. Tratner (1995) describes the ways in which major writers at the turn of the 19th century confronted these issues. Some sought a return to authoritarian structures of the past where paternalistic authoritarian leaders might supply the guidance lost in the impersonal mass socie-ty. Others, influenced by Marx's analysis of capitalism, sought a class-less, socialist solution. But more than anything, the idea of the crowd became a metaphor for the uncontrollable, the unknown and the unpredictable. Lost were both the power of tradition as a stabilizing force and the 'gentile' parliamentary debate as a means for resolving conflict.

By the end of World War I it appeared that the crowd could also be a force for positive change. Thus, as Tratner (1995, p.15) says, "before the war, many modernists and most politicians in government feared being drowned by the masses; after the war, they feared being left out of the mass movements transforming society". Thus, mass society, the characteristic form of the 20th century, would become the object of extensive analysis by social scientists and others, leading to new "techniques of representation and address [that] this analysis made possible" (Tratner 1995, p.21). Capitalism, itself, supplied the inspira-tion for these new techniques, as it sought to forestall economic crises of overproduction by turning society into a mass of consumers. The forms developed by advertising became the forms of modernist liter-ary technique, as they would ultimately become the forms of all the mass media in the 20th century.

> Advertising has shown that the mass mind is influenced by
> utterly bizarre images and words. Politicians have bor-
> rowed such tactics, moving more and more toward the

> Imagist poetry of 'sound bites' as modern media have
> become more and more mass media . . . . If we extract
> 'sound bites' from modernist works, we find moments quite
> as propagandistic, pandering, randomly violent, titillating
> and banal as anything in any ad. Modernist works are full
> of short passages that would be at home in horror movies,
> pornography, or late night TV, just as advertising juxtapos-
> es images from Shakespeare, Wagner, the Bible and T. S.
> Eliot as freely as did Eliot himself (Tratner 1995, p.27).

More revealing was the modernist belief that "if they wrote in clear, easily comprehensible, realistic forms, they would be disconnected from the masses, thus merely serving the nineteenth-century capitalist system" (Tratner 1995, p.27).

This approach to commercial and artistic communication has evolved throughout the 20th century, reaching its most extreme forms in postmodern art and literature. Its purpose is anything but pedagogic, where complex ideas would be simplified in the service of education and democracy. Its purpose is to impress, to dazzle, to confuse, to disorient, so that conscious thought can be replaced by unconscious impulses, which in their commercial form is an impulse to shop, to consume.

Capitalism has a simple, straightforward agenda: to invest capital in the search for maximum profit, to be repeated in a subsequent reinvestment of capital, plus the earlier profit, in the search for more profit, and a continuous accumulation of wealth generally. In this pure form there is absolutely no concern for the human and/or environmental costs of this process. Under industrial capitalism, capital is invested in the production of goods and services with the expectation that they will be sold for more than it costs to produce them. Meanwhile, it is still assumed by most economists - or at last their methodologies betray this assumption - that, as stated by Say's Law, the income generated by labor in the production process would insure that there would be a market for the goods and services produced. Keynes thought otherwise and the welfare state was the product of his and other pragmatic efforts to circumvent or enhance the market so that capital could continue to be invested for a profit.

Korten (1999, pp.47-48) documents the multifarious ways in which the benefits of welfare have been shifted from the people to capital itself over the 20th century in an effort to keep the system afloat. Subsidies range from extensive infrastructure investments covered by local tax-payers, to tax breaks, to extensive health and environmental costs covered by governments, to massive corporate 'bail outs' to protect against bankruptcy, to outright graft and theft by insurance and defense contractors, to say nothing of the extensive use of the war machine to insure 'proper conditions' for investment by US companies overseas. Korten (1999, p.48) cites figures from Estes (1996) that suggest that corporate welfare in the USA may be as much as *five times greater* than corporate profits, amounting in 1994 to $2.6 trillion vs. $530 billion in profits, and these figures do not include direct subsidies and tax breaks. This corporate welfare constituted 37% of US GDP in 1994, and when extrapolated to the whole world would suggest something like a $10.7 trillion subsidy to maintain capitalism as a system. Thus, Korten concludes that:

> . . . although capitalism claims to be an engine of wealth creation, in fact its primary vehicle, the corporation, is more accurately described as a powerful engine of wealth extraction - its profits dependent on imposing enormous costs on the rest of society, so that a few top executives and large shareholders may enjoy unconscionably large financial rewards. If market rules applied, most of the dominant corporations would have long ago found themselves unable to cover their own costs and gone bankrupt or been restructured into smaller, more efficient firms.

Finally, Korten (1999, p.54) explodes the myth that the stock market has anything to do with capitalism as a mode of *production.* In 1993, according to the Federal Reserve, only 4% of capital raised by US public corporations came from the sale of new shares. The rest was obtained from ". . . borrowing (14%) and retained earnings (82%)". Corporations actually spent more money buying back their own shares than they received from issuing new stocks. As Korten (1999, p.54) says,

> . . . the stock market is a sophisticated gambling casino with the unique feature that through their interactions the players inflate the prices of stocks in play to increase their collective financial assets and thereby their claims on the real wealth of the rest of society.

In any case, capitalism has unleashed powerful forces that have both enhanced and threatened life on the planet. The successes and failures are quite well known by now. By the end of World War II there was no longer much hope, except in certain quarters, that a return to traditional 19th century social forms was possible. By the end of the 20th century there seemed to be no viable alternative to capitalism for managing mass society. National socialism of the German and Italian variety was short-lived and most state socialist experiments collapsed under their own weight by the end of the 1980s (with a lot of help from the advanced capitalist countries, of course). These two efforts at managing mass society did solve certain problems such as unemployment and the recurrent crises of realization, i.e., the lack of adequate investment opportunities for capital, that have always plagued capitalism, and they did create a more equitable distribution of (sometimes limited) goods and services than the free market system could achieve. Moreover, in the case of Germany, Hitler not only solved these problems at home but almost instantaneously in the other capitalist countries as well. The 'secret' remedy was war, and the war machine, which has dominated the West, and particularly the United States since that time.

Dwight D. Eisenhower warned in 1960 of the increasing influence of the military-industrial complex in American society, but no American president since then has pointed to this problem. The fall of communism in the late 1980s was supposed to bring a 'peace dividend' to the US, but William Clinton was so ridiculed, publicly, on military matters, that he never gave such an agenda serious attention. The result is that the military budget in the US is now close to $500 billion, and accounts for more than 50% of the federal budget annually. Military armaments also constitute the largest trade item on the world scene, amounting to something between $700 and $800 billion annually (Korten 1999, p.33), followed by narcotics and petroleum at more than $500 billion each.

Needless to say, in a socio-dramatic sense, a war machine requires war, and war requires an enemy. The McCarthy witch-hunt just after World War II was a socio-dramatic event sufficient to serve as a reminder until 1989, and various 'rogue' leaders, 'human rights abusers' and, more recently, international terrorists have furnished the necessary enemies to maintain this war machine into the 21st century. In a practical sense, the war machine also works to resolve conflict amongst competing capitalist nation states. Large scale warfare of the sort presented by the two World Wars in the 20th century is precluded in the nuclear age, but 'low intensity' warfare allows continuous experimentation and 'demonstration' by the US of its willingness to use nuclear-tipped guided missiles, chemical weapons such as Dioxin, or whatever, when necessary, to protect its national 'interests'.

Capitalism is an aggressive, competitive system. The accumulation of wealth in this system requires control over resources, both human and natural. It requires technologies that will enhance this control. Social structures at the turn of the century are, thus, dominated by these requirements. The war mentality plays an indispensable role in these structures, from Hollywood to the football field. War and conflict supply the sensational news sought by all newscasters, they supply escapist entertainment for stressed-out individuals in mass society, satisfying that need for a little extra something that consumerism, nicotine, caffeine, alcohol, sex, food or whatever, leaves unsatisfied.

Depending upon where one or one's parents are in the social hierarchy, he or she will be plagued by a need for security and/or for affiliation (see chapter 10). Either of these needs create a susceptibility to emotional manipulation -- whether political, religious or commercial. This manipulation was described by George Orwell and Aldus Huxley, those mid-20th century authors who had such insight into the social psychology that would come to fruition in the latter part of the century, not under socialism as they imagined, and where the manipulation was crude and clumsy, but under capitalism. Here it has been honed into a refined set of techniques, combining survey and market research with highly sophisticated socio-drama to bring large populations into the proper frame of mind where they can be manipulated and watched over by 'Big Brother'.

But neither the war machine nor consumerism has been sufficient to ward off completely the recurrent crises of realization for capital, though both are still in full force in the increasingly debt-ridden populations of the globalized capitalist world. As a result, financial capital has taken increasing control of the capitalist system, generating a 'casino' mentality and an unbounded regime of speculation (Gowan, 1999). This has been accompanied by an increasing concentration of capital, a natural outcome of competition in any case, as mergers, takeovers and bankruptcies dominate the landscape of the production system. New technologies are indispensable to this process and to its globalization, as centralized control is extended over most of the natural and human resources of the world. The new 'Wizard of Oz' is in the computer, which contributes so many of the 'whistles and bells' that allow this to happen.

Ronald Dore (2000) characterizes this new evolution as 'stock market capitalism', which he attributes as much, if not more to 'political will' as to the forces of globalization and technical change. This political will he sees embodied in a key set of policies put into force in the USA and UK since 1980 (Dore 2000, p.5):

- lower taxes and smaller government
- improved national competitiveness through encouragement of a spirit of enterprise
- belief in the superior efficiency and justice of allocation through competitive markets rather than through politics and administration.

He also adds 'consumer sovereignty' to the last item, hopefully with 'tongue in cheek'. The 'good society' in contrast to that suggested by Keynes and the welfare state, will be ensured by a return to the idea of the 'invisible hand', which has always been accompanied by the war machine and its all too visible fist. Dore (2000, p.10) traces the shift from the values of *stakeholders*, i.e., as the name implies, values of those who have a stake or an interest in the viability of an enterprise, including everyone from employees, to suppliers, to creditors, to customers and local communities, etc, to *shareholder* values, as those to be maximized by the new managerial class. Managers are 'bribed' to change their allegiance from the company to the shareholders through stock options and performance bonuses, as much as by salaries. What this results in is "an economy centered on the stock market as the . . . measure of national well-being, as opposed to an economy which has other, better, more pluralistic criteria of human welfare for measuring progress toward the good society" (Dore, 2000, p.10). It is outside the scope of capitalism to be much concerned about human welfare in any case, and pragmatic adjustments to the contrary in the past are now likely to be washed away by the new rules of the International Monetary Fund (IMF) and The World Bank, as well as by the General Agreement on Trade and Tariffs (GATT) and the World Trade Organization (WTO) (Gowan 1999).

Meanwhile, not all the world has jumped onto this Anglo-American bandwagon. Japan and Germany, as well as the rest of continental Europe, have resisted the total abandonment of the welfare system implied by finance-led Anglo-American globalization. Much of Dore's book is an argument that the shift to stock market capitalism may, in the long run, prove to be more destructive than creative, in the Schumpeterian sense. Unfortunately, this discussion is still within the framework of *growth* as the 'mantra' of all economic theory and business practice, and whatever course the stock market versus welfare capitalist contest takes, it will largely ignore the environmental and deeper human costs of such a perspective.

All of this is played out differently in the Third World, where promises of the good society to be brought about by 'democracy' and the 'free market' system are even more questionable. The 'free market system' is 'free' in many different senses. In Third World countries it is 'free', i.e. open to entrance by transnational capital that is 'free' to compete with smaller, localized capital with all the inequality that such competition implies. Transnational capital is 'free' from any constraints by government at any level. It is 'free' to ignore, or to impose on local governments, infrastructure requirements that accompany its investments. It is 'free' to ignore any social or environmental costs that might be a result of its production activities, e.g. unemployment, health and safety hazards, pollution, etc. It is 'free' to support local political leaders who will grant any necessary concessions. And so forth (Bauzon 1992, pp.9-10).

The result of the 'New World Order' which has been created by the 'free market' system is that most of the Third World is worse off today than it was forty- to-fifty years ago when development first became a concern for international organizations. Bauzon (1992, p.11) reports that Africa has suffered the greatest losses, with problems related to ". . . deforestation, desertification, drought, drop in export earnings, severe indebtedness, and civil wars." Latin America has suffered less but is still burdened by an enormous external debt whose service requires up to 10% of national incomes, with accompanying declines in GNP and resulting severe problems of ". . . malnutrition, infant mortality and disease". Asia is more complex, with substantial growth recorded in the 'Asian Tigers', at least until the mid 1990s' recessions, but with other Asian countries such as the Philippines, Indonesia and Malaysia suffering declines or stagnation in GNP. Bauzon (1992, p.15) claims that the concept of the 'New World Order' is little more than a ". . . rhetorical shroud to conceal . . . hegemonic aims" in a neo-colonial, corporate-controlled world system.

This argument is carried even further in Jerry Mander and Edward

Goldsmith's (1996) and David Korten's (1999) extensive critique of the world capitalist system. As Korten (1999, p.1) says, "In the 1980s capitalism triumphed over communism. In the 1990's it triumphed over democracy and the market economy". On a global scale this has been accomplished through policies of 'restructuring' and deregulation as formalized in the rules of GATT and the WTO, as an extension of the same policies introduced under the regime of Ronald Reagan and Margaret Thatcher in the USA and the UK in the 1980s. These policies succeeded in forestalling the crises of realization in these countries by shifting profit making from the industrial to the financial sector, unleashing a wave of speculative activity that has lasted into the 21st century. This new concentrated capital was available for overseas investment and required a global structure to allow this to happen. While successful, at least temporarily, in narrow economic terms, the social and environmental costs have been enormous, characterized by Mander and Goldsmith (1996, p.4) as:

> the spreading disintegration of the social order and the increase of poverty, landlessness, homelessness, violence, alienation, and, deep within the hearts of many people, extreme anxiety about the future. Equally important, these are the practices that have led us to the near breakdown of the natural world, as evidenced by such symptoms as global climate change, ozone depletion, massive species loss, and near maximum levels of air, soil and water pollution.

It might be well to recall why the American colonies fought their war of independence in 1776. Essentially, they were trying to protect their local industries and local economy from the free entrance of British capital into the colonies, the result of which would have been complete economic domination by Britain (Chang 2003). The southern colonies were already caught in this syndrome as their economy was focused upon the monoculture of cotton, which was exported to the British textile industry. The cost of labor was minimal, since labor was supplied by slaves, and manufactured goods were imported from Britain with virtually no local industry in the South to compete. There was little in the way of social services and no welfare system at all for the poor, outside the 'largesse' of the slave owners. Thus, the northern colonies fought against the extension of this form of domination into the North. If Britain had had the will and a more effective war machine, and communication and transportation had allowed, the USA would probably still be part of the British Commonwealth today. Yet this is precisely the form of relationship that US and other transnational corporations would, and to a large extent, have imposed on the Third World. Indeed, as much as they can, they seek to impose the same conditions on their own populations with the resulting income gaps that are all too well known, especially in the USA and the UK.

In their book, *The Case Against the Global Economy and a Turn Toward the Local,* Mander and Goldsmith (1996, pp.14-16) include a section named "Mechanisms of Self-Delusion", where they outline the various ways in which economists and current economic theory participate in perpetuating this social debacle. As they say, "economists have devised the perfect measurements for gauging their own success and confirming their own self-delusions." For example, GNP and GDP include "depletion of natural resources, the construction of more prisons, and the manufacture of bombs . . .[as]. . . measures of [economic] 'health' ", and exclude such things as ". . . unpaid housework, child care, community service, or the production of food to be eaten and artifacts to be used rather than sold via the formal economy", as if they contributed nothing to the economy. Ted Halstead and Clifford Cobb in the same volume Mander and Goldsmith (1996, pp.197-206) propose a new set of measurements, which they label "The Genuine Progress Indicator", to redress these contradictions. They include in this index all the social and environmental aspects of economic activity that are *beneficial* to society and nature, and that are left out of traditional measures.

The problem with the 'free' market system as currently defined by economic theory is that there are no price signals to indicate environmental or social abuses. Those looking for evidence can find it, of course. For example, Guatemalan newspapers occasionally report that peasants have been severely injured or have even been killed when 'falling off their land". Such bizarre news items are explained by the fact that, 'el pulpo', the octopus, as the natives refer to the United Fruit Company, has taken over all the flat land and left only the, sometimes very steep, hillsides to the native peasants! Nor are there any price signals to indicate that too many toxins are being dumped into the environment, though the health effects can be registered by careful epidemiological research, and so forth.

To further illustrate the extreme distortions in the world economy, Tony Clarke (1996, p.297) cites statistics that emphasize how control is exercised. He writes that if we include the economies of all the nation states, "forty-seven of the top one hundred economies of the world are actually transnational corporations; 70 percent of global trade is controlled by just five hundred corporations, and a mere 1 percent of the TNCs on this planet own half the stock of foreign direct investment." The United Nations Development Program (UNDP) reported in its Human Development Report for 1992 that 20 percent of the world's population in the richest nations receive 82.7 percent of the world's income, while the bottom 20 percent receive just 1.4 percent, averages, that even then mask poverty in the rich nations themselves (Korten, 1996, p.24). The agreements of GATT and the WTO, the policies of the IMF and World Bank, the globalization of finance, and, finally, of culture via cinema and television, will only further serve to encourage this concentration of wealth and increase the gap between the richest and the poorest.

The ultimate irony, of course, is that these developments are not the result of some forces of nature or of natural evolution, as is claimed by neo-classical economics, imbued with the spirit of positivism, but are the product of human intentions, policies and plans, carried out by key actors on the world scene, actors who seek merely to further their own interests. These key actors meet together frequently, having over time institutionalized these contacts in various fora. The July 1944 Bretton Woods meeting, under the auspices of the United Nations Monetary and Financial Conference, was the first of these multinational fora, though Korten (1996, p.21) states that US corporate interests were conceiving plans to dominate the global economy as early as the 1930s under the auspices of the US Council on Foreign Relations. The Bretton Woods meeting established the IMF and the World Bank and provided a framework for subsequent agreements such as those contained in The North American Free Trade Agreement (NAFTA), and the WTO. These oligarchic agreements have largely succeeded in their goals by fostering unprecedented growth in economic activity - output, trade, income, etc. - but have totally ignored the social and environmental costs of this growth.

In May 1954, North American and European leaders established another forum to discuss world political-economic policy, called simply 'Bilderberg' (after the Dutch hotel in which they met). These meetings over the years have included ". . . heads of state, other key politicians, key industrialists and financiers, and an assortment of intellectuals, trade unionists, diplomats and influential representatives of the press with demonstrated sympathy for establishment views. (Korten 1996, p.27). In 1973 the Trilateral Commission was established by David Rockefeller, chair of the Chase Manhattan Bank, and Zbigniew Brzezinsky, its chair until he became Jimmy Carter's national security adviser in 1977. The purpose of the Trilateral Commission was to formalize the meetings of the heads of the world economy, and to recognize Japan as the third side of the trilateral world political-economic oligarchy. Besides political leaders from the three dominant regions of the world economy, the commission has also included ". . . four of the world's five largest non-banking transnational corporations, top officials of five of the world's six largest international banks, and heads of the major media organizations" (Korten 1996, p.27). The G7 and G8 meetings have carried out this tradition in yet another forum in recent years.

While part of a competitive system, these leaders recognize the common need to maintain a certain world framework within which they can operate freely. This framework ensures that the Third World, that labor and the environment, will continue to be available as exploitable resources for use by transnational corporations, and that any costs to society and nature will be borne by the poor and the powerless. Meanwhile, the American 'war machine' insures that the proper hierarchy within this 'club of the privileged' will also be maintained. In other words, this 'absentee' political-economic oligarchy is a *world government* but with a very narrowly defined agenda, an agenda which considers social and environmental concerns only under duress and only as a last resort, and when it is absolutely necessary, to preserve the overall stability of society and nature.

Meanwhile, there are ample signs that the stability of both nature and society are increasingly endangered, though the 'absentee oligarchy' seems blissfully unaware or unconcerned. One clear-cut example of this is the new epidemiology of disease. The Harvard Working Group on New and Resurgent Diseases (1996) summarizes the important changes that have occurred as a result of the global economic strategies of free trade, mono-culture, export-oriented agriculture, deregulation and rapid economic growth (Harvard Working Group, 1996, pp.160-161):

1.   Changed land use, including deforestation, irrigation, monoculture, and urbanization, all of which cause a loss of biodiversity.

2.   Widespread malnutrition, as the gap between rich and poor is widened; loss of publicly provided health care.
3.   Resource depletion and chemical pollution of land and sea.
4.   Migration to escape political turmoil and to seek economic opportunity.
5.   Increased, uncontrolled use of chemical therapies - drugs, vaccines, and pesticides - which turns health care itself into a commodity.

The results of these changes are several and varied but all have led to an increase in exposure to pathogenic micro-organisms, a decline in human resistance to them, and a resulting steep rise in infectious diseases, and this only two decades after the health community was convinced that infectious diseases were a thing of the past! Briefly, the Harvard Group (p.161) summarizes the pattern of these changes:

> The loss of biodiversity means fewer natural predators are available to control disease vectors; people move into new regions [bringing with them and coming into contact with] unfamiliar pathogens; eutrophication of coastal waters (from run off sewage and fertilizer) allows plankton blooms to increase bacteria and viruses.

The World Health Organization (WHO) reported that 16.4 million people died of infectious diseases in 1993, with eight million new TB cases reported in 1991. A third of the world's population is now estimated to be carrying this infection and there are several strains now resistant to all known anti-TB drugs (Harvard Working Group 1996, p.162). Comparable increases in diphtheria, the plague, malaria, cholera, dengue fever and yellow fever have also been recorded.

As described in Chapter 6, human diseases and their changes over time are a result of a complex set of relationships between human activity and the natural environment. The biomedical factors are only one aspect of this complex. The recent increase in the incidence of infectious diseases is one more example of how this complex has worked itself out in the past two decades, as noted by the Harvard Group. Globalization and the 'New World Order' have succeeded in recreating disease patterns that had largely disappeared from human society. Given its single-minded approach to all things, we can expect that the global oligarchy will not seek solutions to this problem by altering profitable interventions into society and nature, however short term this profitability might turn out to be. Rather, we can predict that new 'magic bullets' will be sought, new drugs, new equipment or new techniques, that will insure profits to the pharmaceutical industry, the medical equipment industry and others who might stand to benefit from these new technical fixes. (Harvard Group 1996, p.170).

As stated above, globalization and the new world order are not simply the result of evolution. The human intentions that have created them are supported by certain forms of belief, which in the past we might have labeled as mythology, ideology or religion, but which in the 20th century are now called paradigm assumptions. Positive science with its mechanistic, Newtonian framework, supplies the inspiration for most of modern science and social policy. Within this framework, consciousness and life generally are mere evolutionary accidents, not to be taken seriously in the important work of science, which explains the universe as a giant clockwork governed by universal laws. Thus, the idea that we as human beings could actually change the way in which we confront each other and nature, *by changing the way we explain these things to ourselves* is not a widely held paradigmatic assumption at this moment in history. The idea that we could inspire ourselves and work toward a more cooperative, humane world, is ". . . blocked by a modern equivalent of the dogmatic intellectual tyranny once imposed by the church" (Korten, 1999, p.13. See also Ada 1989).

Korten (1999, p.15) supplies an agenda that would move us toward such a world, once we have overcome this tyranny:

- End the legal fiction that corporations are entitled to the rights of persons and exclude corporations from political participation.
- Implement serious political campaign reform to reduce the influence of money on politics.
- Eliminate corporate welfare by eliminating direct subsidies and recovering other externalized costs through fees and taxes.
- Implement mechanisms to regulate international corporations and finance.
- Use fiscal and regulatory policy to make financial speculation unprofitable and to give advantage to human-scale stakeholder-owned enterprises.

Such an agenda would seek to alter dramatically the world, as we know it. It would confront powerful economic and military interests, and could never be accomplished without a new paradigm that empowers human beings to seek goals and to believe that they could be accomplished by their personal and collective efforts. Indeed, such monumental changes have been accomplished in the past by exactly these means.

Meanwhile, science and technology have so profoundly affected the social scene, that any struggle for change must take place within such a framework. Thus, it is not religious or ideological fervor that must be sought, but a movement that is based upon the spread of information and communication. Just as the education of children is understood as a necessary means to develop a modern society, so the continuous education of adults must be seen as indispensable to the creation of a more humane postmodern society. But this will require a major shift in the worldview of scientists, involving a quite different perspective on the relationship between science and society. Part one of this book outlines ways in which the tyranny of the mechanism could be overcome within the social sciences, so that they could play a more active role in liberating people in the broader society. It remains to be seen whether and to what extent the broader society would be susceptible to such a liberation.

Subjective Reality at the Turn of the Century

As it turns out, there is reason to be hopeful that change is underway, even in the absence of a concerted and responsible intervention by scientists onto the social scene. Of course, there are always those 'rogue' scientists who will insist on abandoning the so-called 'value free posture' of positive science, people like Noam Chomsky, Barry Commoner or Ralph Nader, who will seek to uncover the dangerous effects of modern science and technology as well as the extensive abuse of power and wealth in contemporary society. Indeed, their efforts have often had effects on public policy and the course of human events. For example, Barry Commoner collected baby teeth in the mid-western Unites States in order to establish that radioactive fallout from atmospheric atomic tests in the US was not dispersing into the atmosphere as military and government officials were claiming in the 1950s. Rather this fallout was landing in the pastures where it was eaten by cows whose milk was drunk by babies, with the result that their teeth (as well as the rest of their bodies) contained strontium 90. His work over the past fifty years has continued to expose the deleterious environmental and health effects of corporate activity, and has influenced countless citizens to become active in efforts to address these effects (Commoner 1966, 1972, 1990).

Ralph Nader's efforts to publicize auto safety issues 20 years later resulted in a host of safety-enhancing changes in automobile design, such as seat-belts, air bags, reinforced doors, etc. Recent efforts by Nader and Noam Chomsky and other social scientists to inform the world about corporate abuses of political, economic and military power have been instrumental in inspiring wide-spread protests against globalization and the new world order based upon these abuses, with effects that have yet to be played out on the world social scene.

The efforts of these and many other scientists, journalists and activist citizens, along with a general increase in the level of education and affluence has given the citizens of the developed countries the freedom and the will to be concerned about the overall quality of their existence to the degree that some of the basic premises of late 20th century capitalist society are now being widely questioned. The extent of this questioning is being documented by social scientists, who have been surveying and researching public attitudes over the past twenty years, not in the service of the corporations who seek to exploit this knowledge in order to extend their control over these populations, but in order to emancipate them (and themselves) from the reified structures of thought and action that sustain this society.

One such effort is that by Paul H. Ray and Sherry Ruth Anderson (2000), who interviewed over 100,000 Americans, conducted sixty indepth interviews and organized hundreds of focus groups over a period of thirteen years. They found that 50 million Americans, or 26 percent of the adult population ". . . have made a comprehensive shift in their world view, values and way of life . . . and are shaping a new kind of American culture for the 21st century" (Ray and Anderson 2000, p.4). Since the 1960s, this group, which Ray and Anderson label the 'cultural creatives', has grown from less than 5% to more than a quarter of the adult population, which, as they say, ". . . on the time-scale of whole civilizations where major developments are measured in centuries, . . . is shockingly quick," and they report similar numbers in the European Union.

Cultural creatives are those people who reject consumerism, and materialism generally. They reject greed, racism and social inequality, inattention to the weakest in the name of social Darwinism, and the cynicism and hedonism under which modern sophisticates hide their sense of powerlessness. Politically, they ". . . reject the intolerance and narrowness of social conservatives and the Religious Right", and mistrust all large-scale institutions "including both corporations and government" (Ray and Anderson 2000, p.17). They are middle-aged, under age 70 and over age 25. Their occupations and social class are a cross section of the American population, as is their religious affiliation, except that few would call themselves 'New Age' or dogmatic with respect to any religion. What does set them apart is their gender: almost two-thirds are women!

Ray and Anderson (2000, pp.25-32) contrast the cultural creatives with the 'moderns' who constitute 48 percent of the adult American population and 'traditionals' who represent about a quarter of the adult population. Moderns are more male than female, are accustomed to and support most of the ideas of modern capitalism, including the mechanistic assumptions that govern its approach to understanding and constructing social reality. Thus, they have a high need for achievement and fit the ideal as described first by Max Weber as the 'Protestant (work) ethic', and as propagated by David McClelland (1961) at mid-century as necessary for economic development, the ultimate purpose in life according to most moderns inside and outside of science. The measure of their success is money and the consumer goods that it can buy, as well as the status that it bestows. At the same time, they believe in the principles embodied in the American Bill of Rights: freedom of speech, of assembly, of religion, right to a fair trial, etc, as well as, more generally, honesty, fair play, hard work, the importance of the family and education, the ability of science and engineering to solve most problems, including the ones created by them. They are also likely to be individualistic and not very altruistic, values that have from the beginning been necessary for the competitive mechanisms of capitalism to work properly. Moderns are cynical about politics and unlikely to join movements for social change. This is understandable, since they are quite content with modern, urban, industrial society as it is currently organized.

Traditionals are a declining portion of the American population, dropping from nearly half the adult population at mid-century to their current 25 percent. They are older, poorer and less well educated than the other two groups. They are fundamentalists in their religious beliefs, they believe in the traditional gender separation of roles, with males in the dominant position. They are highly patriotic and xenophobic, and intolerant of difference and change. They support the military, as well as their own right to bear arms. At the same time, they are opposed to big government and to big business and to the ways in which it is destroying the natural environment.

Needless to say, the cultural creatives are the heroines and heroes of Ray and Anderson's book. They are the sign of the future, and much of their effort is spent in analyzing this group. They, "Like mariners of old . . . have sailed beyond the familiar horizon" (Ray and Anderson 2000, p.43). They question the assumptions of modern (and traditional) society. They examine values critically, seeking to escape from the control of the 'thought police' who dominate the mass media and modern culture generally. One of their heroes is David Quinn, whose book, *Ishmael,* is widely read. Quoting from him, they write:

> According to your maps, the world of thought . . . ends at the border of your culture, and if you venture beyond that border, you simply fall off the edge of the world. Tomorrow, we'll screw up our courage and cross that border. And you'll see, we will not fall off the edge of the world. We'll just find ourselves in new territory (Ray and Anderson 2000, p.57 and Quinn 1995, p.91).

In other words, the first step toward gaining freedom is to understand all the ways in which modern society controls us, to understand the socio-drama, the theater within which we are all acting, including its mechanistic aspects, of course, but going beyond them to appreciate the values and intentions which govern our behavior and give the mechanism its direction.

Those who guide the mechanisms of modern capitalist society cannot, themselves, be unaware of the problems that the cultural creatives are exposing, at least not those who were present at their meeting in Davos, Switzerland in 1996. There, Oren Lyons, an Iroquois Indian, described the present world situation in an unmistakable metaphor:

> I see you all as jockeys, and your companies are the horses you ride. You're beating your horses on in a race, but now you can see that you are racing toward a stone wall. You see

some of those ahead of you smashing into the wall, but you
don't turn around or even pause. You're beating your horses
on anyway as fast as you can (Ray and Anderson 2000,
p.57).

Elisabeth Sahtouris confirmed that the problem is widely understood in
a conversation with a Brazilian banker, who claimed that he and his colleagues felt that ". . . we are all going over the edge of a cliff" (Ray and
Anderson 2000, p.57).

Modernists, still half the adult population in the US, are more or less
content with the present capitalist system, or at least are trying to make
their way within the confines of its established values. Traditionalists
are oriented to the past and seek to recover it in whatever ways they can.
The cultural creatives are trying to create a new system, but without any
defining plan or blueprint, such as those guiding leftist politics and revolutionary movements in the past. They have, however, been strongly
influenced by social movements in the 20th century, particularly those
that began in the 1960s. The antiwar movement, the women's movement, the civil rights movement, the environmental movement, the student movements, etc., have all been influential, and, in fact, many of the
cultural creatives have participated in one or more of these movements.

But, as these movements lost coverage in the mass media that are
advertiser-driven and oriented to sensationalism, they began to evolve
into more localized and less 'entertaining', but more sustainable efforts.
Orienting movements to the mass media will always confront the problem that media content is closer to entertainment than information. The
media are superficial and time-constrained, concerned with events
rather than their causes or underlying conditions. Their fixation on audience ratings encourages them to interview prominent politicians and
movie stars, rather than academics and intellectuals. Thus, the analyses
they offer are of the three-minute, if not thirty-second, sound-bite type.
As a result, cultural creatives have been led to believe that they are
alone in the world, though they may join a few others in local struggles
around issues of the sort that were of national significance in the sixties.
The importance of Ray and Anderson's book is to demonstrate how
widespread are the sympathies for something new, for a new culture that
respects nature and fellow human beings.

Their book also cites numerous examples of business enterprises
that are seeking products and processes that are more respectful.

Examples include a line of upholstery fabrics that could be returned safely to nature. William McDonough, Dean of Architecture at the University of Virginia, and his colleagues spent several years designing fabrics and seeking "dyes, finishes, polishes and fire retardants that were 'clean', meaning no mutagents, no carcinogens, no endocrine disrupters" (Ray and Anderson 2000, p.163). Sixty chemical companies refused to work with them, but ultimately Ciba Geigy agreed, with the result that they had to eliminate nearly eight thousand chemicals in order to find thirty-eight that were acceptable.

Another example is a large bank building in Amsterdam, designed by Amory Lovins at the Rocky Mountain Institute. He was instructed to design a building that would be "organic . . . , full of light, air, water, ecologists' plants, nice sounds, and happy people, and it shall not cost one guilder more per square meter [than any other design would]" (Ray and Anderson 2000, pp.164-169). The building, which took several years to design and construct, and required extensive cooperation among designers, artists, engineers, landscape architects and construction people, is an outstanding success, with resulting significant increases in productivity among bank employees. These and other examples are cited by Ray and Anderson to illustrate that the cultural creatives are not romantics or mere idealists. They find concrete ways to implement their ideals and to demonstrate the more intelligent and emotionally satisfying ways in which society could be structured once the current system has 'run into the wall'.

A more sustained example of how the cultural creatives are acting out their ideals is the turn of American people to alternative medicine and organic or natural foods. Industries serving these needs are growing at a rate of 10 to 20 percent per year and are estimated to have earned as much as $75 billion in the year 2000 (Ray and Anderson 2000, p.185). Alternative medicine includes yoga, biofeedback, homeopathic medicine, acupuncture, holistic healing etc., all approaches that view the human being as something more than a sophisticated mechanism with organic dimensions. Capitalist health care, designed to maximize profits for the pharmaceutical companies, medical equipment manufacturers and hospital real estate speculators, is under attack even by medical doctors themselves, a third of whom reported, in 1999, that they would choose another profession if they were to start over again (Ray and Anderson 2000, p.195). It's important to emphasize, of course, that alternative health care does not mean an abandonment of modern medicine but rather a search to supplement something that is absent from it. In 1997, forty-two percent of American adults sought this 'something else', increasing their number of visits to alternative health practitioners from 427 million to 629 million in the years from 1990 to 1997, while visits to establishment physicians actually declined from 388 million to 386 million during the same period (Ray and Anderson 2000, p.330).

These changes and many more cited by Ray and Anderson illustrate the extent to which there is a global change in consciousness among American adults. This change has gone unnoticed in its scale, even by the people who are involved in it. The reason, of course, is the nature of the mass media in the US, as described above, which can find nothing sufficiently sensational to warrant its attention. Thus, like Rachel Carson's *"Silent Spring"*, this revolution, if it is one, is taking place without the fanfare of wider public attention. Nevertheless, a new 'story' is being created, a new image of the future, which may well in time serve to keep modern civilization from 'running into the wall'. And a new story is just that; it is a way of incorporating all the divergent, specialized strands of a given situation into a comprehensible form. As Ray and Anderson (2000, p.229) say, "we need good ways to convey big abstractions in human, relevant and symbolically meaningful terms". In other words, we must stop the destruction of nature and society in the name of profit, and its limited and impoverished scientific rationality, and we must create a story, a vision and a theory of how this may be accomplished. Since the USA is seen by many as composed of the most 'sedated', the most 'colonized', to use Habermas' term, of the affluent populations in the world, it is important to realize that a quarter of that population is engaged in a search for something new.

Another major research effort extends these findings beyond the USA (Inglehart 1997). Combining data from the 1981 European Values Systems Survey, the World values Surveys in 43 societies, the Euro-Barometer Surveys and the two-wave Political Action Study, Inglehart and his long list of collaborators have established that there are major new trends in cultural values extending around the world. He uses the term 'postmodern' to describe new cultural realities in those societies affected by these changes. Furthermore, his analysis is squarely within the context described here in Chapter 10 on human needs, based upon Maslow's hierarchical concept. In other words, where societies have experienced important levels of affluence, people seek to satisfy 'post material' values of the sort described by the need for love and affiliation, esteem and self-actualization. As important, however, is the finding that these value changes are inter-generational, being affected by the pre-adult, especially early childhood, experiences of individuals. Hence, emotional and intellectual development, which depends upon a childhood whose physiological and security needs are well-satisfied, will more or less inevitably lead to the search for higher order need satisfaction in adult life, with many important social, political and economic ramifications.

Thus, while people were able to work hard, even be exploited, as dictated by the Protestant Ethic under modernism, they will no longer offer themselves to this syndrome under postmodernism. They will even be willing to deny themselves the latest consumer goods, if necessary, in order to avoid meaningless and stress-filled work. At the same time, they will seek more meaningful relationships, both at work and in leisure, at least some of which will be of a political nature. Thus, Inglehart found that while participation in elections and general confidence in the modernist political institutions is declining, people are more active than ever in the particular causes that they find important. These causes are first and foremost directed toward ecology and the environment, but also include gender roles, inequality and poverty as well.

Generally, authoritarian institutions that might have seemed important under conditions of poverty and insecurity are no longer tolerated. While an authoritarian science and engineering may have seemed liberating after nearly two thousand years of autocratic religion, they no longer seem so, with the result that more educated and more secure people not only wish, and are in a position to understand the implications of planning decisions and instrumental rationality, generally, but now also wish to be involved in the processes where these decisions are made. This is not a wholesale rejection of rationality and modernity, as some postmodernist writers would like us to believe, but rather a strong desire to be involved in its uses and application. Economic development is no longer seen as an end in itself, one that would justify almost any means, including those propagandized by globalization apologists. Nor is the rationalization of everything in society, as suggested by Max Weber, with its resulting patterns of regimentation and specialization, an acceptable way of life. The alienating effects of this, and of mass society generally, are now well understood, not only as a result of the analyses offered by the Frankfurt School and others in the

50's, 60's and 70's, but also because many people are now secure and educated enough to understand and agree with these analyses. Thus, just as modernization brought the decline of traditional-religious morality and authority, so postmodernism is now bringing the decline of rational-legal authority, or at least its unquestioned and universal use:

> . . . the core societal goal of traditional society is survival under the conditions of a steady-state economy, in which social mobility is a zero-sum game. During the modernization phase, by contrast, the core societal project is maximizing economic growth -- and, in both capitalist and socialist societies, it tends to be carried out by ruthlessly extracting the necessary capital from an impoverished populace, regardless of the costs to the environment and the quality of life. In postmodern society, by contrast, the top priority shifts from maximizing economic growth to maximizing subjective well-being (Inglehart 1997, p77).

Inglehart (1997, p.84) is quick to point out that these multinational trends are by no means universally the same. Each local culture identifies its own relationships to capitalism and modernization and its own dialectical evolution beyond them. Many things play a role in this: "leaders, institutions, climate, geography, situation-specific events, and other unique elements that make up its own distinctive heritage". Nevertheless, there are world-wide patterns associated with economic development that tend to undermine its importance over time, shifting values from growth, acquisition and greed to emotional well-being and justice. These pressures are now being felt in advanced capitalist nations, with resulting demands for participation in decision-making and more democratic institutions in both the public and private sector. This will mean moving beyond the representative oligarchy that passes for democracy in the public sector and the management retreats and workshops that pass for democracy in the corporate sector (Inglehart 1997, pp. 293-323). Unfortunately, as Inglehart demonstrates, these trends can be reversed under conditions of crisis and uncertainty, e.g., the former socialist countries, South Africa, Argentina, etc., and there are short term fluctuations related to economic conditions, particularly inflation and unemployment, in any case. Nevertheless, the longer term trends are quite steady (Inglehart 1997, pp.136-7). Thus, while the students and youth of the 1960's may not be as visible today, at least until

Seattle and Genoa, they still persist in expressing the values that were a product of their early childhood security, though we can expect the mass media increasingly to reduce demonstrations against corporate globalization to sound bites, as they follow their true nature into the future.

One interesting finding by Inglehart and his colleagues was that European Union countries are changing more rapidly in the direction of postmodernism than the United States. His explanation is that this is correlated with higher growth rates after World War II, but one must also recognize the more equitable distribution of income, and particularly welfare benefits in the European Union with resulting higher levels of security. Even the restructuring demands of Anglo-American capital have not yet (?) succeeded in reducing overall welfare to the minimal levels found in the US. Thus, it is not surprising that "the two youngest European cohorts rank well above their American counterparts", though he is quick to add "the United States has shown a significant movement in the predicted direction" (Inglehart 1997, p.147).

What Inglehart's analysis does not address are the autonomous structural forces of capitalism. While it is true that people's values are shifting in a post-materialist direction, there are serious constraints on the level of self-actualization and emotional well being that can be attained without serious structural alterations in the present capitalist system. Somehow, imperialism (at this stage, mostly American) must be tamed and the war machines reined in if the world at large is to attain any overall sense of security. Political organizing for environmental concerns, social justice, gender equality, ethnic and racial tolerance, or whatever, will sooner or later run up against its own wall of corporate power and social irresponsibility. In addition, no one can predict the effects of some major worldwide crisis in the capitalist system itself. The rampant speculative nature of the world financial casino almost insures that some such crisis will arrive sooner or later.

In other words, efforts to alter the institutional rules governing capitalism as a system must be just as much an objective of citizen organizing and demonstrating as efforts to improve levels of individual and collective well being. In that sense, Korten's effort to grapple with what a post-corporate world could look like is an indispensable complement to the analyses of subjective factors as carried out by Ray and Anderson and Inglehart. This is precisely what movements like the World Social Forum are trying to accomplish (www.forumsocialmundial.org). In response to the World Economic Forum established twenty years ago in

Davos, Switzerland for the world economic elite, (i.e., the 'absentee' world oligarchy), the World Social Forum has set out to turn attention to the social impacts of neo-liberalism and globalization. It was decided to hold this forum in a Third World country to emphasize symbolically its anti-Davos orientation. Porto Alegre, Brazil was chosen for the first meeting in January 2001, followed by a second and third meeting in January 2002 and 2003. This forum is not a deliberative body, is not seeking to become a world government or to seek political power in any way. Indeed, according to its charter of principles, it will serve as:

> . . . an open meeting for reflective thinking, democratic debate of ideas, formulation of proposals, free exchange of experiences and interlinking for effective action, by groups and movements of civil society that are opposed to neoliberalism and to domination of the world by capital and any form of imperialism, and are committed to building a planetary society centered on the human person.

In this sense it represents the new consciousness characteristic of social movements all over the world. They are decentralized, democratic, information-sharing and committed to decision making through consensus. They attempt to build a solid base among the people through education and discussion. There is no search for power in the classical Marxist sense, no group or class that would seek to represent the interests of others or of the whole society. They appear to have taken very seriously Lord Acton's famous statement in his April 3rd, 1887 letter to Bishop Mandell: *"Power tends to corrupt and absolute power corrupts absolutely"*, a statement that should be blazoned over the door of every politician and every corporate executive.

This probably goes a long way to explaining why citizens, worldwide, have lost confidence in political institutions and in the ability of political leaders to solve the most pressing problems in their respective countries (Norris, P. 1999). This does not mean that the ideal of democracy has in any way been eroded but rather that citizens are disillusioned in various ways with the manner in which democratic institutions are working. This decline in confidence is probably not unrelated to the way in which the restructuring demanded by the global financial institutions has increased uncertainty in all countries. At the same time, political leaders appear to be less accountable and less subject to electoral defeat, with a growing sense among citizens that there is no way for them to participate in important decision-making. In other words, elections seem not to matter very much, with a resulting decline in voters exercising their rights, and there are no other institutional means available for participation, especially at the national and international level. As a result, ". . . elite-directed forms of participation such as voting are stagnant or declining, [while] elite-challenging forms of participation are becoming more widespread" (Inglehart 1997, p.236). This loss of confidence and trust also erodes the willingness of citizens to comply with laws generally, and makes it more difficult for states to govern without coercion (Norris, P. 1999, p.257). The result of this rise in the number of critical citizens is an expectation that demands for institutional reform will increase, along with those for more meaningful participation at all levels of government.

> Sociologists and political scientists cannot repeat it often enough: the European democracies are facing a demand for renewed participation by citizens in public affairs. A desire for a more participatory democracy, closer to the real concerns of individuals, is gradually emerging. (European Commission 2000, p. ix).

One would think that the new information technologies would offer considerable opportunity for new forms of communication and participation. Indeed, the explosion in information and communications technology is mind-boggling. Numbers become almost meaningless in this context because the moment they are written down they are out-dated. In this sense, it is important to recognize how recent the new technologies are. For example, the first network for sharing documents was demonstrated publicly only in 1991 and was named the World Wide Web (WWW) at that time (Albarran and Goff 2000, p.6). By 1999 there were nearly 45,000,000 Internet hosts, and an estimated 50,000 new Internet users are now being added daily, with an estimated 300,000,000 by the year 2005. (Albarran and Goff 2000, p.7, 14, 18). This, along with the rapid increase in home computers, should make it possible for citizens to communicate with each other and with decision-making centers and thus increase the overall level of political participation.

Unfortunately, while the potential for the more widespread dissemination of uncensored information is there and is being exploited, there are also limitations and abuses that inhibit the realization of democratic goals. First, much of the communication is personal or restricted to specific interest groups. Rita Kirk Whillock (2000, p.167) argues that these interest groups have little need of each other and that ". . . the ideas of the individual continue to be devalued in the political process, depriving them of an effective, deliberative voice and of their individual identity." She further claims that the separation of internet users by time and place further alienates them from political organization which results in "only the illusion of community." Further problems arise because of the ease with which misinformation can be disseminated by hackers and others, thus confounding purposeful uses. Finally, corporate and government control can ultimately be expected to restrict freedom of communication in much the same way that they have with other mass media in the past and present. Indeed, this control may be necessary to limit the range of abuses already present, such as child pornography, cyber terrorism and information warfare. Whillock (2000, pp.185-7) gives examples, such as hackers altering the home page of both the Tory and Labour parties during their latest election campaign, or where a whole different site was established mimicking and ridiculing Bob Dole in the 1996 US presidential election, or where, even more dramatically, ". . . the Spanish government was accused of supporting the e-mail bombing of a web site based in San Francisco that supported Basque separatists."

The future of the use of these new technologies will depend as much upon the ways in which these technologies evolve and the speed with which they become available to the masses of people throughout the world, as well as upon the manner in which they are manipulated by official and unofficial sources. The potential for the wider dissemination of information is there, and for the time being is unhindered by any censorship or control, other than the not inexpensive access to it. If whole books and articles become available it will truly overcome the friction of space in gaining access to the even more substantial forms of information that only well-stocked libraries can supply today. In a political sense, alternative viewpoints on all questions can, for the time being, be made available almost instantaneously throughout the world, including on highly delicate questions such as the bombing of the twin towers in New York, with potentially profound effects on public consciousness and international relations (http://cyberjournal.org). As long as this potential exists, there is a world-wide freedom of information that only visionaries have imagined in the past, a freedom that approaches

Habermas' undominated communication, and perhaps only truly realized in the forum of Ancient Greece (though modern Greece continues to maintain a good deal of this tradition even in the mass media, perhaps more than any other country in the world today).

However, the potential for establishing more democratic political institutions will depend upon more than new technologies. It will depend upon the ability of the majority of citizens to understand truly the issues in all of their complexity, and to actually participate in public affairs. Without this kind of understanding, as Jean-Claude Thebault says, ". . . access to and exploitation of information will be the privilege of an educated minority, who, either consciously or unconsciously, will exercise a form of domination which will jeopardize the very foundations of democracy" (European Commission 2000, p. x). This educated minority must thus be seen as a key factor in the democratization of society. Positivist scientists, as seen in Part I of this book, cannot be expected to offer much hope in this respect; they are self-censored by their own paradigmatic assumptions. We can also gain insight by asking, within the framework of Chapter 10, what were the early childhood experiences of this minority. If these experiences were influenced by insecurity, by deprivation, we can expect that 'exercising domination' would be quite acceptable if it were to further personal gain, and no amount of scientific education would likely alter this. Only a paradigmatic shift in both personal values and social (scientific) outlook of the sort that appears to be taking place in the 'post-autistic' economics movement could accomplish this (www.paecon.net). If democratization is crucial to the stability of modern society, as the research findings seem to indicate, we can begin to appreciate how important the paradigm shift of this educated minority has become to humanity in the 21st century. Nor can the market, or the 'unseen hand', or any existing political process be expected to substitute for the painful process that the 'educated minority' must go through if this is to be accomplished. If "a substantial majority of players must acquire the cognitive faculties which will enable them to play a part in this new society" (European Commission 2000, p.146), then only the 'educated minority' can make this happen, and only a concerted effort on their part to understand *how* this can happen will allow it to happen.

CHAPTER 8

PLANNING THEORY AT THE TURN OF THE CENTURY

Planning is as old as human society; it simply reflects the need to organize behavior for any collective endeavor. Its traces can be seen in all the remains of past civilizations. What has changed the, nature of planning in the past 200 years is the rise of industrial capitalism and the massive uprooting and concentrating of populations in urban centers. Mass society, in other words, has strained the social mechanisms for establishing and maintaining order in the ever-increasing complexity of modern industrial and/or postindustrial society. It is no longer possible for planning to be accomplished intuitively by a handful of male leaders, though this tribal mentality is hardly absent from the current hegemonic class in modern society. Nor was it absent from the group of often architect planners who envisioned the 'big plans' that gave form to nineteenth century Athens, Paris, Washington D.C., Chicago, etc. Nor has the rise of science, which accompanied and facilitated the rise of industrial capitalism, altered this mentality among, especially, male positivist scientists and engineers, who participate, even if only vicariously, in this exercise of domination and control. (Sandercock 1998, p.68)

What has changed in the twentieth century, of course, is the epistemology of planning. Thanks to the enlightenment and the liberation of thought from ecclesiastical authority, nature and subsequently society could be understood in totally different ways. This knowledge has allowed humans to reason about the mechanisms that govern natural and social phenomena, and to establish causal relationships that allow ever more sophisticated systems of planning and control to be imposed. Male hegemons can use these systems even if they don't understand fully their natural and, especially, social implications. Those in positions of power can always find some scientists and engineers to tell them only what they wish to hear about these effects, in any case. Thus, mass society is one that has been increasingly subject to technocratic control as a means to govern organized collective endeavors. This control is largely male dominated and is based in positive science. The rise of a theory and epistemology of planning has also been a positivist and masculine undertaking. According to Leonie Sandercock (1998 p.68, 70)

> Feminists argue that positivist epistemology excludes women as 'knowers' or agents of knowledge and excludes women's life experiences as valid foci of study; that this rise of science is a masculine one; and that history has been written only from the point of view of men of the dominant class and race.

> [Feminists] insist on the importance of discussing the politics of theory and method and the origins and implications of our theoretical hierarchies...[They] insist on paying attention to the political content of knowledge creation, to the ways in which knowledges are institutionalized, and to who benefits from the production of which knowledge.

> [They further] . . . argue that knowledge is not, has never been, gender neutral and that knowledge in planning, for example, is loaded with assumptions about the appropriate relations (of subordination and domination) between the sexes, as well as with assumptions about who is the legitimate knower.

It is worth quoting and listening at length to what Leonie Sandercock says, because it illustrates how profoundly absent has been the female voice in planning and science until very recently. It also helps to explain why and how planning theory had to change over the past forty years, in part because this female perspective came to be heard.

Technocratic (Positivist) Planning

While city planning was not unknown even in the large industrial cities of Europe and North America, it was the experience of Keynesian economics, socialist experimentation and the large scale planning required by the operations of the Second World War that encouraged a shift from design to scientific planning. Wartime reconstruction in Europe and economic 'reconstruction' in the U.S. posed huge planning problems on those two continents. War accounted for the destruction of property in European cities, while sophisticated political-economic 'forces' accomplished some of the same levels of destruction in northeastern, industrial cities in the U.S., though this was little understood even by scientific planners until Marxist structural analysis in the 1970's laid bare the workings of capitalism in urban space[1]. Also little appreciated were the enormous human costs in community mutilation and population displacement as a result of this destruction, something that (technocratic) social science and planning were largely blind to at that time.

Nevertheless, extensive applications of positive science brought new methods into areas like transportation planning, which uses concepts from physics such as the gravity model, and management and programming, which use concepts from systems theory and decision theory. Planning theory was assumed to be rational, objective and clinical. It sought to use theoretical (cause and effect) social science knowledge to regulate and control society for the good of all, good being defined by outside political processes or 'common sense'. It sought to influence decisions, suggest regulations such as zoning ordinances and subdivision regulations to rationalize space. In other contexts it sought to influence social policies and to rationalize the delivery of public services by regulating the public sector for the improvement of social life. It was a planning theory focused upon instrumental rationality, which studied organization theory, decision theory, systems theory, policy making and public choice theory, etc. It put emphasis on controlling and simulating reality, using explanations developed in the positivist social sciences. It was and is a planning theory of *means,* giving less importance to the substance of what is being planned for than to the methods that a proper planning theory should employ.

Positivist (modernist) planning sought to be *comprehensive* (to include all elements in the system being planned for), *rational* (to choose the most efficient means to achieve the stated goals), *technocratic* (to operate as an engineering model), *objective* (to act in no one's

---

1. A German mortgage banker visiting St.Louis in the early 1970's exclaimed that he had never seen such destruction of property as that in central St.Louis, except in Berlin after the war!

particular, but in the 'system's' interest), and *public* (to act in the public sphere and in the public interest). While there was a utopian urge in 19th century planning, this was largely lost under the positivist paradigm where it was replaced by system efficiency and other mechanistic concepts borrowed from the natural sciences. Furthermore, planners, because of their 'superior' knowledge based in positivist social science, were thought to occupy a privileged position in determining the 'best possible future' (see chapter 9) and the best means for arriving there. Needless to say, few practicing planners believe in their privileged position for more than five minutes after they confront the real centers of privilege (power) in their actual planning work[2]. The technocratic model, however, is taking much longer to be seen in its proper light and still appears to occupy premier status in the minds of most planners, practicing or academic, because of its symbolic importance as an occupational emblem. (Allmendinger 1999, pp.3, 250-4).

Scientific or positivist planning was and is closely related to the philosophy of social science from which it sprang in the middle of the twentieth century. Marios Camhis (1979) has traced these connections, suggesting and criticizing the evolution of scientific planning theory in the period since then up to the late 1970's. His first point is to stress the difference between a theory '*of* planning' and theories '*within* planning', the latter referring to substantive areas in which planning is in operation, a distinction drawn by Henry Hightower (1969) in the late sixties. Camhis (1979, p.6) stresses, in this respect, the real danger that an over emphasis on a theory *of* planning will lead to an occupational blindness to the substantive areas *within* planning, which themselves would suggest a planning strategy for leading that area into a better possible future. Ultimately, this raises the question of whether there can ever be a scientific theory of planning, based as it is on the mechanistic assumptions of positivist science, or whether a different set of ontological assumptions might suggest that this notion is naive, if not down right counter productive to whatever progressive impulses professional plan-

---

2. In 1959-60 I toured 20 North American cities, from Tampa to Anchorage and from Los Angeles to Montreal, where I interviewed planning directors, for Doxiadis' 'City of the Future' project. It was amazing how closely these directors already followed the patterns suggested by the phenomenology of planning developed by academics in the 1980's and 1990's, at least insofar as they negotiated with various powerful actors on the urban scene (see below).

ning might contain. But before examining this 'aporia', it would be well to retrace some of the ground covered in Chapter 1 as it relates to a theory of planning.

Camhis examines the scientific pedigree of planning within the ontological dichotomies of rationalism-irrationalism and materialism-idealism. The first dichotomy refers to the broader use of reason and intellect versus the use of the (irrational) supernatural and mystical. Rational here is distinct from the more technical meaning of rationalism as a deductive system based upon *a priori* assumptions, axioms and theorems, which, as we shall see, also can be related to a certain approach in planning. The broader meaning of rational is more general than, and may even be seen to incorporate, the more technical meaning. The latter technical meaning includes both deductive reasoning, where conclusions are drawn in a strict logical way from initial axiomatic statements, as well as inductive reasoning, where conclusions are drawn empirically from observation in the 'real' world.

In the second dichotomy above idealism constructs and tends to reify criteria for assessing an adequate understanding of reality and judges the perception of reality only in relation to those criteria, whereas materialism believes that objects are real and the criteria for understanding them vary according to our improved understanding of them. An example of idealism would be the belief that only those things that can be examined by the scientific method actually exist (at least from a rational standpoint), whereas an example of materialism would be the belief that wolves are different than dogs even if we cannot (at first) perceive a difference between them, or that the world is structured even if we can only see the effects of those structures, etc. The tendency of positivist science to reify method is not unlike the tendency of planning theory to reify instrumentalist rationality; they both lead to a form of idealism. So long as planning theory is a theory of means, a theory emphasizing instrumental rationality without concern for ends or for the substance of that which is being planned for, it is an idealist effort.

Fortunately, neither planning nor science follow the strict rules of their philosophies, with the result that both science and planning are far more flexible pragmatically than their norms would suggest. The results of this variability have not always been for the better, as Camhis illustrates in his examination of the twists and turns of science and planning. He examines one form of 'rational comprehensive planning' as the closest approach to the more narrow *a priori* deductive rationality defined above, where a utopian vision or blueprint is proposed as the axiomatic format for the planning process. This approach generally assumes some form of 'environmental determinism' as the basis for the anticipated success of the implemented plan. A comprehensive plan may also set a number of goals given to it from elsewhere (political processes, market processes, etc.) These goals serve as *a priori* axioms, on the basis of which planning strategies are deduced, i.e., the application of instrumental rationality assures that the most efficient means to achieve the given goals will be derived. Deductive rational planning may work well in a business enterprise because there is one over-riding goal, to maximize profit; all other actions and objectives are subordinate to it. Planning in society, however, has to accommodate a complex variety of goals, not all of which are compatible, a question that is repressed in the deductive planning approach.

Capitalist ideology has given rise to various 'explanations' about how overall (social) rationality is to be achieved. One of these is to assume generally, as does neo-classical economics, that the sum of individuals acting in a rational way will *automatically* produce a rational (social) whole. That different individuals might have different access to information, resources and power and that those who are advantaged with respect to this access could constitute themselves as a group or class that acts collectively to enhance this access at the expense of other individuals, or that business enterprises themselves would at some point declare themselves, legally, as 'individuals', even though their 'individual' budgets are larger than those of some countries, has simply been ignored in much of this subsequent (neo)liberal thought. The other explanation assumes that society is like an organism (or system) and will automatically, as such, rationalize its various parts. These two views are not incompatible and in some ways presuppose each other. Furthermore, they both serve to obscure the differential role of political economic power and, more importantly, have led planners to believe that the interests of the advantaged and powerful class were coterminous with the public interest (Camhis 1979, pp.23-24).

A modification on the strictly deductive approach is one which treats planning as 'advanced decision making', where a general set of goals is established, the means for achieving them outlined, the likely consequences of each examined in relation to the original set of goals, and a final choice of means established on the basis of this process (Camhis 1979, p.30). As Camhis points out, this moves the idea of rational planning towards the more general meaning of rational (as opposed to the irrational) and away from the previous restricted deductive meaning of the term. In fact, he likens this compromise to the hypothetico-deductive approach of science generally, where hypotheses are tested or verified against empirical facts in the same way that alternative planning strategies are tested against the stated goals.

As it turns out the idealist reification of method in planning has suffered the same 'discontent' as the hypothetico-deductive *method* in science, as seen in Chapter 1. Thus, Popperian 'falsification' as an attempt to preserve rationality in science was paralleled by 'disjointed-incrementalism', or 'muddling through' as the British planners called it, as an attempt to preserve rationality (in the more general sense) in planning (Camhis 1979, ch.2). The proposal to abandon large scale utopian engineering in planning is in keeping with Popper's anti-communist sentiments in his political writings, not that such large-scale planning in the Soviet Union was not fraught with difficulties, many of which have been examined in the planning literature as problems associated with trying to establish goals and planning strategies in a complex social system (Braybrooke and Lindblom 1963, and Lindblom 1965).

Nevertheless, incrementalism must be seen for what it is, an attempt to maintain the status quo. It would accomplish this by making only small-scale changes or corrections in the social system, whose effects could be closely monitored. It was, to quote an anti-poverty program director in the mid-sixties, speaking to a group of us eager recruits, planning that "would change something so that nothing need be changed". It is ". . . a problem-directed rather than a goal-directed approach" (Camhis 1979, p.41). If the status quo represents the order of things as desired by those with power in society, and if incrementalist planning will not even examine questions of power, let alone change anything other than that which would enhance the powerful, one can see that any claim to real progress is contradictory to this form of planning. Camhis (1979, p.54) also examines the use of systems theory in planning and directs the same criticism at it:

> [Systems theory]. . . tries to imitate the natural and biological sciences; makes non-valid analogies; includes only those aspects of reality that can be quantified; and ignores what is not susceptible to mathematical analysis. Finally, both systems theory and falsification are ahistorical and conservative.

Efforts have been made to seek a 'happy medium' between the deductive rationality of comprehensive planning and the non-change approach of incrementalism planning, so as to give planning a more realistic role without suggesting such a tightly controlled logic. Mixed-scanning, developed by Amitai Etzioni (1973, 1968), seeks to combine deductive rationalism and incrementalism in an approach that allows both high-level goal setting and incremental planning decisions, with continuous effort to relate these two levels during the planning process. Such an approach to planning allows a good deal of feedback during implementation and mitigates the deterministic tendencies found in comprehensive planning. This approach does not resolve the issue of combining often-incompatible goals, however, or of even arriving at an agreed upon set of general goals in the first place, and thus begs the question of how specific decisions are to be related in the feedback process. Thus planners and decision makers would need supernatural powers of foresight if they were to evaluate effects of specific decisions on the overall course of planning. This is especially true in the application of systems theory and cybernetics to the planning process, given that these techniques are useful in closed or nearly closed systems, whereas social systems are always open, especially in the context of modern capitalism (but even socialism, as the former Soviet Union or utopian religious communities in the U.S. have learned to their dismay).

Mixed scanning is compared by Camhis (1979, pp.65-72) to Imre Lakatos' (1970) 'methodology of scientific research programmes', suggesting that both efforts brought more flexibility and pragmatism to the processes of planning and science. But both were ". . . unwilling to expose further difficulties inherent in the attempt to define 'rational' and 'objective' criteria that can be applied in the process of planning or in the philosophy of science, as well as the difficulties present in trying to solve problems through the specification of a methodology that claims universal applicability" (Camhis 1979, p.72). These and further unresolved problems in the uses of instrumental rationality are summarized by Sandercock (1998, p.88) in a quote from Judith Innes (1995, p.88):

> Rittel and Weber (1973) . . . pointed out 'wicked problems' which could not be solved because the problem definition kept shifting and there was no way to aggregate incommensurable values. The unsolvable puzzles were many, including the tragedy of the commons (Hardin, 1968), the prisoner's dilemma (Rapaport and Chammah 1965), the failure of col-

lective action (Olson 1965), the limitations of Cost-Benefit analysis and other systematic analytic methods (Rivlin 1971), the indeterminacy of the implementation process (Bardock 1977; Pressman and Wildavsky 1973), the inevitability of uncertainty in goal and technology for planning problems (Christensen 1985), the impossibility of aggregating the public interest so that its optimization can be amenable to rational systematic analysis (Altshuler 1965), and the impossibility of relying on the large-scale model for societal guidance (Lee 1973). [For references, see Innes article].

All of these methods and their inherent dilemmas are predicated on the use of monetary values as a measure of benefits and costs, and on the assumption that all human welfare can be reduced to such values. Indeed, this fact may have done more damage to humanity than all the above dilemmas combined. This question will be taken up in Chapter 10, in an attempt to humanize planning theory.

Finally, rational (positivist) planning borrowed not only the deterministic and mechanistic assumptions of positivist social science, but also its misplaced arrogance; both believed that they were real centers of power in modern, mass (capitalist) society, this power deriving from the superior knowledge to be gained from applications of 'certain' scientific methodology to the understanding and explanation of society. This certainty, this arrogance has disappeared to some extent among practicing planners and applied social scientists, at least to a greater extent than it has among technocratic academic theorists. Nevertheless, the effects of this attitude have been strong enough to create a rather dark side of planning history, modified only in part by the 'enlightenment' of the 1960's (Flyvbjerg 1996). This history is marked by the absence of any mention of the contribution of women to planned solutions to social problems in the past (Sandercock 1998, pp.37-38). Even worse the modernist architect- planner embodies:

> . . . an implicit conceptualization of planning as a system of installing patriarch order, a system of gendered control of urban space in which women's place was in the realm of the emotions, the body, the private - that is, the home. In Hooper's (1998) reading, modernist planning is a masculinist order, ultimately, a masculinist fantasy of control (Sandercock 1998, p.24).

Also absent is any mention of the fate of minorities at the hands of state planners, ranging from American segregation policies resulting in a whole system of planned 'reservations' for Native Americans, or public housing 'projects', as they were referred to in postwar American cities, as places where Blacks were 'concentrated'. It is important to reveal these aspects of 'rational planning' because ". . . unless we discuss these hidden intentions and consequences of planning practices, we will continue to perpetuate them" (Sandercock 1998, p.41).

There have been important shifts in planning theory and practice as a result of the critiques elaborated above, but there has apparently been no global shift in professional attitudes. As Allmendinger (1999, p.3) states:

> . . . planning and planners are [not] pushing for any great
> change or re-evaluation of their role. After 50 years, the
> message emanating from academics and professional [in
> the U.K.] seems to be 'business as usual, please'. The 1997
> Royal Town Planning Institute (RTPI) members survey
> found that the main reason for becoming a member was
> career progression while central government was seen as
> the main source of thinking about planning. . .The techno-
> cratic professional seems alive and well.

The reason why this is so is because planning in the advanced capitalist countries has a social status; it has arrived as a profession; and, most of all, it is not a threat to the status quo. Its status is based exactly upon its technical skills, its quantitative methodology, and the mystifying language of mathematics. Most planners are not willing to jeopardize their social (professional) status by suggesting that rational planning is not all that it appears to be. It must give an impression of objectivity and certainty and ward off the fear of anarchy, of chaos. At the same time, it does embody cultural capital; it is symbolically important and socially legitimated. Even if planning is not strictly rational, it must, for sociological reasons, offer the illusion that it is.

The Phenomenological Turn

The dilemmas in technocratic planning theory eventually fostered a search for new ways of explaining the social and professional role of planning. This entailed a phenomenological turn in planning theory which encompassed two separate but related questions: 1) what do planners actually do, a sort of 'ethnomethodology' of planning?, and, 2) what *should* planners do, given a growing understanding of the phenomenology of their activities? The latter has usually been seen to entail a discussion of good communication techniques, often with the framework of a Habermasian ideal speech situation.

A fortunate turn of events in the Unites States prompted this interest in the phenomenology of planning, though it has never been referred to as such in the now extensive literature on 'what is to be done' in planning once the technocratic model had been seen to be inadequate. Because the United States has enormous financial resources to devote to social-political problems, notwithstanding various other economic parameters that accompany any given stage in the evolution of its always troubled capitalist political-economic system, it could create a social mechanism outside the usual channels of local municipal planning, This it did in the 1960's when the Great Society program gave birth to hundreds of community planning projects with funding directly from the federal government. In the process it created a class of planners interested in planning at that level and, to some degree at least, outside the immediate control of the local municipal planning authorities.

These community planners became, in time, a set of 'Guerillas in the Bureaucracy' (Needleman and Needleman 1974), many of whom identified with their communities and often in conflict with the (technocratic) planning agencies that also employed them. While technocratic planners in the U.S. prior to this time had to some extent understood the limitations of positivist planning and had accepted the 'political' and communicative dimensions of planning, they had rarely shifted their identity to the disadvantaged to the degree that community planners did in the 1960's and early 1970's. This identity shift translated ultimately into an opposition between planning conceived as something to be accomplished by trained technocratic professionals and planning which requires the meaningful participation of those affected by the planning, with all that this might imply in terms of both the training that planners should receive, as well as the actual set of professional activities they should engage in. Not only were early community planners unprepared for this type of planning, but neither were the communities themselves, to say nothing of the existing institutional structures of planning in American cities. Indeed, as the Needlemans say, (1974, p.89) "Community planning fits into the community's expectations and the

city's institutional structures like a heretic in church", an idea expressed
by Theodore Roszak (1969) in somewhat more colorful language in the
60's when referring to the introduction of moral questions into the
cathedral of positive science.

Most community planners, therefore, educated themselves on the
job, so to speak. They sometimes found themselves serving as lightning
rods for community anger, which was often the case when they were
identified with the 'establishment'. In more positive circumstances they
would serve as providers of technical knowledge and/or guides through
the government bureaucracies, and, ultimately as allies in community
struggles for community planning objectives or against threatening city
policies (Needleman and Needleman 1974, p. 63-4). In most cases they
were caught up in an exhausting round of meetings and activities with
an emotional involvement that could only be compared to life in the theater. Indeed, community planning is much more closely related to theater and art than it is to science and engineering, suggesting much of
what was to become the new metaphor for planning under the phenomenological perspective.

Community planners thus found themselves thrust onto the urban
stage as protagonists with little knowledge of what to expect. The past
history of undemocratic, technocratic planning had created a backlog of
hostility which often attached to the planner as the nearest target. Only
time and hard work could deflect this hostility to others in the local
bureaucracy, not always necessarily other planners. Here community
education could play an important role, teaching citizens where the true
power actually lay, as it were, assuming, of course,that the community
planners were in command of such a structuralist understanding in the
first place. Other dilemmas were even more difficult to resolve. For
example, communities were more likely to be interested in social priorities, while city planning is directed to physical interventions.
Furthermore, there were often conflicts of interest between community
priorities and overall urban requirements, and, finally, communities and
their planners have usually had limited ability (power) to influence larger events on the urban scene (Needleman and Neeldeman 1974, p.86).

Confronted by the problems inherent in conflicts between community and city-wide planning, some (advocacy type) planners became
guerillas in the bureaucracy, undermining the actions of the official planners, and sometimes engaging in open administrative insurgency
(Needleman and Needleman, 1974, p.120). This posed a more general

problem for planning, both as theory and as practice: should community (or advocacy) planners merely reflect community needs or should they also seek to *educate* communities and their citizens to better understand the political-economic structure of the city and their 'true' needs within it? This question leads beyond the (descriptive) phenomenology of planning and will be taken up in the last part of this chapter. It is important to realize, nevertheless, how moving out of the official institutionalized role of technocratic planning has opened the door to these and other such questions for the profession as a whole.

Community planners confront most of the same sorts of problems that anthropologists confronted as they began to move out of the 'armchair' and into the field since the early twentieth century. Planners who move beyond the 'armchair' of their traditional technocratic role could benefit immensely from the accumulated experience of anthropology and phenomenological sociology in this respect (Junker, 1960; Jongmans, 1967; Williams, T.R. 1967). Fieldwork (and community planning) require gaining entrance to a community, winning the confidence of the local population, listening to and understanding the socially constructed reality of the community, constantly deepening this understanding by checking it against actual situations and with a range of local informants, avoiding leadership roles so as not to disrupt the community upon departure, and so forth.

The Needleman's (1974, Ch.6) applied these phenomenological techniques to a description of the socially constructed reality of planning generally in American cities in the early 1970s. Planning, for all its legitimate place in urban government, has had no clear role in the minds of local political leaders. As the Needleman's say (1974, p.169),

> . . . the concept of rationalized centralized city planning fits awkwardly into the fundamentally irrational value system of a 'liberal' society. . .the physical shape of the city is still determined primarily by private developers who follow the logic of individual profits rather than rational land development, and the administrative policies of city government are usually based on considerations of politics rather than planning decisions.

The Needleman's labeled the planning style which develops within such an irrational context 'counter-irrationality'. Staff assignments, project development and even hiring practices are determined more by political expediency than by any rational organizational plan. Planners act more like librarians, technical advisors and legitimators of political-ly motivated decisions than anything suggested in the professional role model. Technocratic planning itself is fragmented, *ad hoc* and spas-modic in such a context, further contributing to the 'discontent' of the profession. Nonetheless, many technocratic planners have clung to their professional identity, for the reasons discussed above, which often brings them into conflict with community-based planners who are much more politicized, more democratic and more radical in their approach to planning. In fact, the latter consider it to be immoral and professionally irresponsible not to be more interested in the execution or implementa-tion of plans, however much this might involve them in political and even insurgent guerilla activities within the urban administration.

Actual contact with the people has forced community planners to realize that many social problems cannot be solved with physical plans, undermining the 'environmental', or 'physical determinism' that is so common among technocratic planners. Given that the history of city planning since the nineteenth century on has been a history of physical planning, one can see how disquieting this new approach to planning has been for the profession. Nevertheless, an awareness that physical blight is a product of deeper social structural problems is an important insight that community planning has brought to planning thought, one that leaves physically-oriented planners at a loss as to what they should do, indeed, as to what they are, professionally, causing a potential iden-tity crisis of no small proportions.

One response to this insight that physical problems are a product of social or political-economic causes is simply to ignore it. Practicing technocratic planners are quite aware of the tenuous status of planning as a substantive activity within the political economy of capitalism, though they are unlikely to see it in such terms. In any case, they are not willing to jeopardize this tenuous status and the social and economic rewards that it entails by imagining themselves as anything other than 'good' technocrats. But the Pandora's box of citizen involvement, and a deeper level of structural understanding, was opened by the communi-ty planning experiment in the 1960's and early 1970's. Now the ineffec-tiveness of planning can be seen not as a psychological problem for dis-appointed, often cynical professional planners, but ultimately as a social and political-economic problem, with all that this entails for planning thought and practice. Nor is this dilemma restricted to planning; it extends to most of the professions offering services to the people, from health care professionals, to social workers, to child psychologists, to educators, and so on.

The rebellion against systems of authority and discrimination that marked the 1960's, and which gave rise to a complex of thought that would later be called postmodernism, also gave rise to the community planning experiment in the United States as part of a general State reaction that sought to 'change something so that nothing need be changed'. This experiment, along with a general surge in awareness associated with the "Making of a Counterculture", to quote the title of Roszak's (1969) influential book, has resulted in a serious (re)examination of the actual phenomenology of planning within academia and the profession. 'Hidden' forms of discrimination against women, minorities, homosexuals, etc., have been shown to be associated with the positivist theory of planning (Sandercock 1998; Dear 2000). Attention has also turned to the politics and persuasion involved in planning practice (Hoch 1996a, 1996b, Forester 1989, Fischer and Forester 1993), to the question of citizen participation (Pateman 1970, Burke, E. 1979, Fagence 1977, Healey 1997), and to the need to democratize planning and decision-making generally (Zisk 1992; Pierce, et al 1992; Svara 1994; Fischer 1994; Clarke and Rempel 1997; Turner and Hulme 1997; Douglas and Friedman 1998; Steinmetz 1999; Larsen 2000; Estrella 2000; Watson and Barber 2000). Also examined have been questions relating to the ethics of planning (Wachs 1985; Harper and Stein 1992; Hendler 1995).

Each of these new areas of interest suggests new roles for planners and new knowledge and skills that have not been a part of the preparation for the technocratic professional role. Certain skills, like argumentation and negotiation, are necessarily learned on the job, but in the postmodern world of planning the range of voices that has to be heard has increased dramatically. And the more voices that must be heard, the more complex and less technical becomes the planning process. Technocratically oriented planners seek precise engineering solutions, but the socially constructed reality of planning is more like the competing voices of the theater, the parliament, or the 'agora'. In such contexts, humans have to make choices between apparently equally valid claims. These are ethical choices and there are few technical or instrumental means for making them. Positivist social scientists and technocratic planners have sought to escape the painful distress of such choices by regressing to and reifying their methods. The new phenomenological turn in planning theory has argued forcefully against this reification, and has exposed planning thought to the messy reality of argumentation and rhetoric (Fischer and Forester 1993). Thus, Throgmorton, (1993, p.117) suggests that

> . . . *all planning and analysis is rhetorical* [author's emphasis], and that tools such as survey research, computer modeling, and forecasting can be thought of as rhetorical tropes; that is as figures of speech and argument that give persuasive power to the larger narratives of which they are a part. As rhetorical tropes used in practice, such tools also construct the planning analyst's character and the kinds of communities that can be formed between planning analysts and their audiences.

If planning analyses and documents are seen as rhetorical devices (in addition to whatever technical purposes they might serve), then planners must consider what this means. In other words, different audiences might require different presentations, as architects, for example, use models and renderings for lay audiences and sections and plans for audiences composed of fellow architects. Indeed, actual buildings may serve this rhetorical purpose for architects and their clients (Gutenschwager 1996). Furthermore, planning as rhetoric must also then be seen as part of a conversation, as statements directed towards actual or anticipated responses from an audience or audiences relevant to the planning situation. Learning to read audiences and imagining how they will respond requires hermeneutic skills of the sort that politicians either must learn or, more often, possess intuitively. Here ambiguity is frequently more useful than precision, as this allows more flexibility in interpretation by different audiences who will 'read into' utterances what they wish to hear, as a result of the psychology of 'selective perception'. The reason for drawing attention to this rhetorical aspect of planning is not to suggest some Machiavellian use of language, but to emphasize the importance of being understood (and not misunderstood) in the service of more adequate communication during the planning process. In other words, research results, technical documents and planning statements are not neutral, as positivist science and planning theory would lead us to believe. The very same technical information can be used in a variety of ways and for a variety of purposes, all of which must be imagined and understood by planners as they go about their professional activities; the age of technocratic innocence is being eclipsed by a phenomenological sophistication in planning theory.

The understanding of selective perception and reception of communication can be deepened by recalling the importance of paradigms in the history of science or the systems of relevance and multiple social realties as discussed in Part I of this book. At a national or regional scale, these frames of reference are understood as culture, but within planning situations they may be constituted by such things as professional training, class location or life generally. Especially important are those associated with minority status in a larger dominant culture. In this sense, Rein and Schon (1993, p.148) refer to the distinction between 'policy disagreements' and 'policy controversies'. The former refer to conflicts *within* a given frame of reference which can usually be resolved through reference to the commonly agreed-upon rules within the frame, and the latter to conflict *between* frames of reference which cannot be so easily resolved because "the same body of evidence can be used to support quite different policy positions". Conflict resolution in the latter case reminds one of the problems Kuhn describes in the process of paradigm conflict. Because frames of reference, like paradigms, are composed of a complex set of normative and ontological assumptions, as well as sets of evidence and facts related to them, it is often necessary to delve into these subjective depths in order to resolve conflict between competing frames. This generally is a long and sometimes painful process because of the interactions between cognitive, emotional and ethical presuppositions that mark the acquisition of a frame of reference. Thus, it is not unlike the transformational demands placed upon planners who confront the shift from a technocratic to a phenomenological framework in planning theory, itself.

The specter of relativism is never far from a discussion on frames of reference; indeed, postmodernism often glorifies this relativism. However, decisions cannot be made in a totally relativistic world; some closure is always needed if a specific action is to proceed. Specific problems often force an examination of paradigmatic assumptions in this respect, hopefully leading to an understanding that sometimes assumptions, as well as their frameworks, are useful and applicable only in certain circumstances, some of which may no longer even be in force. In this context, the planner's ability to translate across frameworks and circumstances to illustrate the appropriateness of one or the other perspective is a very useful negotiating skill. This is not just a question of translating issues and circumstances into the, sometimes mystifying, language of positivist social science or technocratic planning, a defensive course of action often chosen in earlier, innocent times. Rather, this is the need to be able to interpret and understand the differing social realities and to find some common ground among them, if possible. Just being sensitive to this as an issue is the most important first step to developing this skill.

A more hazardous course for planners is the attempt to de-reify the assumptions and inferences in a given framework, assuming, of course, that they have already been able to do this for their own framework. Here, assumptions are examined for what they are, the product of human thought and experience, not the product of divine inspiration, natural 'law', or some other outside force, something which their taken-for-grantedness is likely to encourage. I say 'hazardous' because de-reification is a more painful experience even than conversion to a new framework; it not only involves great emotional and moral costs, but it also confronts the chaos of social existence. It is the supreme loss of certainty; once again glorified by postmodernism, but not to be taken lightly.

These are all issues raised by the context of this discussion on frames of reference. If positive science is no longer the only framework within which policy and planning controversies can be resolved, then nothing can substitute for a planning theory that is sophisticated in the social psychology of phenomenology and hermeneutics, and in seeking to generate a social context within which such understandings are made possible. This is an important prerequisite to the ideal speech situation to which Habermas' theory of communicative action is directed (Habermas 1984). It is a situation in which different parties may listen to each other's 'stories' and from them understand the sometimes hidden biases in presupposition and belief that guide different judgements and behaviors (Dryzek 1993). Dryzek makes an important distinction between clients and audiences in this respect. Persuading clients, the typical situation in the architectural design model of planning, for example, is quite different from persuading an audience, many of whom may have no interest in implementing a given policy or a plan. Indeed, they may see this as threatening to some of their own policies and plans.

In the past these potential conflicts of interest would have been resolved by reference to 'objective' facts and scientific (positivist) reasoning. In the United States, at least, it was the failure of this approach to succeed in most of its major efforts in the 1960s and 1970s that caused a change in the approach to national policy-making and planning. Dryzek (1993, p.219) quotes DeLeon (1998, p.96) here: "If the Great Society programs, Vietnam and the energy crisis taught anything to policy scholars and practitioners, it should have been humility regarding both the power of their tools and their roles in actual decision making". While these statements suggest a structural analysis of these 'failures', one which would place them in the context of the world capitalist system (see below), they can still be examined within a phenomenological framework, which is necessary, in any case, in order for a critical planning theory to be advanced. The call for an ethic of communication in planning and policy discourse is of unusual importance in any system that calls itself democratic, and is probably indispensable if planning is to succeed in such a framework. An ethic of communication would involve ". . . exposing and counteracting manipulation of agendas, illegitimate exercises of power, skewed distribution of information, and attempts to distract attention . . . Dialogue in the ideal speech situation is free from deception, self-deception, domination, strategizing, and any exclusion of participants or arguments" (Dryzek 1993, p.228).

These rules should lead to a search not only for a new critical approach to planning, but to democracy in general. Current 'democratic' systems are rife with the violation of these rules, which would account for the growing discontent with established political institutions. Planners have to work in the face of this antipathy, as well as in the face of ignorance. Thus, in addition to their skills as learners (in the anthropological sense) and as communicators, they must also develop skills as educators.

Education is a special case of translation, but also, as we shall see, a special case of learning as well. Unlike the translation among competing frames of reference in a policy debate, education is involved in translating complex, technical information into common, everyday language. Citizen participation, in particular, but even participation by business or political leaders, may require extensive education about the likely effects of any given course of action, such as the implementation of a plan or the application of a policy. Given the variation in paradigmatic suppositions outlined in Part I of this book, one can appreciate that this is not simply a matter of translating scientific (mechanistic) explanations into everyday language; it is a problem of allowing social reality to be presented in all of its positivist, phenomenological and structural complexity. This problem of translation takes us far beyond the idea of the 'report' and the 'presentation', however clearly formatted with audio-visual techniques they may be.

Besides the methodological variation suggested by differing social science paradigms, planning research, itself, is a form of directed learning for planners. As such, it could be directed in part to anticipated planning actions themselves (Argyris, et al, 1985). This would entail, among other things, participation of those affected by the research in the actual design of the research (Argyris, et al, 1985, p.xiii). In this way the research process would be a learning experience for citizens as well, while also ensuring that the results of the research would not be 'alien' to those citizens. Such an approach to research would direct attention to those things that might need to be changed, i.e., subjected to planning or policy actions, something which neither positivist nor phenomenological research is necessarily aimed at accomplishing (Argyris 1985, Ch.8). Meanwhile, a communicative, participatory approach could further alter the way such planning-oriented research intentions were realized, when contrasted to the technocratic approach.

Another teaching-learning technique that could be used in planning and policy analysis is focus groups (Kreuger 1994). Focus groups are small groups of 8-10 people, hopefully representative of a larger community, who meet to discuss a specific topic. They have been used mainly as a marketing device, but constitute an approach that lends itself to social research and participatory planning as well. Focus groups require a moderator who guides the discussion and some means of keeping a record. While they have been used mostly as a research technique, there is no reason why they cannot also be used to educate, or to experiment with ways of educating citizens on planning problems and issues. If the focus groups are representative of, or even include, citizens with leadership roles in larger communities, the effects can be amplified. At the same time, valuable in-depth information can be gained about how best to communicate to larger communities on any given set of issues.

A more complex learning device that could be employed in citizen education is the simulation game. Simulation games can not only abstract on and summarize important aspects of any planning situation, they also require participation and human interaction, valuable attributes in any learning situation (Boocock and Schild 1968). They also allow attention to focus on the importance of the rules that govern the game and, thus, on the aspect of social reality to which they refer. In this sense, games are free to allow exploration of any form of maximizing behavior for individuals and/or groups, and not just those related to monetary values to which most planning situations are reduced. Thus, important human needs, such as security, self-esteem, or even self-actualization can be played out in the gaming situation allowing insight into some of the 'hidden' benefits and costs of planning situations. Group needs for democracy, participation and justice, or the destructive (or constructive) effects of competition or conflict, can also be built into and evaluated in the gaming situation.

Simulation games have the ability to combine both mechanistic and/or systems aspects of social reality with more humanistic attributes such as those on which phenomenology and/or theater are based. If the puzzle is the prototypical positivist form and theater is the prototype for artistic form, the simulation game has the unique ability to combine these forms in a particularly satisfying way.

> [The simulation game]. . .combines both theater and puzzle. It accommodates both dramatic and mechanistic forms of behavior, and perhaps more importantly, it may be perceived in both of these forms by the players. The result is that while players attempt to solve the puzzle or mechanism that underlies the game, as the author of the game had to solve and validate the 'puzzle' in the real world in order to construct the game, they are also aware that the game may have a variety of outcomes. They may also be helped to understand . . . that the rules governing the play of the game are representative -- and reasonably so -- of the real world rules. Nevertheless, the rules governing the game mechanism are largely a scientific convenience designed to produce the appropriate outcomes in relation to the range of possible decisions by the players. The players play against the 'black box' of the game mechanism much as they play against a real world only partially known to them. In that respect, the game is 'real'. At the same time, they interact with other players within a moral context of things to do and not to do, and in the end judge the outcomes as good or bad for themselves or others. In this

respect, also, the game is 'real'. Solving the puzzle, however, and judging the play and its outcomes (as both action and theater) are two quite different acts of knowing, and they derive from the ability of the game to reflect reality from the two different points of view expressed above. The puzzle has but one solution, the one built into the mechanism of the game, but the outcomes deriving from the goal-seeking actions and interactions of the players can be many. Judging the outcomes is generally based upon criteria existing outside the game itself, though the game experience ought to illustrate the implications of the judgements underlying the rules of play and the effects of these rules on the players' judgements and on the outcome of the game. This in turn is much like the experience of watching the outcome of a play [or story], where the audiences, and actors, experience the effects of the actors' moral judgements and their derived actions (Gutenschwager 1979, p.30-31).

It is important to emphasize that simulation games be used as heuristic and not as problem solving devices. In this sense, computerized simulation games are not very useful; they obscure more than they illuminate and educate. They place too much emphasis on the mechanistic and not enough on the sociodramatic. Players need to be able to see the game transactions taking place and the human emotions that accompany them. Only in this way may such experiences approach 'ideal speech situations'.

Simulation games, focus groups, action research, street theater, devised theater, posters, pamphlets, comic books, etc., are some examples of the many techniques that may be used to implement the idea of a participatory, democratic approach to planning. Once the theoretical issues have been worked out, the profession can draw upon the widespread experience of those interested in education and communication to complete its phenomenological purpose. Meanwhile, this purpose, itself, may need to be strengthened and broadened by a structural understanding of planning and its role in the larger social, political, and economic scene on which it plays out this purpose.

The Social Structure of Planning

The essence of structuralism, as seen in chapters 3 and 6, is the study of relationships. Structural analysis would thus *locate* planning as an activity, as well as theories about, or *of,* planning in the social structures of the time and place where they are found. Interest in structuralism in planning theory has been reflected mainly in an increase in the applications of Marxist theory in the social sciences since the 1970's. Structuralism has not really been taken up to a large extent by planning theory, however, at least in the English-speaking world. Part of the reason for this is that it gives no clear direction to professional planning activity; its methodology calls for 'reflective abstraction', a not very satisfying approach for the pragmatist mind-set in either technocratic or communicative planning. Furthermore, it is likely to move planning thought beyond the radicalism embodied in the participatory approach into the more disquieting waters of national, even international, political activism. Thus, the many reviews of the history of planning and its theory that has occasioned and/or been occasioned by the phenomenological turn do not refer in any systematic way to the changes in the political economy of capitalism that have inspired these changes.

Planning is embedded in the structures of capitalism, the system which has increasingly defined life on this planet over the past several hundred years, and even longer if we consider mercantilism as its antecedent structuring force. The shift of planning from a design to a scientific orientation half a century ago was a product of the crisis in the world capitalist system, a crisis in over-production and over-accumulation that brought a wave of speculative activity, which ended in the Great Depression. This was not the first (or the last) such crisis in the capitalist system, but it was the most threatening up to that time. There was a bright and a dark side to the resolution of this crisis. The bright side was the application of Keynesian economic theory and the creation of the welfare state, a development that suggested that people in a mass society could live with some level of satisfaction of their basic needs, including especially a minimum sense of security, hence the name 'Social Security'.

The dark side of the resolution was war. War, of course, has not been unknown to capitalism; it is its very essence, both literally and metaphorically. The massive destruction of human life and property that resulted from the advanced weaponry of the two world and subsequent wars in the twentieth century has modified the degree to which it can be imagined as an ultimate means to resolve the metaphorical war that is represented by the competitive nature of the system, though, as seen in Chapter 7, this has in no way altered the desire to develop new, more destructive weaponry, nor the importance of the war machine in the economic structures of capitalism.

In any case, these responses to the Great Depression in the U.S. created both the idea and the need for a more broadly based scientific approach to planning at all levels of society. Thus, the subsequent history of the idea of planning must be related to the structural needs of capitalism. For example, the Second World War and the sudden increase in industrial production needed to sustain it also produced a need for additions to the labor force, needs that were met in the U.S. by recruiting drives in the South and in the 'suburbs'. The result was a substantial increase in the migration of rural populations, especially blacks, to the industrial belt cities of the North, and of housewives from the central and peripheral areas of those same cities into industrial employment. These two populations tasted the independence and self-esteem brought about by well-paid and more or less satisfactory employment. Their sudden dismissal at the end of the war sent 'Rosie the Riveter' back to the suburban homestead where she would constitute a reserve of consciousness to inspire the subsequent feminist movement, and unemployed blacks into the ghettos where they would create a set of planning problems for the newly 'scientized' profession of planning. Unemployed wives could be seduced by the new cornucopia of consumer goods, including the 'good life' in new towns and new suburbs, where they were once again 'subordinated' to their well-paid husbands who benefited from the post-war boom in the world economy.

Suburban development, meanwhile, as the critical, usually Marxist, geographers and sociologists would demonstrate, was not unrelated to the structural forces of capitalism as they worked themselves out in urban space. Insurance companies and banks engaged in 'red-lining' practices where central city areas were outlined and 'outlawed' for the insurance and financial assistance that is necessary to protect property values. Meanwhile, federally assisted financing in the form of Veteran's Administration and Federal Housing Administration loan insurance in the U.S. included regulations that allowed only lower density suburban housing to qualify. The combination of these factors stimulated economic activity in all the sectors related to suburban development, including especially the automobile industry. This created the need for planning of these new suburbs and of new transportation systems, particularly superhighways to accommodate them, which in turn called for the application of many of the newly developed scientific planning techniques, related especially to urban infrastructure and land use and transportation modeling. Inner city banks (among others) in the meantime, were siphoning off deposits from central city dwellers to finance this suburban development, even while denying this financing to those same depositors.

At the same time, the other populations of 'redundant' workers, to use the colorful British euphemism, i.e., the blacks and other Latino populations who had migrated north to take advantage of the war industry, were simply left to fend for themselves. One result was the race riots in American cities in the late 1940's and the resulting birth of a planning specialty in 'race relations'. The newly enforced poverty experienced by these populations also, in time, created new scientific planning approaches in social work, education, health care, and so forth. They also created the need for new scientific planning applications in housing and urban renewal, as the massive destruction in exchange-values of inner city property resulting from red-lining in time also resulted in the massive destruction of use-values, prompting the comment on the 'bombed out' look of inner cities by the German mortgage banker mentioned above.

The fate of housing for the minority populations was described by Meyerson and Banfield (1955) in their book entitled *"Politics, Planning and the Public Interest"* where 'politics' would substitute for the interests and workings of capital on the urban scene. These public housing projects, as I discovered myself while working on a report for the Chicago Plan Commission in the mid-fifties, were remarkably different from similar projects designed to house rural white or sometimes Native American populations prior to World War II. Those pre-war projects were low density, low-rise projects, integrated into existing neighborhoods. The post-war housing projects were high-rise, high density, and highly segregated. Pruitt-Igoe, a prototype, architectural-prize-winning project in St Louis that was blown-up twenty or so years after its construction, was much studied by sociologists in an effort to understand its failure as a planned solution to low income housing (Rainwater 1970). 'Politics' had again resulted in many architectural design modifications that rendered the projects unlivable for the low- or non-income families that occupied them.

This dark side of urban and social planning exposed its racism and discrimination and was one important factor that prompted awareness among blacks and a sufficient number of whites to inspire the Civil Rights Movement of the early 1960's in the U.S. This movement was part of an extended world-wide insurgence against authority structures that depended upon and used scientific planning as a means of fostering economic (technological) development, while controlling people (and nature) in the name of progress (Leiss 1974). It evolved quite naturally into, and paralleled, the anti (Vietnam) war movement in the U.S. in the late 1960s, marking the first time that young people refused to participate in the imperial adventures of the American war machine. Both the Civil Rights and the anti-war movement raised awareness about capitalism, prompting a resurgence in reading and writing about Marxist structuralism on both sides of the Atlantic. Meanwhile, the rest of the (Third) world had experienced enough of the darker side of capitalism so as not to require such 'enlightenment', though there was a burst of writing on 'dependency' coming out of Latin America and Africa especially, which helped explain to First World audiences how capitalism actually worked in the periphery. As explained above, the Great Society Program resulted in large part from these movements and gave many young planners the opportunity to come even closer to the dark side of planning. One result was the phenomenological turn in planning theory over the past quarter of a century, as evidenced by the large number of writings attesting to this transformation.

Meanwhile, there is a danger that learning to communicate and negotiate more effectively will simply add a layer of phenomenologically oriented instrumentality to the former technocratic mentality. Thus, if planning theory is still understood as a set of rational methods specific to the situation at hand, now bolstered by rhetorical techniques referring to the manner of negotiating the application of these techniques, and if the measure of success is the ability to execute plans according to their 'sponsor's' interests, even if these are localized interests, then planning theory is still relegated to the same apolitical and amoral status as that propagated by the earlier 'value free' positivist approach. Thus, in order to transform itself, to move beyond an effort to find a universal method, it must also include and be governed by a social theory in the broad sense, one that would explain existing reality in a form other than as propaganda that serves the status quo. It must, in other words, encompass a 'counter-analysis' (Sandercock 1996, p.85), which would also include a theory of 'social transformation'. This was the practical purpose of Marxism, but the social transformation it sought was too dependent upon authoritarian structures, adequate, in some sense, for an underdeveloped largely uneducated population, but not possible to sustain when the complexity of the system and the demands for participation increased. Thus,

> . . .a broader, more political definition of planning domains and practices [its structure] . . . will have to include mobilizing constituencies, protests, strikes, acts of civil disobedience, community organization, professional advocacy and research, publicity, as well as the proposing and drafting of laws and new programs of social intervention (Sandercock 1998, p.204).

A dialectic structuralism sees this (re) definition of radical planning as an effort to place planning and social theory within the process whereby theory confronts reality and is shaped by it, even while it is helping to shape it. Changes in theory do not occur separate from the reality that it seeks to explain, and this reality and the changes in it inspire changes in that theory.

> Theoretical transformations (especially in the social sciences. . .) are neither the unfolding of independent ideas in the mind, nor simply the outcome of contradictions within a theoretical domain between theory and a static reality. They are strongly related to and affected by changes in reality itself. This position is not to be taken as advocating some kind of materialist determinism. Ideas or theories are themselves part of reality, and at the same time are instrumental in structuring and restructuring this reality (Camhis 1979, p.126).

The modern world system is in the process of being deconstructed, even dismantled, by capital, in a desperate search to maintain profit levels. Workers at every level in the socio-occupational hierarchy are forced into an equally desperate search to find security, often by migrating within and/or among countries. Finally, those in the humanities and the social sciences seek to explain all of this. The efforts of capital can be seen in a combination of 1) Reaganism/Thatcherism or neo-liberalism that has sought, and to a remarkable degree achieved, the dismantling of the welfare state, including any restrictions on the search for profit at home, and 2) globalization, which seeks the elimination of any restrictions on the search for profit overseas, especially in the Third World. The efforts of workers can be seen in the migratory flows from the countryside into the cities and into the advanced capitalist countries from the underdeveloped countries, but also between and among the cities of those developed countries. There is nothing new about all of these sorts of migration, which is simply to attest to the fact that people have responded to their dissatisfaction and insecurity, both before and during the rise of capitalism. What is not so much appreciated, or at least stressed, are the human costs of migration. Migrants are uprooted and their families and communities disrupted as a necessary by-product of their actions. Migrants are always 'homeless', even when not necessarily 'houseless', and their estrangement is often visited upon their children and grandchildren, especially if their skin color identifies them as an 'other'.

The efforts of philosophers, artists, historians, linguists, social scientists, etc., to explain all of this is broadly encompassed by the term postmodernism. Postmodernism is often representational, as in literature, architecture and the arts, with the purpose of creating a sense of vertigo, of uncertainty, as a reflection of the all too common experience for people witnessing the destructiveness of modernist capitalism. This sort of art is not very useful when it simply leaves its audience with a sense of helplessness and powerlessness. Philosophy and social science may use some of these same techniques, by writing into their 'explanations' the same linguistic uncertainty, but other efforts are also marked by desire to understand these phenomena and to explore the many dimensions of postmodernism outside of language itself.

In the future, postmodern planning theory, now characterized mainly by the phenomenological turn as described above, will need to reinforce its structural analysis in order to avoid some of the same problems it has criticized in modernist theory (Lauria and Whelan 1995). This will entail a study of how capitalism is likely to evolve within the coming decades, so that planning as activity and theory can be located within that evolutionary path, which in turn will require that planners write a new 'story' about society and their role within it. This is a project which is well underway with the effort over the past two decades to recast planning in its postmodern role. In this new story the planning 'actor' is given new *purpose,* new *agency* and new *action.* What remains is to fill out the *scene,* to incorporate other powerful actors with their *purposes* and *agencies* and acts, insofar as they have a bearing upon the role of the planner. Thus, it is not only knowing how to *act* that is important to planners, a subject which has been examined extensively under the recent phenomenological approach to planning theory, but it is also knowing theoretically the context or structure of the political economic system within which planning must operate. This means knowing the *forces* (i.e., the *actors, purposes, agencies* and *acts)* that are at work beyond the obvious exercise of power in the political arena. It means knowing how *actors* (i.e., capitalists) in a capitalist system are working within and through the institutions of the state and society to accomplish their single-minded profit-seeking goal *(purpose).*

Structural analysis, or the radical political economy model, has served to expose the sometimes confused role that planning actually plays in the capitalist system. While planners have believed that they were acting in the public interest, the unintended consequences of their actions have often only served the interests of capital. Planners did this, on the one hand, by arranging for the provision of goods and services that the 'market' could and would not supply, because either they were unprofitable when supplied to everyone or inadequate when supplied only to those who could pay. This is the abiding problem of privatization, one that is simply ignored under current neo-liberal theory and practice.

On the other hand, planning, as Harvey (1985) has shown, helps to resolve contradictions among the various circuits of capital that individual capitalists cannot accomplish. The latter include resolving conflicts among the different branches of capital, as well as those between capital and the larger social system, through negotiation, legislation, mediation, and, where necessary, repression. Sandercock (1998, pp.91-2) reduces this analysis to an exposition of the class struggle, which in the final analysis it certainly is. It is, however, at the same time, a good deal more. Structural analysis serves to demonstrate the ultimate irrationality of a totality, a system, which is generated by individual actors acting in a perfectly rational manner (i.e., a victory of instrumental over substantive rationality). Besides being a blow to instrumental rationality, it also destroys the 'myth' that an 'unseen hand' will ensure the 'best common good', the cornerstone of neo-classical economics and of its mathematization of all things. As Harvey (1973, p.190) says in a revealing passage about the operation of capital in urban space:

> In capitalist economies rent arises in monopoly, differential
> and absolute forms. Once it has arisen, rent serves to allo-
> cate land to uses. When use determines value a case can be
> made for the social rationality of rent as an allocative
> device that leads to efficient capitalist [spatial] production
> patterns (although the aggregate quantity of rent paid seems
> an extraordinarily high price for society to pay for such an
> allocative mechanism). But when value determines use, the
> allocation takes place under the auspices of rampant specu-
> lation, artificially induced scarcities, and the like, and it
> loses any pretense of having anything to do with the effi-
> cient [spatial] organization of production and distribution.

There are a myriad of other ways in which the process of planning, at whatever level or locale, is influenced, i.e., enabled or restricted, by the structure of capitalism: how surplus is extracted and invested, how the contradictions among production, consumption, and the realization of profit are worked out in any given time or place, etc. (Dear and Scott 1981). It is not so much that planners will be instructed by structural analysis as to how they should act in any given time and place, as it is that they must understand the context (the *scene*) within which they are acting, if they are to act with wisdom *(phronesis)*. Structural analyses, including Marxist ones, don't in themselves allow or deny planning a course of action with respect especially to social transformation, nor need they necessarily have a 'paralyzing effect on policy debates' (Sandercock 1998, p.92). Structural analyses are paralyzing only if they are presented in a determinist way. Marx's structural analyses may appear to be deterministic, but only if they are taken out of the context of his entire work. A dialectic structuralism is not paralyzing because it has ever in mind the human origins of structures; structures are con- structed (and they can be deconstructed).

Structural analyses provide a context *(scene)* within which planners (and everyone else in society) acts. They do not necessarily prescribe courses of action, any more than most new insights do. Knowing that there are gender and racial biases in technocratic (positivist) planning theory does not 'instruct' planning activity. Such activity will always be processed through a judging mind. One hopes that better, more informed, judgements will result from better knowledge, even if the scope of the problem is enormous; does anyone think that overcoming sexism or racism is going to be any easier than 'overcoming' capitalism?

The 'power' of planning, once the engineering model has been placed in proper perspective, is the power of judgement. Revealing contradictions is not to be taken lightly in such a context, especially if the contradiction is between what actors, e.g., planners, think they are doing and what they are actually doing (as revealed either by the technical, political or bureaucratic knowledge that planners share with clients, or as revealed by a careful structural analysis of the larger context or scene within which they are all working).

What is the postmodern *scene* of today and towards which tomorrow seems to be heading? It is a *scene* dominated by flexible accumulation, or flexism in short,

> a pattern of econo-cultural production and consumption characterized by near instantaneous delivery and rapid redirectability of resource flows. Flexism's fluidity results from cheaper and faster systems of transportation and telecommunications, globalization of capital markets, and concomitant flexibility - specialized just-in-time production processes enabling short productive and production cycles. These result in highly mobile capital and commodity flows able to out-maneuver geographically-fixed labor markets, communities, and bounded nations/states. Globalization and rapidity permit capital to evade long term commitment to place-based socio-economies, thus enabling a crucial social dynamic of flexism . . . (Dear 2000, p. 152. See also Harvey 1989).

This dynamic has produced the much celebrated 'vertigo of uncertainty' (Moretti 1987) that characterizes postmodern culture. It has also produced a growing income gap between the rich and the poor (people and nations), a separation between 'absentee' capitalists and the dispersed labor force that is subject to it, an explosion in corruption, violence, crime, drug-trafficking, arms dealing, white slavery, and so forth, that characterizes the contemporary world scene. Its urban spatial form, with Los Angeles as its prototype, is a disjointed, disconnected (except by automobile), widely scattered set of household (real consumer) units which are joined solely by an electronic '(dis)information' highway (Dear 2000, p.159).

All of this has now been much explored and exhibited in academia, as well as in the theater of the big and little screens, in painting, in architecture, and so on. But where is it all headed? Will capitalism 'run into the wall', will it implode, will it 'blow itself up', (both literally and metaphorically)? Will it make the planet uninhabitable for Homo sapiens and other species and simply dissipate itself? There are those who believe that we will simply 'live happily ever after', enjoying the 'end of history', or that any disturbances in our technological utopia will be easily re-addressed by new increments in science and engineering.

Ray and Anderson (2000, p.37-40) suggest three possible scenarios out of the not-so-blissful present into the unknown future: Scenario one they label "Falling Apart". All of the dire predictions about ecology, poverty, overpopulation, nuclear, chemical or biological war will result in the 'disintegration of civilization' as we know it into chaos. Nobody likes to think about this possibilty because it is too depressing, though it is a real possibility, in fact the more likely the less people want to think about it.

The Second Scenario they label "The Highly Adaptive World". In this scenario a sufficient number of 'important' people do reflect seriously about Scenario One, and they do act upon this reflection so as to move the world towards a more sustainable future, *before the social and ecological problems become insurmountable*. This, Ray and Anderson believe, would require a rapid adjustment in consciousness and intention at a rate something like the rate of increase in Internet users over the past five years.

Scenario Three they label "Muddling Our Way to Transformation". Here that minority population they identify as 'cultural creatives' gradually increase in number, solving problems as they do, but not probably fast enough to avoid several disastrous social and/or environmental 'episodes' that are in danger of carrying humanity over the brink into chaos. Postmodern planners and scientists, i.e., those informed by the phenomenology of science and planning, as well as by a structural understanding of society, could well be in the vanguard of the cultural creatives, offering their technical and communicative skills in an effort at collective survival. Structural analysis in this respect would not lead so much to a change in *agency,* in what planners actually do, as to a change in *purpose,* i.e., to what they turn their considerable knowledge and skills.

If we are in a transitional period, as many believe, then how can we best understand this process and therefore plan for a better future? Many turn to complexity studies and chaos theory as suggestive metaphors for what confronts us as a social system. System shifts and transition periods are accompanied by seeming chaotic behavior as the system moves away from a period of equilibrium to some future more 'steady state'. This process has been labeled 'hunting',

> where a system seeks a new equilibrium at a different level in its evolutionary path, one which will resolve the contradictions in the old equilibrium, much like Kuhn's new paradigms resolve anomalies in older ones (Ray and Anderson 2000, p.249).

Hunting may also produce crises in the form of problems that cannot be resolved under the old equilibrium, and may, indeed, even lead to the extinction of some living species (Wilson, E.O., 2002). Human systems have a considerable evolutionary advantage over other systems, of course; their 'hunting expeditions' may be informed by *knowledge*. This knowledge gives a structure to human existence in its sociodramatic form. The rebellion of the 1960's could not be a revolution ". . . because you can't just stop being in a story, you have to have another story to be in . . . and you can't start wanting something till you know it exists" (Quinn 1995, p.264, as quoted in Ray and Anderson 2000, p.254). Thus, the 'hunt' for a new 'steady-state' in human systems will also be a 'hunt' for new structures of knowledge, given that knowledge is inexorably tied to social structures in a socially constructed reality.

Wallerstein (1999) addresses this issue directly in his book, *The End of the World as We Know It*, where he divides his discussion into two parts: "the World of Capitalism" and the "World of Knowledge". The world of capitalism, he argues, will change profoundly over the next half century, to be eclipsed by some as yet unknown future system, and after an undoubtedly painful and destructive transition. Capitalism will have to change primarily because the environment, the biosphere, will no longer be able to support human life at the current rate of its alteration[3]. Wall Street demands and will dismiss any executives that do not increase profits more than 10 per cent per year, "But nothing in the physical world can match such growth rates for long - they simply cannot be sustained" (Ray and Anderson 2000, p.317). What Ray and

---

3. I use the term 'alteration' rather than destruction to suggest that it is no more proper to impose social metaphors on nature than material ones on society. Nature cannot be 'destroyed', only altered. Whether humans can survive in this altered nature is of no concern to nature; it will continue to exist in its altered form.

Anderson refer to here is the 10 per cent increase in the demands on the ecosystem that such corporate growth rates entail. Capitalism is in a bind because there is no known solution to this problem within the current structure of capitalism as a system.

There are three possible solutions to this problem, according to Wallerstein (1999, p.81):

1) make the corporations pay, i.e., internalize the costs of environmental pollution. If the total externalized (public) costs, not including tax breaks and direct subsidies, of subsidizing capitalism as a system in the U.S. were $2.6 trillion a year in 1994, and the total corporate profits for that year were only $530 billion, one can easily see that even a zero rate of profit would only cover 20 per cent of these costs (Korten 1999, p.48).

2) Government pays for all these costs via taxation. If the government were to actually pay for these costs, it would have to raise taxes to such an extent that a) it would squeeze profits on business enterprises, or b) it would so reduce income for everyone else that they would no longer be viable consumers, leading to a crisis of realization of capital, assuming that citizens would not revolt against such tax increases in the first place.

3) Do nothing.

Aside from some token efforts by governments, the last alternative has been in force since the environmental 'crisis' was discovered half a century ago, except that the ecological burden has to some degree been shifted out of the advanced to the lesser developed countries in Africa, Asia and Latin America by moving heavy industry to these countries and/or actually shipping waste products to them; "We'll let the other side of the ship sink ", as Eugene McCarthy used to say, ironically.

Other factors leading to the eclipse of capitalism, according to Wallerstein (1999, p.130-131), include the 'deruralization' of the population, which leads to a loss of desperate workers who could offer themselves as victims to 'superexploitation', defined by the 'dependistas' as receiving such a low income that they cannot 'reproduce themselves' as a labor force. As long as there were other desperately poor rural workers to take their place, capital did not have to worry about the reproduction of existing labor. Urbanization, however, leads to a rise in awareness reflected in union organizing, etc., and a demand for (relatively) higher wages, so that the loss of rural workers will in time squeeze corporate profits. In addition, the movement for democracy which began in the 1960's has reached a critical threshold in the advanced countries. In time it should tip the balance in favor of the people in opposition to capital, though the road will be long and painful.

The rise of democracy should not only tip the balance of the people against corporations, it should also tip the balance against an exclusive dependence upon technocratic planning and instrumental rationality generally. The struggle of the democratic movement can be observed (even measured) by the worldwide increase in "educational facilities, health facilities and a higher income base" (Wallerstein 1999, p.99). It can also be seen in the rise of multiculturalism, as seen in the phenomenological turn in the planning literature. An improved standard of education and of living would in itself account for the movement for greater democracy, as people have the wherewithal to demand more participation in making the 'socially constructed rules' that govern their lives.

In the world of knowledge, Wallerstein sees an erosion of the structures that have dominated science since the enlightenment. It is quite natural for knowledge to change if capitalism itself is to change. Modern science is the child of capitalism, locked in a dialectical relationship with it. By accepting the Cartesian separation, science, including social science, has been able to ignore the 'discontent' of complexity studies and the 'arrow of time', the idea that nature is not a fixed, timeless mechanism, but that it too is evolving and its laws are no longer reversible. As a result of this, natural science may look more to social science, rejecting determinism and trying to understand nature and natural science as part of the same 'socially constructed reality'. In this sense the study of a possible, even a better possible, future, is quite within the role of science. Planning a better possible future can only occur "when we have mastered the structures, yes have invented 'master narratives' that are plausible, relevant, and provisionally valid, that we can begin to exercise the kind of judgements that is implied by the concept of agency [planning]" (Wallerstein 1999, p.218). Then will we be able to see, as best we can at any given moment, how any given planning action will relate to all the other actors and their purposes and agencies who compose the complexity of the social reality in which we work, and have some sense of what we are accomplishing as the intended and sometimes unintended consequences of our actions.

PART FOUR

TOWARDS A HUMANISTIC THEORY
OF PLANNING

CHAPTER 9

CREATING A BETTER POSSIBLE FUTURE: THE SOCIODRAMATIC DIMENSION OF PLANNING [1]

Introduction

To review the argument to this point, it is claimed that planning is a form of social intervention designed to help (re)organize society, often, though not always, in its spatial effects. Its purpose is to improve the state of society in some significant way. Often enough it does not give sufficient attention to the possible inequitable effects of its actions, i. e., some people might benefit while others suffer as a result of planning interventions. Usually these benefits and costs are measured in political-economic terms, though there are other social and psychological benefits and costs that could be accounted for if planning were conceived in a more humanistic framework.

As an intervention, planning has an obligation to know the social world into which it is projecting itself. As I have argued in the above chapters there is more than one way of knowing the social world. The 'outside' view of positivism gives vital descriptive information on a large scale, and this information is indispensable for proper planning strategies. At the same time, knowledge from within the phenomeno-

1. Revised edition of Gerald Gutenschwager, "Planning a Better Possible Future: Towards a Humanistic Theory of Planning, Paper presented at "Confer-In", Conference of The American Institute of Planners, Boston, MA, October 7-11, 1972

logical framework helps planning to appreciate that the social world is composed of people who do things in meaningful and purposeful ways, i.e., that descriptive patterns, however complex and unintended they might be, are always the product of individual actions, thoughts and purposes. Furthermore, there is a differential and unequal distribution of power to achieve one's purposes. That is, different people have different political-economic abilities and resources to accomplish their goals.

Ultimately, however, even powerful individuals are locked into the same structure of institutionalized behavior that controls everyone in the social world. In short, they cannot act in any way they please. They must use their power according to the structured rules, formal or informal, of the social system to which they belong. Indeed, they gain their power because, in their social roles, they represent these structured rules. However, as this structured system is not a mechanism, i.e., does not in the final analysis succumb to natural law, planning must understand how these structures are created and maintained socially. They must understand the use and manipulation of symbols, and the rhetorical importance of all communication in this respect.

Planning enters this 'conversation', as Burke calls the social struggle, with its own communicative resources. An engineering view of this process will permit only the use of a technocratic language, a language that has its own rhetorical impact, of course. But a technocratic language, though filled with mystery, hence power, is also alienating; it is ill suited for democracy. Assuming that the latter is important, i.e., that planning, itself, is not alienated from its social (as distinguished from its scientific) role, then it must sharpen its understanding of these different perspectives on society. It must use all the epistemological resources it can to attain this understanding, and then learn how to share this knowledge so that planning may contribute to, rather than inhibit democracy.

Revising planning theory would require attention to aspects of the social world otherwise neglected in current social theory with its heavy bias toward the physical and mechanistic. One of these neglected aspects, as seen in Chapters 2 and 5, is found in phenomenology, and among those who strive for 'inside' or 'intersubjective' understanding of the social world. This perspective defines society through its shared meanings and images, not through forces or vectors. It sees individuals as acting purposefully together through accepted beliefs and expectations and explains the dynamics of society as efforts to create and maintain or legitimize these beliefs.

This aspect is complemented by a socio-linguistic and socio-dramatic perspective that explains why statements, including scientific ones, about the present and future social order are inescapably moral. This morality derives from the fact that humans alone in nature create and experience their world linguistically, representing and communicating about nearly all things symbolically. Insofar as these socio-linguistic symbols constitute reality they are always subject to interpretation and critical judgment.

Planners along with most social scientists have fallen enthusiastically into the trap of scientistic (positivist) mysticism with its price-based, benefit-cost perspective on the social order. One result is often a failure of the profession to satisfy either itself or its clients in this respect. Moreover, the very legitimacy of planning (and many other professions) has been threatened by movements such as advocacy planning, civil rights, minority pressures, 'post-autistic economics', or simply the 'generation gap', and so forth. The basis for understanding this dilemma must be found within a social and planning theory that would account for this dissatisfaction. Such a theory must be humanistic, for these are human problems, and it must not so readily discard the accumulated wisdom of philosophy and art. Unlike scientific theory, it must develop a capacity to openly confront ambiguity and morality and accept them as necessary dimensions of any social reality. It must further develop principles of communication that will speak to the symbolic basis of the social order so that significant changes, when necessary, can be imagined and carried through.

Much of current planning, like the social theory that inspires it, evades these issues through the myth of objectivity, with the result that it constitutes little more than an elaborate apology for the status quo. Insofar as the status quo has proven incapable of solving the pressing urban and social problems in the West -- indeed, it is now busily exporting them to other countries around the world under the guise of globalization -- one must question the adequacy of this 'apologetic' theory, and seek where possible to improve and change it. The effort in this and the following chapter will be to review these issues and suggest a direction for such improvement and change.

The Many Faces of Planning

Definitions of planning have varied over the past century, depending on the perspective and training of the definer, the pressing issues of the times, the audience appealed to, the technology of calculation, etc. Looking back, for example, we see that planning was at one time almost synonymous with *mapping or design;* as for some it remains today. The future is graphically portrayed as a blueprint, and the various social, economic and political organizational forms are subsumed under the spatial form.

As a more dynamic perspective developed and the co-ordinative difficulties became more apparent, planning was forced to include the time dimension and became more synonymous with *programming.* This dimension of planning has developed steadily throughout the New Deal, the Second World War, and the post-war effort at national development, and has been aided immensely by the rapid improvement in computer technology over the past decade or two. After some rough treatment at the hands of laissez-faire economists during the '30's and '40's, because of an uncomfortable association with totalitarianism, programmatic planning was elaborated into the high status social science 'systems design', and is now actively employed by the military and large scale business concerns as the appropriate definition of planning for their purposes. Some academics have also urged this definition of planning on the profession, though there doesn't appear to be widespread application in city planning, except perhaps in primitive forms such as capital budgeting, etc.

The combined effects of recalcitrance in the face of programmatic authority and the success of Von Neumann and Morgenstern (1947) in elaborating a mathematical theory of games, has suggested another definition of planning as a form of *strategy.* Strategic planning directs attention to conflict and conflict resolution (under the strict logic of game theory, of course). With a continuous rise in levels of social conflict during the civil rights and Vietnam war protests in the 1960s and 1970s, and with the planner often in the middle of this conflict, 'strategy' superceded 'program' as the preferred metaphor for organizing planning thought for several decades. However, as there are dangers inherent in following the systems metaphor too literally (Boguslaw 1981, McDermott 1969), so also are there dangers in following the gaming metaphor to its extremes (Louch 1966, p.209): human behavior can be deterministically defined *only to the extent that the humans involved don't take note.*

The attention given to participation is related to this question about determinism, which leads to a possible fourth definition of planning as *art* and more specitically as *dramatic* or *narrative art* in the broad sense of the word. From time to time persons have offered the suggestion that planning be defined as art, though it appears that no one has taken this definition seriously, or at least seriously enough to explore the implications for planning theory and methodology. This is unfortunate, I think, because there are important philosophical and theoretical reasons for looking more closely at planning as art, and it is to this definition that the following discussion will be directed.

Planning is, In Effect, a Concern for the Future

To say that planning is, in effect, a concern for the future is, of course, to repeat a truism. Yet it is at this basic level that one must begin to develop a more humanistic definition of planning. Most planners will accept the qualification on the future described in their plans as one of the many possible, although this varies according to how early in the planning process and in what way ambiguity is eliminated to accommodate various demands for precision. But planners do speak about possible futures, about hypothetical pictures or images referring to certain goals or states in the human condition after the passage of time. They furthermore include plans on how to arrive at those possible futures, plans which include or account for system statements or statements of relationship and implied or explicit directives for action, all of which are generally deemed necessary to planning of any kind.

What is also necessary, though likely for various reasons to remain implicit, is the assumption that the possible futures outlined in plans are 'good' futures, futures 'better than the present'. Quite apart from the criteria used to establish the goodness or 'better-ness' of a future, this moral component is inescapable, being built into language, like gender or tense or any of the many aspects of linguistic form.

To understand how this is true one must understand that all images of the present, past and future are learned *with their moral connotations.* It is in the nature of humans to learn about (especially social) reality through the symbols used to describe it. That portion of reality learned through direct experience is extremely limited, and even then is subject to linguistic interpretation. Our first exposure to the world around, a world presented to us by our early socializers, usually our parents, has a crushing authority, deriving from our total dependence upon those primary socializers. That reality is objectively true and proper because it is the first and only reality presented to us at that time (Chapter 2). All subsequent interpretations of the world must grapple with the eminence of that set of images, modifying, elaborating, changing where possible, but always within a moral context; new images, new interpretations must be established as better, more appropriate, for whatever reason, than prior definitions of reality. All education in this sense is the establishment or re-establishment of the appropriateness of a way, however simple or complex, of perceiving, defining, and *judging* reality. The process is not unlike that described by Kuhn (1970) whereby new paradigms are added to the repertoire of science, sometimes after a hassle that shakes the intellectual and social structure of the scientific community itself. Plans of the future, especially those that deviate very much from the present, pose exactly this kind of dilemma for their readers and implementers.

Meanwhile, the present, however inadequate, inefficient, unjust and possibly unloved, carries all the weight of past legitimation in its mere existence. Even though seriously eroded, the seeming appropriateness of the distribution of authority and the ability of those who use that authority to sustain the status quo are usually enough to inhibit radical change. Thus is the continuity and integrity of societies maintained. When injustice, inefficiency, and inadequacy grow (usually as a result of excessive exploitation of the 'system' by those in positions of authority) and the advantages to some outweigh their legitimate 'rewards', new, more radical plans for the future are tolerated. But it is the erosion and/or rejuvenation of the *legitimacy* of the present through which judgement is expressed, not the inadequacy, or injustice, or inefficiency per se.

This process of judgement is continuous, as individuals and groups decide whether the present is as they know it to be (or *not* to be) and hence whether it is as it *ought* (or *ought not)* to be. Perception is never free from judgement because reality can always potentially be *not what it ought to be.* Thus are plans formulated to bring the future into harmony with what we feel the present ought to be. Thus are all plans moral statements about the present (and future).

The moral dimension of planning, because of its symbolic or linguistic origins, serves to emphasize the importance of communication in planning. In fact, planning may be (re) defined as 'communication about better possible futures'. The 's' on futures is not incidental; it accompanies 'possible', and is necessitated by the ambiguity of symbolically created realities, and the 'better' is, as seen above, an inescapable part of all human communication about the past, present or future.

The conventional medium of planners is the 'plan', a statement in graphic, programmatic or strategic form of purpose or intention relating to the future. Other actors speak about the future through other media, through curriculum, through ritual, through spectacle, through art, etc. All statements about the future must have their socio-linguistic referents, however, if they are to be understood and acted upon in a social manner. And these socio-linguistic referents are bound to the communication groups who create and sustain them as meaningful in their social context.

Some would contend that positive science transcends these sociolinguistic constraints by virtue of having created a language of its own. But in fact scientists become part of a separate reference group, linguistically speaking, whose definitions of reality are no less symbolic and no less socially learned, for all their claims to 'a-sociality' or objectivity. Their world-view and paradigms are essentially *mechanistic* though hedged by deference to probability (which is the scientific metaphor for ambiguity), and their moral values are generally reducible, following Bentham, to some version of price (Burke 1965, p.194). In any case, all plans constitute socio-linguistic communication about the future.

The moral dimension of communication about futures derives from perspectives on the present. These perspectives emphasize either acceptance or rejection (Burke 1959), and plans are designed either to perpetuate (accept) or change (reject) the present. Futures are thus seen in communications about the present, communications that are either positive or critical; as with Burke, it is important to recognize that we are all poets, framing our analyses and plans in these poetic categories of acceptance or rejection.

Planners are 'Inside' the Present

The strange sounding statement, 'Planners are inside the present', refers to the fact that planners are social actors and insofar as planning is a social phenomenon it is this 'inside-ness' that is most important (Benveniste, 1972). Objectivity or outside-ness is important for understanding, of course, although even here there is an aspect rarely considered in the education and practice of planners: little attention is given to subjective analysis, to the interpretation of events and their aggregation in the course of planning. During professional training much time is devoted to the learning and application of appropriate models. These models constitute higher order metaphors used to understand and explain social, economic, political and spatial relationships, and often provide the basis for operational planning for the future. Most of these models or metaphors are heavily biased to the mechanistic, drawing as they do upon a long tradition of success (with nature) among the physical sciences. The emulation by planners and social scientists of physical science is both instrumental and social; the mechanistic metaphors are suggestive, particularly in highly aggregated social situations, and they do largely account for the success of physical science and the resulting high status of their users in the social and academic hierarchy within the modern(ist) world.

Nevertheless the social world for which and in which planners perform their professional tasks is composed of human actors whose perceptions and intentions do, after all, produce that social world. If their actions were fully determined by the physical forces posed in the mechanistic models there would be no explanation for social change; indeed, this aspect of social science is one of the least developed (see Chapter 5).

Understanding how the social world is a product of human perception and intention, and how it changes (or does not change) as a result of these perceptions and intentions, requires a further elaboration on objectivity or outside-ness as empathy, a knowing or understanding (*verstehen*) of how others perceive and act in relation to the present (hence future). The lack of empathy, and of training in this form of 'objective' analysis, which could lead to a better understanding of 'intersubjectivity', has often handicapped planners by separating them from their clients; hence the accusation of a 'middle-class' bias, for example. But this lack also separates planners from their 'employers', the policymakers, often resulting in a failure to implement planned solutions when it would seem otherwise (socially) rational to do so.

With a growing interest in participatory democracy and advocacy planning in the planning profession, there is a critical need for developing skills of the kind necessary for empathetic understanding. While *verstehen,* as a form of this understanding, was first sought as a methodological goal by Max Weber, it is equally to the phenomenologists and particularly Alfred Schutz (1970) that we owe much for detailing the type of analysis and modeling necessary for understanding our fellow humans in their social setting (See Chapters 2 and 5). Planners concerned with effectiveness would seem to have no alternative but to ground themselves in the phenomenology of everyday life and in the theory and research necessary to develop an understanding of this phenomenology for the social situations in which they have and will find themselves. For, while planning, as communication is only possible from 'inside' the present, this 'inside-ness' must be informed by a careful 'outside' analysis of the kind that allows intersubjective communication to be understood in the first place.

This 'inside--outside-ness' is perhaps best illustrated by what social science has labeled 'participant-observation'. Planners must become participant-observers in the present. They must recognize that they are inescapably a part of the present, that their actions and communications are one of many contributions to the future, but that a certain detachment of the kind found in the educated but concerned observer should enhance this participation. Learning to become an educated and concerned observer requires as much special training and at least as much difficult abstract thought as is required to master the physical models so popular in the positive sciences. Hopefully, the image of 'untroubled' social scientists applying their 'methods' to social analysis will become a thing of the past, as succeeding generations of academics and professionals force the issue of 'praxis' beyond the rhetoric of the classroom, although the very real issue of how one is to act, even symbolically, through communication is still for the most part only intuitively understood.

One thing, however, is clear: the *value-free* image of planners 'inside' the present is a paradox, if they are seeking something like a 'better possible future'. A critical perspective and hence critical communication is simply denied the planner under this rubric, which is why the 'better futures' portrayed in so many plans are but empty rhetoric: no one takes them seriously and the plan 'stays on the shelf'. In effect, if planners are 'value-free' professionals, they are morally disarmed even before they begin to communicate. Of course, moralizing scientific planners would be in an equally paradoxical situation in their social setting, where they are expected to act as value-free technicians, and where a critical approach would be likely to threaten their professional status. But this is a social paradox, whereas the former effort to indoctrinate planners into a value-free self-image has created a psychological paradox. Morally concerned professionals, who know that it is philosophically correct, indeed inevitable, that they take a critical perspective on the present, are able to manage their critical communication to accommodate the expectations of those who employ them. When they have been socialized to believe that a critical or value-laden perspective is evil in itself, then they are faced with a far more difficult dilemma.

One of the results of this condition has been the generally conservative nature of social science, at least in the Anglo-American world (Gouldner 1970). Value-free or amoral objectivity is so deeply rooted in this worldview as to take on the character of a myth (Roszak 1968). Positive social scientists and planners have been effectively alienated from society by imposing a barrier of technique between themselves and reality. One result of this has been an almost total orientation to the existing, and an explicit distaste for working with the possible. Pragmatism and empiricism serve to provide the philosophical base for this conservative positivism because of their supportive perspective on the present (Horkheimer 1947). Empirical truth can only be grounded in the existing, not in the possible, and the pragmatic attitude assigns moral goodness (along with utility) only to that which has worked.

Thus, one of the problems facing social scientists and their related professionals is to re-establish themselves 'inside' the present, and to explore the nature and implications of their roles as actors on the social scene. The higher order metaphors that have been developed to explain social reality are thought provoking in their perspective on the present, in spite of their generally mechanistic properties, but the search for better futures must lead beyond this to encompass the phenomenology of acting and communicating in everyday life.

Planners Must Understand How 'Presents' and 'Futures' Are Created and Maintained

A 'present' social order or social reality is a hierarchy closely related to the distribution of property or wealth (Burke 1965). Power to control others by manipulating rewards and punishments is generally consistent with this hierarchy, i.e., it rests disproportionately with those higher up. Other functional and organizational dimensions of the social order are also subordinate to this hierarchy, any disclaimer about pluralism notwithstanding, which suggests that social change must ultimately be judged in relation to this hierarchy. Power and property determine the 'nature of things' during any period of social history, but the 'order' that sustains them derives from their general acceptance by society as a whole. The hierarchy is deemed appropriate or *legitimate* for the times, and those who benefit most, of course, attend closely to the maintenance of this legitimacy (Chapter 2).

Various forms of technological change may or may not affect this hierarchy, quite apart from the ways in which everyday life is changed. Technological and organizational changes may simply serve to enhance the legitimate power of those at the top of the hierarchy, particularly when consistent with the prevailing myths about the meaning and quality of life (Carey and Quirk 1971). In this sense nothing in the history of the past two hundred years would seem to have threatened the basic social premises of efficiency, mechanism and control, at least until recently, or to have eroded the hierarchical position of those most successful in accommodating themselves to these premises. It is hard to accept the claims about rapid social change in this light or to see that any significant critical planning has ever been carried out.

The apparent inertia of any social hierarchy is not only a product of control; or, at least, the notion of control is a far more complex one than is supposed at this level of societal scale. Control is not only a matter of manipulating material rewards and punishments, which is a necessary but not sufficient means for maintaining the present, but is also a product of sociodramatic techniques used to maintain the legitimacy of the hierarchy and the type and distribution of rewards that prevail in that social order.

Sociodrama refers to the social paradigm most common to the arts and most completely developed into a perspective on social theory by Kenneth Burke and Hugh Duncan (See Chapter 3). It draws a critical distinction between society and nature, emphasizing the difference between 'things moving' and 'humans acting'. The sociodramatic paradigm likens social reality to *theater* in contrast to *mechanism,* and derives theoretical explanation from the artistic rather than scientific likeness of humans. This is not to say that humans are not rational, but rather that human rationality seeks perfection in the symbolic of which science is but one, albeit persuasive, version. Thus, the search for fulfillment is grounded in that which is deemed important, and social goals are a product of this.

Science is the most powerful *symbolic* system motivating western society today, although it usually claims only instrumental value. Mechanism, efficiency and control, as stated above, are among the basic premises of this system and they permeate social relationships down to and including the most intimate. But they are established social premises, not solely because of their utility, but also because of the sociodramatic techniques that persuade of their appropriateness.

Burke (1965) defines the sociodramatic ritual of maintaining legitimacy as consisting of two complementary efforts: *mystification* and *victimage.* As discussed in Chapter 3, mystification arises from social distance, especially between classes and across the division of labor in society, and is grounded in claims about the 'naturalness' of the social order. Certain 'rights', while actually socio-linguistically created and maintained, are claimed (especially by those who benefit) as 'natural', or as divinely given. Examples include the 'right' to royal status in medieval society or the 'right' to all the private property one can amass in our own. Mystification helps us sustain this so-called natural order through the trappings of class, status and rank. We are 'embarrassed' (to use Burke's term) by our inability to understand even the 'mysterious' language of our status equals, or to understand the basis of an authority that is socially equal to our own. The 'embarrassment' up and down the social hierarchy must, therefore, be even more profound. It is in this sense that Burke likens it to absolute guilt of the sort arising from 'Original Sin' and finds it, along with *victimage* and its rituals for catharsis and redemption, seemingly indispensable to the maintenance of the social order.

In *victimage* public 'villains' are sought out and sacrificed, as in scapegoating, often by public 'heroes,' an inescapable essence of all theater on and off the screen. This serves as both a warning to, as well as a cleansing of guilt about those villainous thoughts in all of us that would question the appropriateness of the existing social hierarchy. In this way the social order is maintained by those who command the symbols of authority. One might refer to these sociodramatic techniques as special forms of reward and punishment, forms deriving from the peculiar social character of existence. We all engage in and witness mystification, observing symbols of dress, manner and language designed to separate rather than unite. We know the bureaucratic tricks that are used to protect status and office. And we are all conscious of the various forms of victimage exercised by those in power, from teacher to national leader, and from the symbolic cowboy-and-Indian versions of Hollywood to the all too real versions of Dachau and Vietnam (to say nothing of Iraq, Kosovo, and Afghanistan in recent years).

Yet we also know that mystification and victimage cannot sustain indefinitely a social order whose legitimacy has been seriously questioned. If nothing else, our experience with history should teach us that. Nor are humans likely to stop questioning their social order, nor stop communicating their thoughts about it. What is important here is the choice of *form* for communication about the present social order, particularly when that communication is critical. And if planning is 'communication about better possible futures', it too must explore this question of form.

The problem of form returns to the original question of how 'presents' and 'futures' are created and maintained. The excesses of mystification and victimage would seem to argue against dependence on these particular forms of communication to establish (or break down) legitimacy. They have in fact been responsible for some of the least acceptable moments in human history. The alternative would seem to be a more careful search for less destructive forms available to sociodramatic communication about 'presents' and 'futures'. This leads to the (until recently) unusual suggestion that planners ought to be more familiar with poetry and poetic categories.

Poetry is broadly used here and by Burke (1959) to refer to all linguistic syntheses or statements about the present or future. Since we are not likely to think of the poet or artist, and hence their categories, as appropriate in a discussion about planning, it might be well to remind that the poet, too, is engaging in communication about the present and possible futures. (The importance given during the Cold War in the American media to the Russian preoccupation with what their poets were communicating ought to suggest that art is not socially and politically separated from the material and instrumental in either Russian or American society, though it has been effectively 'victimized' under the crushing authority of science and technology in both.)

Thus referring to poetic categories in a critical book about scientific planning should not (after some thought, perhaps) be so strange after all. As Duncan would say (1969, p.287-8):

> Among all institutions in society, art alone sustains a wide,
> constant and searching criticism . . . Even the American uni
> versity, supposedly dedicated to free inquiry, seems unable
> to create and sustain free criticism of its own work.

Perhaps the inspiration from art can suggest a way to possible futures 'better' than those offered to date by a narrowly defined science.

Returning to the contention that communication about the present or future is inescapably moral, we recall that acceptance or rejection is inherent in all such communication. Added to this is the transitional or 'maybe' category which rounds out the possible perspectives on the social order. Burke, as indicated in Chapter 3, places tragedy, comedy and epic, in the *supportive* category, satire, burlesque and elegy in the *negative,* and the grotesque and didactic in the *transitional.* After studying each category for its ultimate historic implications, Burke concludes that the comic frame is the most humane, resting delicately as it does between tragedy and the negative categories of satire and burlesque and thus preserving the ambiguity necessary to inhibit the excessive uses of mystification and victimage.

The comic frame is a quasi-conservative one, suggesting that no political system is free from the human weaknesses that ultimately encourage the uses of mystification and victimage. Every system brings advantages to some over others and with it the temptation to exploit that advantage for selfish gain. Even some of those who followed and supported the profound social reforms implemented through the communist revolution must have recognized that those systems did not escape these temptations. Unlike the degradation inherent in satire and burlesque and the too heavy burden of guilt intrinsic to tragedy, the comic frame

> . . . should enable people to be observers of *themselves*
> *while acting.* Its ultimate would not be passiveness, but
> *maximum consciousness.* One would transcend himself by

noting his foibles. He would provide a rationale for locating the irrational and the non-rational. (Burke 1959, p.171, author's emphasis)

Burke goes on to explain that the 'non-rational' is a neglected quality in the vocabulary of our overly rational scientific world view, which dichotomizes the world into rational and irrational, and ignores the important possibility of non-rational experience totally outside this dichotomy.

But the comic frame is also critical, pointing up the mistakes that must be corrected to keep the social order viable. And it is in this sense that planning communication can stand to gain in poetic insight, for the mechanistic approach to planning can never be comic, or even poetic; it treats humans as integers not actors. It does not address itself at all to critical insight but assumes the appropriateness of the present in combination with whatever physical models are employed to carry that present into the future. Nevertheless, plans are social artifacts, and in their social context are used primarily as didactive techniques, or tend to be used communicatively as such, particularly when rewards and punishments are scheduled to be consistent with them. But planners have limited control over rewards and punishments; these tend, as stated above, to rest disproportionately with those higher up in the social hierarchy. As long as planners pay no attention to questions of legitimacy, and give no attention to the sociodrama that sustains legitimacy, they are not likely to effect any critical changes in the real world.

What this suggests is that a new planning methodology as communication would have to follow from a broadened theory and image of the professional role, a role which would use the full range of communication techniques and poetic categories. Planning theory would have to encompass much more than the purely technical and conventional wisdom about mapping, programming and strategy. Taking seriously the definition of planning as art would require an understanding of the planner as a social actor joining with others in a constantly evolving sociodrama in which the present is critically observed and out of which the future is created. This sociodrama mixes the deterministic with the humanistic - 'forces' with 'interests' - in a synthesis of social form. To the planners 'tool kit' would be added (or perhaps only edited) new communication techniques: games, public events, videos, formal drama, displays, adult education, devised theater, etc. Advocacy and community planning had already moved in this direction by attempting to break down the technical mystifications of planning, often working with prior 'victims' of planning, and placing planners at the service of their clients in dramatically different ways. The emphasis on 'participation' is a further example of this phenomenon and Lisa Peattie (1970), in an article on community drama, suggested that the 'disadvantaged', too, were finding their own sociodramatic techniques for planning better possible futures (Rap Brown claimed during the turbulent 1960's in the U.S., "Every riot brings a new poverty program!").

One final dimension in this humanistic perspective or planning theory has to do with the basis for change in a democratic society. One of the primary efforts of democracy is to vest authority in rules rather than status, the effect of which is to counter some of the tendencies to mystification and victimage. A cardinal premise, however, is that *all* must participate in making those rules. Needless to say, if the 'rules' that govern social theory are derived from physical models, there is little social recourse to those rules. Their legitimacy has been established outside of society. Their success derives from their ability to explain the natural world; who would ever think of *changing* the laws that govern the gravity model, for example! Yet a democratic society should change in precisely this way: through a change in the rules. Planning a better possible future in a democratic society is thus not a task of bringing society closer to an ideal state of equilibrium, for example, but is rather one of opening discussion about the rules and broadening the participation in their formulation to the greatest possible extent. Critical discussions about zoning, for example, ought to touch upon its use as a social segregative device, in addition to its seeming explicit purpose of separating incompatible uses; discussions on urban renewal should (as they already have) speak to the enormous profits accruing to developers while claiming that slums were being cleared; etc.

Since the 1960's some planning professionals have been responding to 'sociodramatic' communication from those who wished for more democratic participation in making the rules. It appears that planning theory is now broadening to incorporate those significant moments in the social and professional world. For it is one thing to say that a democratic social order should maintain an open discussion on the rules in which all would participate, and quite another thing to find the means for allowing this to happen. It appears that as these become more significant professional planning goals, planning theory will necessarily have to become more humanistic, looking beyond traditional social science concerns to a more philosophical perspective on society. The classic works of social thinkers and humanists that could help in this effort have been neglected in professional education and, even more distressingly, in most of the educational experiences that precede this level as well. Establishing the importance of wisdom beyond mere technocratic technique would seem to be one of the most important challenges facing the planning profession at this time. Hopefully, this book will contribute to such an effort. Meanwhile, we need to look more closely in the following chapter at what planning could ultimately seek to accomplish *at the human level.*

CHAPTER 10

BEYOND MONETARY VALUES: PLANNING FOR HUMAN NEEDS [1]

Among the many legacies of the 1960's has been a profound questioning of the mechanistic assumptions inherent in western social theory up to that time. Growing out of this has been a series of critiques on planning and development theory ranging from Schumacher's (1975) *Small Is Beautiful,* to dependency theory, the North-South debate, and more recently, Norgaard's (1994), *Development Betrayed.* One important contribution to this discussion was the work of Paul Streeten (1981) and his associates, who observed that not only had post-war economic growth not guaranteed basic subsistence needs for the mass of people in the developing societies, but, by implication, that development theory itself was remiss in not addressing this apparent contradiction. In other words, the economistic categories of growth in GNP, GDP, etc., or even per capita income, did not necessarily give evidence to the abiding inequalities in those developing societies and their apparent inability to satisfy the most basic needs for substantial portions, if not the majority, of their populations. The same issues are now being raised within the discipline of economics, itself, especially by the graduate students in Western Europe, as evidenced by the movement for a *post-autistic eco-*

1. Revised edition of Gerald Gutenschwager "Social Theory in Development Planning: The Elusive Needs Hierarchy", Paper presented at the 20th World Conference of the Society for International Development, Amsterdam, 6-9 May 1991.

nomics (pae_news@btinternet.com, www.paecon.net). The term refers to the endoscopic nature of neo-classic economics, especially in its highly mathematical forms, and a lack of attention to the real socio-economic problems of 'actually existing' capitalism.

Streeten called attention to the need to consider these problems and to address the political-economic prerequisites for dealing with them. For example, development planners, as well as political leaders, would have to foster changes in the ownership patterns of physical assets (or means of production), especially land; resource allocation priorities would have to change; there would need to be changes in the balance of political power, usually involving some decentralization of decision making; and so forth.

This issue of basic needs has been widely discussed and the discussion may even have had some effect on the fate of populations in the Third World. Also, thanks to the untiring efforts of Mahbub ul Haq (1999), there is now a Human Development Report published annually by the United Nations Development Program, which addresses these issues in a formal way. But the theoretical issue has not been developed much beyond an obvious agreement about the importance of these subsistence needs. In particular the question of defining needs in a more comprehensive way has not been addressed at this level, especially in relation to the broader issues of planning and development theory.

Needs in relation to consumption is an important problem in planning and development at all levels of affluence, and two contemporary factors would seem to accentuate this point. One is the obvious ecological limitation to ever-expanding levels of consumption: if the entire world consumed energy and polluted the environment at the rate of the developed countries, we would probably have already exceeded the capacity of the earth's biosphere to support human existence. Obviously, the current forms of production and consumption, which represent the 'ideal' direction of development in the world today, cannot be sustained, either theoretically or practically (Wilson, J.O., 1980, Durning 1992). The issue of what is to be produced, and how, must be related to the question of what should be consumed and why. Hence, theories of consumption beyond the simple 'rational man' concept must gradually complement if not replace the production-oriented economic theories that have dominated planning and development thinking up till now.

The second factor is the apparent failure of the socialist systems to transcend the consumerist mentality that characterizes the capitalist mode of development. In other words, need satisfaction has been an overt goal of socialist theory and policy since the inception of socialism in the early 20th century. In spite of this, or perhaps because of it, widespread consumer dissatisfaction appears to be one factor that contributed to the abandonment of socialism in Eastern Europe and the Soviet Union, and its replacement by a 'free market system', as a hopeful panacea to these problems. Hidden behind the issue of freedom are important theoretical issues related to human needs and the appropriate political-economic means for satisfying them, for neither liberal-bourgeois nor Marxist theory has adequately addressed these issues at the social psychological level (Preteceille and Terrail 1985).

Maslow's Developmental Need Hierarchy -- Its Use and Abuse

Abraham Maslow's (1970) need hierarchy is a possible starting point for elaborating the full range of human needs in a dynamic framework. Unfortunately, Maslow has had mixed (often negative) reviews, since empirical research has been unable to establish a basis for accepting his theory (Fitzgerald 1977, Lederer 1980). This is partly a product of the complexity of the theory, which proceeds on the basis of the following hierarchy:

1. *Physiological needs* - hunger, thirst, sex, temperature control, etc.
2. *Safety needs* - security, stability, dependency, protection, freedom from fear, anxiety and chaos, need for structure, order, law, limits, strength in the protector, etc.
3. *Belongingness and Love needs* (need for affiliation) - need for affectionate relationships with friends, spouse, children and community.
4. *Esteem needs* - two types
   a. *Self Esteem* - strength, achievement, adequacy, mastery, competence, confidence, independence and freedom
   b. *Social Esteem* - reputation, status, fame and glory, dominance, recognition, attention, importance, dignity or appreciation
5. *Self-actualization* - need to become more and more, idiosyncratically, everything that one is capable of becoming, from ideal mother or father, to athlete, musician, carpenter, or whatever

The first four levels are often referred to as deficiency needs (without the satisfaction of which an individual may be considered psychologically deficient or less than fully human, etc.) and the fifth level as the 'being' or growth need (or the ultimate basis for realizing oneself as a human being). To this hierarchy Maslow adds another two (non-hierarchical) needs:

1. Cognitive needs - the need to know and understand
2. Aesthetic needs, which are found in all cultures at all times

According to Maslow the hierarchical needs must be seen in their entirety as an interrelated system in which the drives overlap and interact, but within a framework in which *lower needs must be generally satisfied before higher needs come into play.* The latter is summarized in the concept of prepotency and is one of the most controversial aspects of Maslow's theory of needs. The idea of prepotency is difficult to operationalize for research purposes and is often misunderstood. For example, the idea that needs at one level must be more or less satisfied before those at the next higher level are felt or recognized as unsatisfied by the subject, leaves open at least two empirical questions. First, should an *unrecognized* need be counted as satisfied or unsatisfied, and, second, should the researcher or the subject(s) identify needs and/or their satisfaction. Various attempts to verify Maslow's theory have used differing, often implicit, interpretations of these questions, with varying, sometimes conflicting, results. Furthermore, while Maslow is quite explicit in maintaining that prepotency is only a general rule with many well-known exceptions (by usually exceptional people), many critics use these exceptions as a refutation of the theory (Antsyferova 1974).

A second, more serious misunderstanding of Maslow's theory, one that invalidates much of the empirical research attempting to verify it, is related to the fact that, according to Maslow, needs are developed and the level in the hierarchy established *throughout the childhood, adolescence and early adulthood* of the average individual. Quoting from Maslow,

> . . . in the fortunate life history the safety needs are salient and satisfied during childhood, the affiliation needs during adolescence, and the esteem needs during early adulthood. Only as a person nears his 50's, generally, will self-actualization needs become strongly salient (Hall and Nougairn 1968, p.32).

In other words, to test Maslow's theory adequately, complex longitudinal studies would be required. Cross-sectional analyses that attempt to relate need and/or satisfaction to a position in an organizational hierarchy in the workplace, for example, would have to be very carefully designed to identify this dynamic of psychological developmental; great care would be required in identifying the independent versus dependent variables in such cases.

Finally, much of the more rhetorical criticism of Maslow focuses on the issue of self-actualization, ignoring or glossing over the prior levels and the prepotent character of the hierarchy. Critics on the left accuse him of ignoring the extent to which need satisfaction, generally, is a social rather than psychological (individual) problem (Antysferova 1974, Lethbridge 1986, 1989, Nord 1977), whereas critics on the right accuse him of being a socialist (McInnes 1977) or Marxist (Springborg 1981, p. 276). Although Maslow did not develop a comprehensive social theory, he was certainly sensitive to social (psychological) issues. He emphasized, for example, the fact that the *social and cultural conditions* for realizing need satisfaction were as important as the needs themselves. In any case, it is fairly obvious that all need satisfaction is socially contingent. Maslow recognized this, though he did not attempt to spell out what the social organization for need satisfaction should be, which is a quite different issue in any case.

It is true that self-actualization appears as the most personal and individual need, but it is actually the last stage in the hierarchy. Unfortunately, according to Maslow, few people reach this level, *mainly because the social conditions do not permit it.* Individuals reach this level generally in their 50's and they must, according to the theory, have more or less satisfied all the needs at the other (apparently more) socially contingent levels before embarking on self-actualization. The emphasis on this top level of the hierarchy and lack of attention to the other levels and to the important contingency of the prepotent or hierarchical nature of all needs leads to a misrepresentation of Maslow's theory (Smith 1973). This is to say nothing of the greater danger of abusing the notion of self-actualization by using it to justify self-indulgent behavior at any age. A possible example of the latter is described by Adrianne Aron (1977) in her discussion of the hippies of the 1960's. Even though her research did not uncover any evidence that the hippies knew anything about Maslow, she suggests that

> Since the hippie experience is above all a quest for the kinds
> of peak experiences that Maslow describes, and since every
> person who aspires to or achieves the sort of thing that
> Maslow terms self-actualization moves wittingly or unwit-
> tingly onto Maslow's turf, the hippies, whether they know it
> or like it, must be considered Maslowians (Aron 1977, p.11)

However, the issue here is: Who is to be criticized for this distortion, Maslow or the hippies? Aron admits that Maslow warned against this danger and the need to distinguish between a ". . . psychologically healthy self-actualizer" and a ". . . selfish person, seeking his own personal, salvation . . . " (Aron, p.10), but this does point to a deeper tension in Maslow's theory relating to the abiding unresolved dialectic in social theory (and its applications): the individual versus the social. Here Maslow's theory is certainly incomplete if not inadequate.

In fact, if Maslow's theory is reframed in terms of the classic duality between the individual and the social, we can see that his need hierarchy is set directly within this context. Unfortunately, Maslow focused upon emotional development and gave little attention to cognitive development, which he referred to as existing outside the needs hierarchy. Yet self-actualization, the ultimate need, must depend as much upon cognitive as it does upon emotional development. In this sense, cognitive and emotional self-actualization or self-realization is the life force expressed from the first moment of life. It is this striving to realize oneself from infancy on that characterizes the human individual. It is a striving that involves the development of one's emotional and intellectual self, a development that requires the mastery of the symbols (Gardner 1993, p. 242, Torff & Gardner 1999, p. 142-3), which represent the collective and social intelligence that characterizes human existence (Stonier 1992).

Collective intelligence, according to Stonier, is something we share with other species and relates to our ability to work together as a system, to take information, as a collectivity, from the environment, and to organize our behavior in response to this information. Collective intelligence enhances our ability to survive and to reproduce, i.e., to survive as a species. Collective intelligence characterizes a whole range of species from ants, bees and dolphins to humans. Social intelligence, characteristic of humans and some higher primates, is " . . . an advanced form of intelligence which allows an animal . . . to analyze and respond correctly (intelligently) to possible behavioral responses of other members of the group" (Stonier 1992, p. 72).

What is critical here is the importance of the group, the collectivity, for human development. Maslow's identification of needs for safety, affiliation and esteem at critical points in the childhood, adolescence and early adulthood of the individual is also an identification of those important moments when individuals strike out, cognitively, on their own, and when they are most in need of structure and emotional support from the social environment. In the first instance the child discovers its being apart from the mother. Here it needs a behavioral structure to begin replacing and enhancing its genetically defined biological structure. This period Maslow defines according to the need for safety, security, stability, dependency, protection, etc., needs that are normally satisfied by the family or its surrogates. Samuels (1984, pp. 91-2) defines these as 'first order needs', whether physical (food, warmth, etc.), emotional (security, self-esteem, etc.), or cognitive (knowing, understanding, etc.), because they " . . . originate with the individual".

Needs for social support during adolescence are more complex and differentiated. Individuals confront puberty, demands for more sophisticated cognitive skills, and the need to define an identity apart from the family. The social location of these processes is usually a group of age peers, i.e., of other individuals confronting the same psychological challenges. Here Maslow identifies the support needs as those for belongingness, for affiliation, for love, etc., needs that must be satisfied to a great extent in a group larger than the family but smaller than the whole society. Samuels (1984, pp. 92-95) refers to these as 'second order needs' because they arise " . . . precisely in social interaction" and " . . . *exist because there is a group*" [author's emphasis]. Their satisfaction is necessary to the group so that it may function socially, and they are realized at that level through the establishment of rules or norms, which structure behavior within the group. Satisfaction of affiliation needs is thus necessary to both the group and the individual, which further serves to emphasize the dialectical nature of human existence.

Finally, esteem needs characterize early adulthood and are related cognitively and emotionally to one's social and/or occupational role. One needs support from one's professional peers, support in the form of recognition, attention, importance, reputation, status, etc. This social psychological support is different from that earlier in life; the collectivity acts in a more impersonal and functional way to ensure that the highest levels of collective intelligence will be attained. Samuels (1984, pp.

95-97) refers to these, as 'third order needs', satisfaction of which is necessary to the functioning of the whole society or culture. As such, they are more time and place specific, and are subject to change.

For the individual, second and third order *emotional* needs recall the dependent state of human existence during infancy, where need satisfaction is emotionally framed. This emotional framework is carried over into adulthood, where it serves both to motivate the individual and to facilitate the operation of collective and social intelligence. One unfortunate by-product of the human need to belong is the formation of an identity, which often *excludes* other groups, other religions, other cultures and other races. The security and recognition that one's own group provides often leads to the denigration of other groups and their assignment to an inferior ontological status, which permits forms of inhumanity that can reach extreme proportions. This emotional 'well' has been repeatedly tapped by everyone from gang leaders to political leaders, who seek their own geo-political goals by exploiting the need to belong. The challenge of this century will be to enhance the ability of all humans to extend their need to belong, their identity, to the entire species of Homo sapiens, indeed, to the entire ecosystem. Our collective intelligence will need to expand to include the entire universe if we are to survive what Carl Sagan has called our 'technological adolescence'.

Only later in life, according to Maslow, will individuals be free to seek true self-actualization, after they have attained self-esteem and confidence in their abilities as social beings. Only at that time will they be able to explore their own capacities to their fullest, but even then always within a social context. Meanwhile, it is important to re-emphasize the extent to which emotional and cognitive intelligence develop simultaneously within the individual. One might visualize the two strands of the DNA as a metaphor for the way in which cognitive and emotional development reinforce each other (Gardner 1993, p. 254). Humans are always trying to realize, to actualize themselves emotionally, but they must conquer the cognitive world and enter the symbolically constructed reality of their collectivity to do so.

Failure to mature at any given stage in a child's life may leave residual emotional and/or cognitive needs in adulthood. Thus, it is important to distinguish between *objective* adult needs for subsistence, for safety, affiliation and esteem, which do not exist in any sort of hierarchy of prepotency, and residual *subjective* adult needs of the same sort, which do.

For example, *objective* needs for security can be met by already known programs in social welfare, the social safety net, etc. The problems here are associated with the erosion of this net by the globalized attack on human welfare under the neo-liberal policies in effect since the early 1980's, though one must also be sensitive to the problems associated with too much security and the corresponding lack of incentive to work, or even act, at all, in this respect. The issue here is to find a proper balance, however difficult this may be. *Subjective* needs for security, on the other hand, as a residual from inappropriate or missing childhood conditions for meeting security needs at that time, can not be met by increasing the objective conditions of security, according to Maslow's theory. Here adult education and counseling would be required, the effort being to help adults understand the origins of their feelings of insecurity as a psychological insight into these emotions.

The same strategy would need to be followed for adult affiliation needs, differentiating them from 'manufactured' needs spawned by modern urban society, whose alienating and fragmenting effects have been documented for well over a century by artists and social scientists alike. The satisfaction of these *objective* needs could be met by more humanistic urban planning and design of the physical environment, taking it out of the hands of contractors, land speculators and banks, on the one hand, and by planning efforts to create the social conditions for human contact to replace that which has been lost from the former small scale society, on the other. The point here is not to romanticize the village, as has often been the response to this problem in the past, but to create an urban system with both the time and the accessibility that would allow these personal contacts to take place.

Residual *subjective* needs for affiliation that are the result of an inappropriate social environment during adolescence could be satisfied in the same manner as subjective safety needs, through adult education and counseling. Ironically, this is already being done within corporations, not only for safety and affiliation needs, but also for esteem needs, to the extent that these corporations are sensitive to emotional needs as a strategy for increasing productivity. Here the full range of needs may be addressed in an effort to create emotional intelligence, at least among management staff, though there is every reason to believe that the insights could filter throughout the corporation's working force, with positive effects on the entire organization. I would say 'ironically', because the ultimate purpose of the corporation is to out-compete its rivals, often leading to their destruction and absorption through mergers and takeovers, hardly a formula for creating an over-all socio-economic environment in which human needs could be satis-fied, either objectively or subjectively. This contradiction relates to the neo-classical belief that individual rationality, the corporation being treated in a perverted way as an individual, will produce a social ration-ality through the agency of some sort of equilibrium-providing 'unseen hand'. This economic 'fundamentalism' is the root cause for the inabil-ity to meet human needs adequately wherever global capitalism holds sway. Any 'residual' emotional problems are neatly rationalized away by assuming that

> Failures in human social behavior - violence, alienation and injustice are . . . a burden from our animal origins that civi-lized society is still learning to cope with, through education, bribery or coercion. With but a few exceptions, writers argue that humankind has yet to invent the social institutions that will conquer, once and for all, this shady side of our evolu-tionary past. Almost never is the problem cast in terms of a failure of the institutions of civilized society to meet intrin-sic needs of the human organism (Clark, M. 1990, p. 37).

In the hard-nosed world of economic rationality, on which most of scientific planning is based, this discussion of human emotions and human psychological needs would likely engender skepticism, if not down right derision. How can one measure need satisfaction? How can you operationalize these emotional concepts? Are these concepts universal? Are there 'hard' science bases for emotions? For needs? Etc. Actually, there is a good deal of effort to answer just these questions. For example, the four basic emotions, fear (anxiety), anger, depres-sion, and satisfaction, have each been consistently identified by facial expressions in cross-cultural research (Ekman and Friesen 1975, cited in Goleman 1995, p. 290), and have also been associated with hor-monal discharges. Kemper (1987, p. 272 and 1978, cited in Sites 1990, p.8) records fear to be associated with epinephrine, anger with norepinephrine, both originating in the sympathetic nervous system, while depression and satisfaction depend upon the parasympathetic nervous system and are associated with the varied activation of acetyl-choline.

Goleman cites research linking these emotional discharges with specific medical effects via the immune system. Excessive and recurrent anger is associated with heart disease, fear or anxiety, which is produced by stress, is a well-known risk factor for a host of diseases, and depression has been found to exacerbate and delay recovery from most physical diseases, with satisfaction or positive feelings generally having no deleterious medical effects and, in fact, seen to assist in the recovery from other diseases (Goleman 1995, pp. 168-185). The inference here is that unsatisfied needs will trigger negative emotions, chiefly fear, anger or depression, depending on the psycho-synthesis of the individual, as well as on the accepted manner in which such emotions may be expressed in any given socio-cultural setting.

Meanwhile, the overall social importance of need satisfaction and emotional health is becoming increasingly well understood as a result of Goleman's book on *Emotional Intelligence* (1995). Applications are now being studied in education (Salovey and Sluyter 1997), in management science (Cherniss and Goleman 2001) and generally throughout society (Bar-on and Parker 2000). Emotional Intelligence refers to the ability of individuals and groups to manage their emotions effectively, so as to avoid dysfunctional behavior. This research is matched by, and somewhat overlaps, research on cognitive intelligence. Early understandings represented by the concept of IQ (Binet and Simon 1905, 1980), and subsequently the much more theoretically and developmentally elaborated work of Piaget (1950, Mussen 1970), is now being augmented by work such as that on 'multiple intelligences'.

Gardner (1993) has argued that there are seven intelligences. In addition to the linguistic and logico-mathematical intelligences that are measured by IQ and most achievement tests, and which constitute the subject matter of most formal schooling. Gardner (1993, p. xi) also identifies " . . . musical intelligence, spatial intelligence, bodily-kinesthetic intelligence, and two forms of personal intelligence, one directed toward other persons, one directed toward oneself". Musical, spatial and bodily-kinesthetic intelligences are well known, are often referred to as 'talents' rather that intelligences, and are associated with music performance and composition, architecture and the visual arts, and dance and athletics, respectively, etc. They are not generally seen to be of primary importance in formal education, so that they are developed in special programs and only in those individuals who are outstanding, and/or in families or communities where these intelligences may be especially valued. The last two, personal or interpersonal intelligences, are closely related to emotional intelligence, as well as to Maslow's need hierarchy. For Gardner, these intelligences are of vital importance and, like emotional intelligence, are largely ignored in formal educational settings. Yet he feels that they may be the best predictors of ultimate success in life, better than IQ or general intelligence, as defined in the western world.

In any case, Gardner's main point is that different intelligences require different learning environments and different interactions between innate individual abilities and the social constraints under which they will be realized and formed. Furthermore, the earliest environment of the child may the most critical in this respect:

> 'Constraints' research has revealed that, by the end of early childhood, youngsters have developed powerful and already entrenched theories about their immediate worlds: the world of physical objects and forces, the world of living entities, the world of human beings, including their minds. Surprisingly, and in contradiction to the claims of Jean Piaget (Mussen and Kessen 1983), these naive 'conceptions' and 'theories' prove difficult to alter, despite years of schooling. And so it often happens that the mind of the five-year-old ends up unaffected by the experience of school (Gardner 1993, p. xviii).

To emphasize this point, Gardner (1993, p. 379) cites the book, *Kindergarten Is Too Late* by Masuru Ibuka, the founder of SONY, as an example of how important the Japanese feel are the first five years of (pre-school) life.

All of this serves to illustrate that human emotional and cognitive need satisfaction is most importantly a *developmental* problem, beginning with the moment of birth, and to show how inadequate any quantitative measure of years of schooling or monies spent on education, or whatever, will be in capturing the essence of this process. Measures of basic subsistence need satisfaction - food, clothing, shelter, etc. -- are always important, of course, and their inadequate satisfaction in so many parts of the world after so many years of 'development' planning is merely a testament to the colossal inadequacies of current political-economic systems to meet even these most elementary needs. But once such subsistence needs are met, the full force of the *developmental* character of need satisfaction must be faced. Neither adult education nor social welfare theory seems to be sufficiently attuned to this understanding (Galtung 1980, Gough 2000), or at least they seem to minimize it in their search for a theory of adult needs and their satisfaction. But if this is true, there would seem to be no point in mentioning Maslow in this respect, since his theory is focused almost exclusively on the developmental aspects of need formation and satisfaction. Furthermore, even an exclusive focus on adult needs would have to make reference to the role that adults play in the satisfaction of the developmental needs of children; this dimension would appear to be an inescapable aspect of any discussion of human needs, in any case.

Empirical Research on the Needs Hierarchy

What is surprising about most of the discussion of Maslow's hierarchy is the general lack of empirical research. Ross Fitzgerald (1977), who pretty much dismisses Maslow's hierarchical concept as unscientific (in a positivist sense), states that, "Predictably, there has been no sustained effort, on the part of academic psychologists, to follow up and develop Maslow's theoretical leads" (p.42), and, "Certainly there has been little serious study of hierarchies of needs as elaborated by Maslow . . . " (p. 43), and, "As we have seen, needs lying above the safety ones have seldom been studied" (p.45), though he does go on to state that, "The stunting of emotional growth when human beings are denied warmth and contact *during their formative years* has been well documented" (pp. 45-46). The emphasis was added to illustrate how the developmental aspect can be fairly obvious to one who is looking for it, but quite invisible to one who is not.

Gerard Huizinga (1970) was not necessarily looking for this dimension when he embarked upon a study of the workplace in the Netherlands. Huizinga *was* very sensitive to the dynamic nature of the need hierarchy and to the importance of realizing that satisfaction at one level is a prerequisite for need development at a higher level, but he came to appreciate more fully the developmental aspect of the hierarchy and the prepotency concept as his study unfolded. Since only when fulfilled does a need level tend to be forgotten, psychological health as self-actualization or growth assumes that deficiency needs are fulfilled. Furthermore, it became clear to him that few people reach the growth potential for self-actualization. Growth is usually blocked by unfavorable conditions during childhood, such that one or more deficiency needs remains chronically unfulfilled, with the result that some adults may actually regress as they age, even to the lowest levels.

Huizinga identified many problems in the modern family, such as divorce, frequent moving, absent parents, etc., as well as spoiling and permissiveness, as often overlooked and special kinds of need frustration. Without stability, as well as consistent and clear rules needed to structure behavior, basic security needs are frustrated. Need for immediate gratification leads to irresponsibility, inability to cope with disappointment, and a persistent tendency to perceive others as means-to-ends, etc. This syndrome often constitutes a special problem for two-career families; parents don't have the time (or energy) to create structure. Thus, according to Huizinga, it is not uncommon for individuals, even in affluent societies, to fail to grow out of deficiency needs. They often lack courage, with the result that the need for security outweighs the anxiety associated with growth; growth needs are less prepotent and therefore more dispensable.

Turning to Huizinga's empirical results, we see that he found, as have other organizational researchers, a relationship between level in the occupational hierarchy and level in the need hierarchy. However, his research indicated that ". . . most psychological growth *through the deficiency needs* [author's emphasis] is accomplished by the time biological maturity has been reached" (Huizinga 1970, p. 153). In other words, psychological growth may be an age-related phenomenon, but for childhood and adolescence only, which serves to confirm Maslow's contention to the same effect cited above. Further tests showed that ". . . *all* psychological growth (and not merely growth through the deficiency needs) is ended by the time the lowest age bracket which occur[red] in [his] sample is reached" (p. 153). In his *adult sample there was no change in growth level by age;* in fact ". . . more people seemed to regress with age than to grow in this sense", which is ". . .in good accord with Maslow's finding that real self-actualization is so rarely encountered" (p. 153).

What Huizinga concluded from these findings was that occupational level was probably the *dependent* variable caused by level of attainment in the need hierarchy rather than the other way around. What this implied was that changes in the work environment would not necessarily change the level of need achievement for the workers. Childhood development would appear to predispose individuals to certain levels.

Changes in the work environment would tend to be interpreted (or misinterpreted) according to one's pre-existing level of psychological growth, (though, one would hope that individual counseling and education could alter this in many cases). More specifically, Huizinga found that among Dutch workers greater job satisfaction was correlated with higher level needs. If higher needs were prepotent, this would mean that lower needs had been satisfied and were no longer important as a result, which is not surprising given that Dutch workers exist under general conditions of affluence, with the exception noted that specific childhood experiences could cause considerable variation among even affluent populations.

What was unexpected in Huizinga's results was the finding that workers at all levels were frustrated in their higher needs. This has been generally emphasized by management theorists for lower occupational levels but it appears to be true, surprisingly, for higher occupational levels as well. Job enrichment, including more planning and control functions, would thus appear to be important for all levels in the occupational hierarchy. To the extent that lower needs were stronger at lower occupational levels would suggest that they had been fulfilled to a lesser extent. Thus, material incentives may be more important for lower occupational levels; and, as Huizinga suggests, for the lower occupational levels not included in the study even greater emphasis would need to be placed upon lower need satisfaction.

Another more age-sensititive attempt to research needs empirically is represented by the work of Frederick Samuels (1984, Chapters 7 and 8). In the 1970's and early 1980's he sampled populations in the U.S., in New Hampshire -- ranging in age from seven to 'probably one hundred', and in a more age-restricted sample from Hawaii. His New Hampshire data showed that, except for early adolescence where physiological needs were strongest (perhaps some combination of puberty, peer pressure expressed in dress codes, or even food as a sublimated expression of a need for belonging), in all other age groups belongingness and love was the dominant need, and this was true at all age groups in his sample. It appears that little has changed in the U.S. since the 1960's (See below). The same was true of the Hawaiian sample of college students, but not of adults living in Honolulu, where safety needs were rated as highest. These data would seem to support both Maslow's and Huizinga's contention that most adults are burdened with unresolved or residual lower order needs. Esteem needs, for example, even in the adult populations were never very high, and almost always less important than belonging, safety and even physiological needs. These populations could hardly be characterized as mature in Maslow's terms, or as 'emotionally intelligent' in Goleman's terms.

Thus, what is suggested by this analysis of Maslow's theory and the empirical research relating to it is that it should be seen as *focused not so much upon adult psychology as upon childhood or developmental psychology.* This shifts the emphasis from the problem of how to satisfy adult needs in any given population to that of understanding how economic, political and socio-cultural conditions give rise to a characteristic schedule of needs as a result of childhood experiences. The hippies were obviously responding to a lack of satisfaction of their need for affiliation salient during childhood or adolescence. The 'peak experiences' sought by the hippies, and as described by Aron above, were not so much a misinformed search for self-actualization as they were an attempt to experience the illusion of, and in many cases act out, a different reality where need for affiliation could be satisfied; thus was an emphasis placed upon 'love' throughout the 60's. The lower order needs for subsistence and safety had obviously been chronically satisfied and were no longer prepotent such that, as Maslow would indicate, the hippies were willing to endanger those lower order needs even by 'dropping out' of the career track much valued by their parents.

The 1960's were a particular reaction to the general alienation mentioned in the earlier part of this chapter, a reaction that has been almost totally abandoned since the 1980s (except among the cultural creatives - see Chapter 7), as consumerism has again grown into all-time excesses. More than ever, shopping is now seen to substitute for affiliation and esteem needs, to the extent that for some it has become a form of addiction, leading to the formation of special organizations in the United States (e.g., 'Spender Menders'), patterned after Alcoholics Anonymous and designed to assist women, in particular, to recover from this addiction. Because the hippies were romantics and their actions under theorized, and for the most part uninformed, their protest was easily co-opted by consumer capitalism: the peace symbol could soon be found on bathroom rugs; long(er) hair became stylish (and expensive to maintain); and the blue jeans turned from worker attire to $100 Gucci symbols! These remarks are not just an interesting aside, for the global village has made the demand for these consumer symbols the essence of the aspiration for development the world over, including in socialist countries. Judging how this consumerist phenomenon relates to human needs and, in particular, to Maslow's hierarchical theory, is critical to any understanding of the course that this aspect of globalization is likely to take in this century.

Need Satisfaction under Capitalism and Socialism

Both capitalism and socialism have promoted significant levels of development in spite of various degrees of distortion fostered by the conflict between them. Nevertheless, there has been considerable evidence of dissatisfaction in both systems, with all the psychological implications of this term. Under capitalism, need satisfaction has been largely reduced to commodity fetishism in a process that has been extensively analyzed by Marxist theorists beginning most importantly with Marx himself. Based upon this background, Kate Soper (1981,1985) has developed a thoughtful analysis of the effects upon need satisfaction in modern society. Soper argues (with Marx) that the pattern of needs in a society arises not only in *response* to a production system, i.e., we need and are able to obtain those commodities that are made available, but also in *reaction* to a production system, i.e., needs displaced by a production system. Drawing upon Marx's analysis of alienation, she emphasizes the extent to which modernization via capitalism has caused us to abstract on the process of realizing ourselves through our *objectivations* (See Chapter 2). The point can be seen by comparison with peasant and pre-industrial societies. There one can easily observe the effects of one's labor or effort. The artisans and farmers owned the means of production (tools, buildings, etc.), and finished the products they started. Since we are what we are because of what we produce, and our sense of value (esteem) derives from the valuation of those products (objectivations) by ourselves and others, there was little misunderstanding about one's position and worth in such a society.

In modern society what we produce for ourselves (and others) is *money*. The means of production are owned by others (capital, the State) and the objects of production are not identifiable as our products, let alone owned by us in any sense of the word. The only mark of success (esteem) on the production side is *money* (earned) and essentially what that money can buy. We are forced by this abstraction to realize ourselves ultimately through consumption, not production

(Lasch, 1979). Thus, according to Soper, our leisure (non-work) activities take on a great significance. Our consumer goods and our leisure activities are our chief means of realizing ourselves and of satisfying our esteem needs. It is also in this sense that postmodern theorists speak of the *image* value of consumer goods (Ewen 1999), a value existing alongside Marx's classic distinction between use value and exchange value.

Capitalism has clearly exploited this alienation and resulting abstraction on esteem-need satisfaction to its own advantage as a mode of production. Socialism, on the other hand, has sadly ignored its importance -- sadly, because capitalist consumer society, for all its successes, is unable to satisfy the basic subsistence needs of sizeable minorities in the advanced countries and of the majority of those in the underdeveloped countries. Meanwhile, the utopian promise of socialism has apparently been forestalled by its neglect of this issue, for alienation would appear to be as much a problem at the mass scale of all modern society as in its particular capitalist form. Socialist workers have been apparently no more able to realize themselves in production than capitalist workers, in spite of the attempts to alter theoretically the nature of the abstraction, whereby the party would serve as the vanguard of the proletariat and the state its surrogate owner of the means of production.

Capitalism has always promoted insecurity. It is formalized in economic theory, glorified in business schools and seen generally as the source of incentive, productivity, and labor discipline at all levels of the economic system. Socialist countries, on the other hand, addressed the problem of insecurity directly, largely eliminating it from their internal economic order, except for the dissidents. Of course, older generations in Eastern Europe and the former Soviet Union still lived with the psychological memories of the past, memories of war, hunger and deprivation, while younger generations had experienced the abiding, though somewhat abstract military threat from the capitalist West. The European socialist systems had also fostered the satisfaction of affiliation needs, as workers in these countries probably now fondly recall.

But the external military threat and the concern for national security inhibited severely the realization of the full promise of socialism with respect to the whole range of needs in Maslow's hierarchy. This threat forced exorbitant human and material resources to be wasted in military research and production, with the result that productivity increases in civilian industry were never sufficient to provide the full range of consumer goods available in the capitalist West. Furthermore, technology transfer from the military to civilian sectors was severely restricted, for reasons of national security. More importantly, militarism and national insecurity forbade the satisfaction of esteem needs, except in the form of party privilege, usually expressed as a search for consumer goods, i.e., the mark of 'distorted' esteem as it is known also under capitalism. Creating this 'distortion' was, of course, the cornerstone of western psychological warfare theory, and the collapse of socialism can be attributed to the success in the application of this theory as much as to anything else.

A further complication to realizing oneself under socialism can be found in the tension between altruism and individualism. As Soper points out, (1981, p. 162) communism (much like Christianity) calls for sacrifice of self for the good of the whole society. This often creates a tension between self-affirmation and self-sacrifice, which is as likely to lead to psychological tension under socialism as it does under Christianity. This leads

> . . . to the question regarding the extent to which human happiness requires a denial of what one is, in the interests of that which one might become; from the question, that is, of the dependency of satisfaction upon the dynamic creativity that can only proceed at the cost of the single reproduction of the pleasures of sameness (Soper 1981, p. 161),

which in turn leads to the question of how a society designed to maximize human happiness and fulfillment is to accommodate the need for *dissatisfaction,* which as Rousseau, Nietzsche and Freud all observe, is the source of much creativity, artistic and other. It is clear that there is a lack of popular interest in needs that are already satisfied, happiness having as much to do with 'lacking as with having', and socialism and development theory generally have not confronted this philosophical problem. This paradox could account for the insatiability of consumerism in capitalist societies, especially as it seeks to become a substitute for other forms of gratification. Also, in light of the types of dissatisfaction that contributed to the collapse of socialism, it would suggest a belief in those countries as well that 'commodities' can gratify all needs. Any theory or utopian vision, which fails to confront this tension between having and wanting, will fail to grasp the dynamic character of human needs.

Implications for Social Theory and Planning

Maslow's hierarchy may yet offer a way to transcend the seemingly irresolvable dilemma of 'true' versus 'false' needs, but not without some careful attention to how his theory (and social theory generally) is to be used. To illustrate I will turn to a recent essay by Patricia Springborg (1981) who, in her analysis of needs, offers a forceful corrective to the messianic claims made by critics of capitalist need production and manipulation in modern society. She rightly argues that capitalist societies

> . . .are a haphazard conglomerate of different entities, some of which are a product of historical accident, others of human design, but all of which are integrated more highly in thought than in reality (p. 217)

In addition, she points out that to the extent to which radical critics succeed in persuading their readers that capitalism is highly proficient in manipulating its subjects and in creating and exploiting 'false' needs, they encourage a sense of powerlessness that would inhibit correction through political means (pp. 241-2). Finally, critics of commodity fetishism under capitalism may have placed too much hope in the ability of revolution to resolve these issues, or, more specifically, in the ability of the proletariat or its vanguard party to correct once and for all the human evils of greed and exploitation (pp. 235 - 37).

These points are well taken and serve to caution about the normative assumptions that are often hidden behind descriptive and analytical accounts. She also claims, however, that

> The scientific explanation of behavior in terms of needs is more or less doomed to failure because. . .[t]o attribute overt behavior to hidden needs for security, relatedness, self-actualization, or any of the many needs that have actually been postulated, presupposes that there is conclusive evidence to establish this link objectively. But, of course,

> there is not. The processes of human motivation are private,
> and to some degree unconscious processes; the only person
> in a position to have any knowledge of how this behavior
> relates to underlying principles is the subject himself, but
> according to the cannons of scientific objectivity we cannot
> take his word for it (p. 196).

Here Springborg is arguing from the position of the Cartesian world-view and its positivist applications to social science (Capra, 1982). However, social scientists, including especially psychologists, are often, if not always working with such 'private' information, supplied, sometimes reliably and sometimes not, by the subject. If this is not acceptable scientifically, then there is no such thing as social science (at least in the Newtonian sense), to say nothing of society itself! (See Chapter 2)

If we attempt, therefore, to validate Maslow's theory in the conventional positivist framework of science, we are probably doomed to fail. Indeed, much of the empirical research on his theory has proven inconclusive, quite apart from the inherent difficulties of framing an empirical test in the developmental and cross-cultural form that would be required to do so. This harks back to the question of whether social science should be in search of universal laws, i.e., ahistorical and transcultural laws, perhaps as implied by Maslow himself, or in search of historically contingent heuristic devices (Gillwald 1990). Is Maslow's need hierarchy a universal (even biological) law governing human behavior, or is he simply offering an historical insight? If it is the former it will probably be impossible to verify, even in a probabilistic framework, though this is not an argument for abandoning empirical research. If it is the latter - a heuristic device - then it should not be

> . . .regarded, positively or negatively, as [a] proposition of
> 'science', but analyzed as [a] legitimization of a very peculiar and probably highly significant construction of reality
> in modern society. Such analysis, of course, would bracket
> the question of the 'scientific validity' of these theories and
> simply look upon them as data for an understanding of the
> subjective and objective reality from which they emerged
> and which, in turn, they influence (Berger and Luckmann
> 1966, p. 188).

Berger and Luckmann (pp. 119 - 20) suggest that social theories are validated not by empirical research but by 'social support', i.e., they become 'standard, taken-for-granted knowledge in the society in question'. This is a much more modest ontological claim for social theory than that made by Springborg, who, from her position, rejects Maslow's theorizing as incapable of scientific validation.

Thus, postulating a need for security, affection or esteem does not necessarily imply a universal depiction of what those satisfactions are or how those needs may be satisfied, definitions of which would be culturally contingent in any case. More important, the definitions of needs and satisfactions are usually taken for granted by the socio-political-economic system within which individuals find themselves. For example, neo-classical economics postulates certain utility-maximizing behavior as typical, a necessary normative assumption in order for the theory itself to proceed. What is important here is not whether such theory can be verified, but that policies, programs, and even private decisions inspired by this theory establish reward and punishment schedules, including purely psychological ones, that return as self-fulfilling prophesies; they may literally determine the results of any empirical psychological research seeking to establish universal laws about human behavior and human needs. It is not that these neo-classical assumptions are universal scientific law; rather they have been extremely persuasive, philosophically and politically, and large numbers of (important) people act them out *as if they* were universally true. This is consistent with Marx's observation that liberal economists *believe and act as if* utility-maximizing individuals pursuing their own self-interests in a war of all-against-all would result in the common good, rather than a general negation. This in itself is mildly ironic, but he found greater irony in the fact that " . . .private interest is itself already a socially determined interest, which can only be achieved within conditions established by society and through the means that society affords. . ." (Marx 1971).

When social theory is treated as heuristic, it may be viewed as carefully crafted metaphor, which would not only serve to guard against the ever-present dangers of reification, but would be consistent with newer understandings in the philosophy of (natural) science that have resulted from relativity theory, quantum theory, and complexity studies. Science in this view would not seek an eternal objective truth. Rather it would seek an understanding of what a theory couched in the form of a probe, or jetty as Derrida (1990) refers to it, into nature (or society) would provide in the way of knowledge. Knowledge would be viewed as para-digm-contingent rather than universally true, especially in the case of social science where theory, itself, is so inescapably a part of the social reality being studied. Needless to say, most discussion about attempts to verify Maslow's theory have been conducted in the Newtonian frame-work and have often failed to find conclusive empirical support of the needs hierarchy in that framework, though Maslow may have been as guilty of presenting his theory in this way as his critics (Galtung 1980).

Whether or not this violates Maslow's initial intent or the intent of those who have pursued an empirical test of his theory, viewing his the-ory in a holistic, or dialectic, or heuristic framework seems a more appropriate path to take, although it does not simplify the task for those who seek to use it in that way. The theorist in this view should not be seen as bringing Maslow's need theory to the planning situation as if it were some sort of engineering device which might only require adjust-ment for local circumstances. Social scientists and planners 'engaged with', or 'inside', the social reality under study, would be seeking not so much to apply an ontology of needs as to uncover an ontology of social communication. The issue of the relativity of needs would have to be joined in the medium where they are established. The theorist would view himself or herself not as a prestiged holder of universal knowledge but as a participant in the construction of a social reality. The task would be to educate, not mystify, to present arguments in a comprehensible manner, and to allow the subjects of planning to determine their own needs in an informed way. If advertising is secretly manipulative, this manipulation must be exposed. If Maslow's need hierarchy appears to have heuristic value, it also must be exposed. The task is not to impose a theory but to expose a discourse, a formidable task given the language gap between the experts and the populace. But this is the challenge of a revised more humanistic planning theory and, in a broader sense, of a holistic philosophy of social science. None of this is to argue that empir-ical research should in any way be abandoned; simply it also must be made a part of the public discourse in a much more meaningful way than it has been up to now.

How, then, would one proceed to apply Maslow's theory to a plan-ning situation? Apart from the general dissemination of the theoretical ideas, one would have to develop operational definitions for the needs and some measure of satisfaction appropriate for a given socio-cultural setting. Among other things, this would require a transposition and synthesis of the vocabularies used by planning experts in the various disciplines. Economists, in particular, who are key decision makers but the most removed intellectually and emotionally from the human and psychological, would have to be involved in this discourse. Once involved, they would hopefully appreciate the value of this set of criteria for judging planning success. They should be able to observe, for example, as two authors demonstrated for South Korea, that rapid rates of growth in per capita income and GNP do not necessarily translate into greater need satisfaction for the population. Shin and Snyder (1983) defined and measured need satisfaction within Maslow's framework, grouping physiological and safety needs under quality of physical life, affiliation and esteem needs under quality of social life, and self-actualization under quality of personal life. Using 50 indicators to measure change in quality of life in South Korea from 1963 to 1979, they found (paradoxically?) that while the country experienced remarkable rates of growth in per capita income and GNP, and substantial improvement in physical life, that social quality and personal quality of life actually declined during that period. With all the caveats about the significance of empirical research, these results still must cause some reflection on the path if not the meaning of development planning in such terms.

As the discourse on need satisfaction as a measure of success unfolds, one could imagine substantial research to identify just such contradictions in the planning and development process. Research and discussion would focus not only on needs and their satisfaction, but ultimately upon the conditions under which needs at various levels in the hierarchy could be satisfied (Samater 1984). These conditions would also have to be defined operationally in an ongoing effort to plan in a more meaningful and dynamic way. While neither theory nor research has been sufficiently articulated in this context to be able to state what these definitions would be, certain priorities are suggested from the previous discussion of Maslow and his critics. For example, if the growth and satisfaction of needs take place almost entirely during childhood, adolescence and early adulthood, one would have to focus attention and research on the conditions faced by populations during this period in their lives. While it is a truism that productive workers are important to a society, and equally true that productive workers are a product of psychological development under specific social conditions, little work in planning theory addresses this critical issue.

In addition to the above, one could gain a greater understanding of *where* an actual adult population was, psychologically, at any given moment in the planning process, and an understanding of the set of needs and expectations that would characterize that population as a result of the childhood, adolescent and early adulthood experiences that they had already endured. This would help to identify appropriate incentives for the adult population, on the one hand, and the agenda for public discussion of needs, on the other. Thus, for example, if a population or a portion were predominantly concerned about safety because this need had been chronically undergratified during childhood, this need would be prepotent for this population and would dominate its motivations and expectations within the planning context. Their judgement of the success of planning would be closely related to the extent to which this need was being satisfied; other rewards or incentives in the work or social environment available to *satisfy* other higher order needs would be either ignored or misinterpreted.

What complicates this picture more than anything else, however, is the problem that different segments of the population, whether they be social classes, age groups, socio-occupational groups, or whatever, could very well be at different stages in the need hierarchy at the same time and in the same place and, that over periods of time, these combinations could be constantly changing, in part because of the success of the planning process itself. This almost inevitably would give rise to conflicts of interests, conflicts which might be understood in other terms by political scientists, but which greatly complicate the task of establishing planning priorities in a dynamic framework. The need hierarchy, and theories of cognitive and emotional development could help to illuminate and resolve many of these conflicts, but only if made a part of the public and planning discourse.

Conclusion

The value of a heuristic theory is that it suggests explanations that would not otherwise be thought of. With the help of Marx's theory of alienation it would appear that Maslow's theory could offer useful insights on the phenomenon of consumerism and the role of commodity fetishism even, perhaps, within a socialist structure. In the former socialist countries, for example, some of the (powerful) people were apparently willing to forego guaranteed employment for a chance to experience the consumer paradise they believed 'free market' societies to be. Chronic gratification, as Maslow's theory would predict, had made safety and affiliation needs no longer prepotent in these societies, and people were willing to endanger them in a search for the satisfaction of esteem needs that, as we have seen above, are now realized not at work but in leisure, particularly through the image value of consumer goods. Thus, it is no (psychological) accident, that for most people, shopping is the great sociodrama of the twentieth century (See Chapter 3). On the other hand, the hippies of the 1960's eschewed this form of gratification, recognizing, perhaps, the deceptions involved. In any case, they were by and large the children of affluent families where physiological and safety needs were chronically gratified, while their needs for affection apparently were not.

Although there are obviously many other dimensions to the examples mentioned here, it is apparent that the heuristic value of Maslow's theory can help to improve understanding and help to articulate a whole range of issues associated with modern society. Even if it is used only as a checklist, as Galtung (1980, p. 70) suggests, it could serve to caution against satisfying some needs at the expense of others, or the needs of some segments of society at the expense of others, with often serious political repercussions. The question posed is how development and planning theory can be flexible and dynamic enough to accommodate the different needs of different groups. Such theory must also be able to adjust over time when these groups and/or succeeding generations themselves change as a result of the success of planning and development.

The emphasis on material output in almost all economic theory tends to bias attention away from certain categories of need, particularly affiliation and esteem needs, because, especially within the very limited psychological vocabulary of economics, they are so difficult to measure. Indeed, a shortcoming of both neo-classical and Marxist economics is their disregard for the changing nature of needs over time. Neither theoretical tradition has shown much awareness (at least in application) of how to build in, theoretically or practically, the satisfaction of higher order non-material needs as a society develops.

Thus, a planning theory that included the need hierarchy would have to foresee changing institutional structures over time especially in relation to developmental (or child) psychology. It would have to include a theory of institution building and transformation that would accommodate changing needs as lower order needs were becoming satisfied. A sense of the scope of this problem can be appreciated in a quote by Luis Alberto Machado (1980, quoted in Gardner 1993, p.370), the then Minister for the Development of Human Intelligence of Venezuela:

> We [Venezuelans] are going to completely transform our educational system. We are going to teach how to develop intelligence everyday, from kindergarten to college, and we are going to teach parents, especially mothers, how to teach their children from the moment of birth, and even before, how to develop all their capabilities. In this manner we will be offering our people and all the peoples of the world a real new future.

Humanistic planning would have to include a monitoring system that would indicate degrees of need satisfaction at each level and suggest institutional transformations designed to satisfy new needs at higher levels as they arose, while at the same time not disrupt the production system and the distributive mechanisms. This would be a difficult task given the disciplinary boundaries in academia and the professions, boundaries that encourage intellectual provincialism and inhibit theoretical formulations that incorporate more than the accepted lore from the home discipline. This academic provincialism, combined with the elitism that characterizes most academics and professionals concerned with planning, rightly gives importance to the concern by many critics of Maslow about the hidden normative assumptions in his theory. Working within the Cartesian-Newtonian framework, which assumes that universal laws concerning human behavior can be discovered through empirical research, they refuse to endorse any theory in the absence of such proof. Treating social theory as heuristic rather than deterministic would go a long way towards resolving this dilemma. If all social theories were treated as suggestive metaphors *to be used in public discourse about collective social goals,* there would be no issue of imposing normative theories on unsuspecting subjects. Then planning could realize its human as well as scientific goals.

EPILOGUE

Σα βγεις στον πηγαιμό για την Ιθάκη,
Να εύχεσαι νάναι μακρύς ο δρόμος,
γεμάτος περιπέτειες, γεμάτος γνώσεις. . .

Κι αν πτωχική την βρεις, η Ιθάκη δεν σε γέλασε.
Έτσι σοφός που έγινες, με τόση πείρα,
Ήδη θα το κατάλαβες η Ιθάκες τι σημαίνουν

Κ. Π. Καβάφη, *Ιθάκη*, 1911

As you set forth for Ithaca,
pray the road is long,
full of adventures, full of learning. . .

And if you find her meager, Ithaca has not deceived you.
Thus wise as you have become, with so much experience,
you'll already have understood what Ithacas mean.

K. P. Kavafis, *Ithaca,* 1911

Planning is almost by definition an idealistic endeavor. It seeks to improve, even alter the world in order to further the progress of humankind. Its technical knowledge, however, is necessarily placed at the disposal of those in authority, those with the political economic power to bend society (and nature) to their will. Often the conceptions of progress held by those with authority, hypocrisy and cynicism notwithstanding, are not the same as those suggested by scientific planning, however 'scientific', itself, may be defined. If and when planners become aware of this contradiction they face a choice: either they compromise their (scientific) ideals, called 'working within the system', or they leave, seeking a 'better' place to exercise their skills, or perhaps to join a 'movement' to displace the powerful, or even some combination of all these.

At some point such encounters may lead to a feeling of nihilism, and, at least for some, the feeling that any effort to improve the world, indeed, to find any meaning at all in life is absurd. While philosophers have often visited this dilemma in the past, it has become particularly acute over the past century, as the 19th century promise of science has been crushed by the horrors of its application in exploitation, war and environmental devastation. Existentialism formalized these feelings in a philosophy of the absurd that has been accompanied by a widespread feeling of nihilism, particularly among artists and writers. This feeling was eclipsed by the idealistic fervor of the 1960s, at least among the young, only to be born again in its current postmodern and deconstructionist forms where the philosophical problem has been (semi-consciously) transferred to language and other forms of artistic expression, supplying grist for the mill of much academic parricide and the propulsion of the cult of the 'new' so important to consumer capitalism.

In any event the sense of absurdity and nihilism remains, and an idealist profession such as planning is particularly susceptible to its despairing effects. Quite apart from whether planning becomes more humanistic or not, it must confront this philosophical problem directly. Thus, a sense of the absurd, otherwise treated as a conclusion, perhaps because it often arrives later in life after some considerable experience with the 'real' world, must be treated, as Camus said, as a starting point. A sense of the absurd, it's coming into consciousness, is what makes this problem tragic, because of the loss of meaning that accompanies it. Camus (1955) confronts this problem in his brief essay on the Myth of Sisyphus. Sisyphus is for him ". . .the proletarian of the gods, powerless and rebellious, [who] knows the whole extent of his wretched condition". Sisyphus knows that good and evil are never far apart, just as satisfaction and absurdity are born of the same breath. The many failures of planning to change the world for the better may also contain the seeds of hope; for Sisyphus, it is the effort that matters.

If we think for a moment even about our successes, if we revisit our plans after time has passed, we may discover that sometimes the differences between success and failure are not as great as we imagined. Time has a way of altering both our plans and our interpretation of them. This does not mean that we stop judging our plans, even when we are confronted by the possible absurdity of even our best efforts. For it is after all the effort that matters and if Camus can judge Sisyphus as happy, then we also must believe that ". . .the struggle itself towards the heights is enough to fill. . .[our] heart[s]".

BIBLIOGRAPHY

Ada, Michael (1989). *Machines As the Measure of Man: Science, Technology and the Ideology of Western Dominance.* Ithaca, NY: Cornell University Press.

Adorno, Theodor (1984). *Aesthetic Theory.* Translated by Greta Adorno and Rolf Tiedemann. London, Boston: Routeledge & Kegan Paul.

Albarran, Alan B. and David H. Goff (2000). *Understanding the Web: Social, Political and Economic Dimensions of the Internet.* Ames, Iowa: Iowa State University Press.

Allmendinger, Philip (1999). "Planning in the Future: Trends, Problems and Possibilities" in Philip Almendinger and Michael Chapman, eds., *Planning Beyond 2000.* Chichester, New York, Weinheim, Brisbane, Singapore, and Toronto: John Wiley & Sons, pp. 241-274.

Antsyferova, L.I. (1974). "The Psychology of the Self-Actualizing Personality in the Work of Abraham Maslow," *Soviet Psychology,* Vol. XII, No. 3, pp. 21-39.

Argyris, Chris, Robert Putman and Diana McLain Smith (1985). *Action Science.* San Francisco and London: Josey-Bass Publishers.

Aron, Adrianne (1977). "Maslow's Other Child," *Journal of Humanistic Psychology,* Vol. 17, No. 2, Spring, pp. 9-24.

Bar-on, Reuven and James D.A. Parker, eds. (2000). *The Handbook of Emotional Intelligence: Theory, Development, Assessment, and Application at Home, School and in the Workplace.* San Francisco: Jossey-Bass.

Bauzon, Kenneth E. (1992). *Development and Democratization in the Third World: Myths, Hopes, and Realities.* Washington, Philadelphia, London· Crane Russak, Member of the Taylor & Francis Group.

Benveniste, Guy (1972). *The Politics of Expertise.* Berkeley, CA: The Glendessary Press.

Berger, Peter and Thomas Luckmann. (1966). *The Social Construction of Reality.* Garden City, N.Y.: Doubleday & Co.

Bernstein, Richard J. (1978). *The Restructuring of Social and Political Theory.* Philadelphia: University of Pennsylvania Press.

Bertalanffy, Ludwig von (1962). "General Systems Theory - A Critical Review". *General Systems Yearbook,* Vol. 7.
    (1952) *Problems of Life: An Evaluation of Modern Biological and Scientific Thought.* New York: Harper Bros.

Binet, Alfred and Theodore Simon. (1980). *The Development of Intelligence in Children.* Nashville,TN: Williams Printing Co (originally published in 1905).

Blair, Swenda (1979). "Why Dick Can't Stop Smoking: The Politics Behind Our National Addition" in *Mother Jones*, January, pp. 31-42.

Boocock, Sarane S., and E.O.Schild, eds. (1968), with a Preface by James S. Coleman. *Simulation Games in Learning*. Beverly Hills and London: Sage Publications.

Bloomfield, Gerald (1978). *The World Automotive Industry*. Pomfert, Vt.: David and Charles.

Boguslaw, Robert (1981). *The New Utopians: A Study of System Design and Social Change*. NY: Irvington Publishers.

Bookchin, Murray (1974). *The Limits of the City*. New York: Harper and Row.

Boudon, Raymond (1971). *The Uses of Structuralism*. Translated by Michalina Vaughn. London: Heineman.

Boulding, Kenneth (1964). "The Image and Social Dynamics", in Geroge K. Zollschan and Walter Hirsch. *Explorations in Social Change*. Boston: Houghton Mifflin.

Boyden, S.V., ed. (1970). *The Impact of Civilization on the Biology of Man*. Toronto: University of Toronto Press, 1970.

Braybrooke, D. and C.E. Lindblom (1963). *A Strategy of Decision*. New York: Free Press.

Brenner, M. Harvey (1973). *Mental Illness and the Economy*. Camdridge, Mass.: Harvard University Press.

Brown, Richard Harvey (1987). *Society as Text: Essays on Rhetoric, Reason, and Reality*. Chicago & London: University of Chicago Press.

Burke, Edmund (1979). *A Participatory Approach to Urban Planning*. New York and London: Human Sciences Press.

Burke, Kenneth (1959). *Attitudes Toward History*. Boston: Beacon Press (First published in 1937).

_____ (1965). *Permanence and Change*. Indianapolis: Bobbs-Merrill Company, Ltd. (First published in1935).

_____ (1968a). *Counterstatement*. Berkeley: University of California Press.

_____ (1968b). *Language as Symbolic Action*. Berkeley: University of California Press.

_____ (1969a). *A Grammar of Motives*. Berkeley: University of California Press.

_____ (1969b). *A Rhetoric of Motives*. Berkeley: University of California Press.

————— (1973). *The Philosophy of Literary Form: Studies in Symbolic Action.* Berkeley: University of California Press

Caldicott, Dr. Helen (1979). "Health Hazards of Nuke Power". *The Guardian*, May 23, p. 9.

Camhis, Marios (1979). *Planning Theory and Philosophy.* London and New York: Tavistock Publications.

Camus, Albert (1955). *The Myth of Sisyphus and Other Essays.* New York: Alfred A. Knopf. Translated from the French by Justin O'Brien. Originally published in 1942 as *Le Mythe de Sisyphe.* Librarie Gallimand.

Capra, Fritjof (1982). *The Turning Point: Science, Society and the Rising Culture.* New York: Simon and Schuster.

Carey, James W. and John J. Quirk (1971). " The Mythos of the Electronic Revolution", *The American Scholar.* Vol. 39, No.2, pp. 219-241.

Chang, Ha-Joon (2003). "Kicking Away the Ladder: Neo-Liberals Rewrite History", in *Monthly Review,* Vol 54, No. 8 (Jan), pp. 10-15.

Cherniss, Cary and David Goleman, eds (2001). *The Emotionally Intelligent Workplace: How to Select for, Measure, and Improve Emotional Intelligence in Individuals, Groups, and Organizations.* San Francisco: Josey-Bass.

Chomsky, Noam (1957). *Syntactic Structures.* The Hague: Mouton.

Clark, Mary E. (1990). "Meaningful Social Bonding As a Universal Human Need". John Burton, ed. *Conflict: Human Needs Theory.* N.Y.: St. Martin's Press, pp. 34-59.

Clark, Terry and Michael Rempel (1997). *Citizen Politics in Post-Industrial Societies.* Boulder, CO and Oxford: Westview Press, A Division of Harper Collins, Publishers.

Clarke, Tony (1996). "Mechanisms of Corporate Rule", in Jerry Mander and Edward Goldsmith, eds.. *The Case Against the Global Economy and a Turn Toward the Local.* San Francisco, CA: Sierra Club Books, pp. 297-308.

Collins, Randall (1989). "Toward a Theory of Intellectual Change: The Social Causes of Philosophies", *in Science, Technology and Human Values.* Vol. 14, No. 2 (Spring), pp. 107-140

Commoner, Barry (1966). *Science and Survival.* New York: Viking Press.

————— (1972). *The Closing Circle: Nature, Man and Technology.* New York: Bantam Books.

_____ (1990). *Making Peace with the Planet.* New York: Pantheon Books.

De Grazia, Sebastian (1962). *Of Time, Work and Leisure,* New York: Twentieth Century Fund.

Dear, Michael and Allen J. Scott (1981). *Urbanization and Urban Planning in Capitalist Society.* London: Methuen.

Dear, Michael J. (2000). *The Postmodern Urban Condition.* Oxford and Malden, MA: Blackwell Publishers, Ltd.

DeLeon, P. (1988). *Advice and Consent: The Development of the Policy Sciences.* New York: Russell Sage Foundation.

Derrida, Jacques (1981). *Positions.* Translated and annotated by Alan Bass. Chicago: University of Chicago Press.

_____ (1990). "Some Statements and Truisms about Neo-logisms, Newisms, Postisms, Parasitisms, and other Small Seismisms" in David Carroll (ed.) *The States of 'Theory': History, Art and Critical Discourse.* New York: Columbia University Press, pp. 63-94.

Diesing, Paul (1991). *How Does Social Science Work: Reflections on Practice.* Pittsburgh: University of Pittsburgh Press.

Doctorow, E. L. (1994). *The Waterworks.* New York: Random House.

Dollars and Sense: A Monthly Bulletin of Economic Affairs (1979). "Big Brother in the Work Place", No 45, March, p. 17.

Dore, Ronald (2000). *Stock Market Capitalism; Welfare Capitalism: Japan and Germany Versus the Anglo-Saxons.* Oxford: Oxford University Press.

Douglas, Mike and John Friedman (1998). *Cities for Citizens: Planning and the Rise of Civil Society in a Global Age.* Chichester, New York, Weinheim, Brisbane, Singapore and Toronto: John Wiley & Sons.

Doyal, Lesley and Imogen Pennell (1976). "Pox Britannica: Health, Medicine and Underdevelopment", *Race and Class*, Vol. 18, No. 2, pp. 155-172.

Dryzek, John (1993). "Policy Analysis and Planning: From Science to Argument" in Frank Fischer and John Forester, eds. *The Argumentative Turn in Policy Analysis and Planning.* Durham, NC and London: Duke University Press, pp. 213-232

Duncan, Hugh D. (1962). *Communication and Social Order.* New York: The Bedminster Press.

_____ (1965). *Culture and Democracy: the Struggle for Form in Society and Architecture in the Middle West During the Life and Times of Louis H. Sullivan.* Totowa, N.J.: Bedminister Press.

_____ (1968). *Symbols in Society.* New York: Oxford University Press.

_____ (1969). *Symbols and Social Theory.* New York: Oxford University Press.

Durning, Alan Their (1992). *How Much Is Enough? The Consumer Society and the Future of the Earth.* N.Y., London: W.W. Norton & Co.

Durrell, Lawrence (1963). *Prospero's Cell, and Reflections on a Marine Venus.* New York: Faber & Faber.

Easlea, Brian (1973). *Liberation and The Aims of Science: An Essay on the Obstacles to the Building of a Beautiful World* Totowa, N.J.: Rowman and Littlefeld.

Ekman, Paul and Wallace Friesen (1975). *Unmasking the Face.* Englewood Cliffs, N.J.: Prentice Hall.

Ellul, Jacques (1964). *The Technological Society.* New York: Vintage Books.

Estes, Ralph W. (1996). *The Tyranny of the Bottom Line: Why Corporations Make Good People Do Bad Things.* Emeryville, CA: Berrett-Kochler, Publishers.

Estrella, Marisol, et at (2000). *Learning from Change: Issues and Experiences in Participatory Monitoring and Evaluation.* London: Intermediate Technology Publications, Ltd. And Ottowa, Canada: International Development Research Center

Etzioni, Amitai (1968). *The Active Society.* London: Collier-Macmillan and New York: The Free Press.

_____ (1973). Mixed Scanning: A Third Approach to Decision Making" in Andreas Faludi, ed. *A Reader in Planning Theory.* Oxford: Pergamon Press.

European Commission, Forward Studies Unit (2000). *Democracy and The Information Society in Europe.* New York: St. Martin's Press.

Ewen, Stuart (1976). *Captains of Consciousness: Advertising and the Social Roots of the Consumer Culture.* New York: McGraw-Hill.

_____ (1999). *All Consuming Images: The Politics of Style in Contemporary Culture.* N.Y.: Basic books.

Eyer, Joseph and Imogen Sterling (1977). "Stress-Related Mortality and Social Organization", *The Review of Radical Political Economics,* Vol. 9, No.1, Spring, pp. 1-44.

Fagence, Michael (1977). *Citizen Participation in Planning.* Oxford, New York, Toronto, Sydney, Paris and Frankfort: Pergamon Press.

Feyeraband, Paul K. (1975). *Against Method.* London: New Left Books.

_____ (1978). *Science in a Free Society.* London: New Left Books.

_____ (1987). *Farewell to Reason.* London: Verso

Fischer, Robert (1994). *Let the People Decide: Neighborhood Organizing in America.* Updated Edition. New York: Twayne Publishers and New York, Toronto, Oxford, Singapore and Sydney: Maxwell Macmillan International.

Fischer, Frank and John Forester, eds. (1993). *The Argumentative Turn in Policy Analysis and Planning.* Durham and London: Duke University Press.

Fitzgerald, Ross (1977). "Abraham Maslow's Hierarchy of Needs - An Exposition and Evaluation". Ross Fitzgerald, ed. *Human Needs and Politics.* Elmsford, NY: Pergamon Press, pp. 36-51

Flyvbjerg, Bent (1996). "The Dark Side of Planning: Rationality and 'Realrationalitat'" in Seymour Mandelbaum, Luiggi Mazza and Robert W. Burchell, eds., *Explorations in Planning Theory.* New Brunswick, NJ: Rutgers University, Center for Urban Policy Research.

Forester, John (1989). *Planning in the Face of Power.* Berkeley, CA: University of California Press.

Foucault, Michel (1972). *The Archeology of Knowledge.* Translated by A. M. Sheridan Smith. New York: Pantheon.

Fraser, Colin and Sonia Restrepo-Estrada (1998). *Communicating for Development: Human Change for Survival.* London and New York: I.B. Tauris, Publishers.

Fromm, Eric (1941). *Escape from Freedom.* New York: Rinehart.

Galtung, Johan (1980). "The Basic Needs Approach" in Katrina Lederer (ed.). 1980. *Human Needs: A Contribution to the Current Debate.* Cambridge, Mass: Oelgesch-lager, Gunn & Hain, Publishers, pp. 55 - 123.

Gardner, Howard. 1993. *Frames of Mind: The Theory of Multiple Intelligences.* N.Y.: Basic Books.

Gellner, Ernest (1984). "The Scientific Status of the Social Sciences", in *International Social Science Journal.* Vol. 36. pp.567-586.

Giddens, Anthony (1984). *The Constitution of Society.* Cambridge: Polity Press.

Gillwald, Katrin (1990). "Conflict and Needs Research". John Burton, ed. *Conflict: Human Needs Theory.* N.Y.: St. Martin's Press, pp. 115-124.

Goleman, David (1996). *Emotional Intelligence.* N.Y.: Bantam Books,

London: Bloomsbury Books.

Gough, Ian (2000). *Global Capital, Human Needs and Social Policies: Selected Essays, 1994-99*. London: Palgrave.

Gouldner, Alvin W. (1970). *The Coming Crisis of Western Sociology*. New York: Basic Books.

Goulet, Denis (1971). *The Cruel Choice: A New Concept in the Theory of Development*. New York: Atheneum Press.

Gowan, Peter (1999). *The Global Gamble: Washington's Faustian Bid for World Dominance*. London: Verso.

Gunder Frank, Andre (1981). *Crisis in the Third World*. London: Holmes and Meier.

Gutenschwager, Gerald A. (1969). *Awareness, Culture ared Change: A Study of Modernization in Greece*. Unpublished Ph. D. Dissertation, Chapel Hill: University of North Carolina, Department of City and Regional Planning.

―――― (1970). "Social Reality and Social Change". *Social Research*, Vol. 37, No 1 (Spring), pp 48-70.

―――― (1973). "The Time Budget - Activity Systems Perspective in Urban Research and Planning". *Journal of American Institute of Planning*, Vol.39, No.6 (November), pp. 378-387.

―――― (1979). "Gaming, Education and Change". *Journal of Architectural Education*. Vol. 37, No.1 (September), pp. 30-32.

―――― (1989). *The Political Economy of Health in Modern Greece*. Athens: National Center of Social Research (in Greek).

―――― (1984) "The Social Stucture of Health and Disease" in *Greek Review of Social Research*, Vol. 53, pp. 24-49 (in Greek).

―――― (1996). "Architecture in a Changing World: the New Rhetoric of Form", in *Journal of Architectural Education*, Vol. 49, No. 4 (May), pp. 246-258.

―――― and Mary Gutenschwager (1978), "Research on the Use of Time", *Review of Sociological Research*, Athens Centre of Social research, Vol.33-34, pp.335-348 (in Greek).

Habermas, Jurgen (1970). *Toward a Rational Society: Student Protest, Science and Politics*. Boston: Beacon Press.

―――― (1971). *Knowledge and Human Interests*. Translated by Jeremy J Shapiro. Boston: Beacon Press.

―――― (1984). *The Theory of Communicative Action*. Translated by T. McCarthy. Boston: Beacon Press.

Halfpenny, Peter (1982). *Positivism and Sociology: Explaining Social Life.* London: George Allen & Unwin.

Hall, Douglas T. and Khalid E. Nougain (1968), "An Examination of Maslow's Need Hierarchy in an Organizational Setting," *Organizational Behavior and Human Performance,* No. 3, pp. 12-35.

Hall, Ellen (1979). *Inner City Health in America.* Washington, D.C: Urban Environment Foundation.

Halstead, Ted and Clifford Cobb (1996). "The Need for New Measurements of Progress" in Jerry Mander and Edward Goldsmith, eds. *The Case Against the Global Economy and for a Turn Toward the Local.* San Francisco, CA: Sierra Club Books, pp. 197-206.

Hanson, Victor Davis, and John Heath (1998). *Who Killed Homer?: The Demise of Classical Education and the Recovery of Greek Wisdom.* New York: The Free Press.

Haq, Mahbub ul (1999). *Reflections on Human Development.* Delhi: Oxford University Press.

Harper, Thomas L. and Stanley M. Stein (1992). "The Centrality of Normative Ethical Theory to Contemporary Planning" in *Journal of Planning Education and Research.* No. 11, pp. 105-116.

Harvard Working Group on New And Resurgent Diseases (1996). "Globalization, Development and the Spread of Disease", in Jerry Mander and Edward Goldsmith, eds. *The Case Against the Global Economy and a Turn Toward the Local.* San Francisco, CA: Sierra Club Books.

Harvey, David (1973). *Social Justice and the City.* Baltimore: The Johns Hopkins University Press and London: Edward Arnold Publishers, Ltd.

———— (1985). *The Urbanization of Capital.* Baltimore: The Johns Hopkins University Press.

———— (1989). *The Condition of Postmodernity.* Oxford: Basil Blackwell Ltd.

Hendler, Sue (1995). *Planning Ethics: A Reader in Planning Theory and Research.* New Brunswaick, NJ: Rutgers University, Center for Urban Policy Research.

Healy, Patsy (1996). "The Communicative Work of Development Plans" in Seymour Mandelbaum, Luiggi Mazza and Robert W. Burchell, eds. *Explorations in Planning Theory.* New Brunswick, NJ: Rutgers University, Center for Urban Policy Research.

Hightower, Henry C. (1969). "Planning Theory in Contemporary

Professional Education" in *Journal of the American Institute of Planners,* Vol. 35, No. 5.

Hoch, Charles (1996a). "A Pragmatic Inquiry about Planning and Power" in Seymour J. Mandelbaum, Luiggi Mazza and Robert W. Burchell, eds. *Explorations in Planning Theory.* New Brunswick, NJ: Rutgers University, Center for Urban Policy Research, pp. 30-44.

———— (1996b). "What Do Planners Do in the United States" in Seymour J Mandelbaum, Luiggi Mazza and Robert W Burchell, eds. *Explorations in Planning Theory.* New Brunswick, N.J.: Rutgers University, Center for Urban Policy Research, pp. 225-240.

Hofstadter, Richard (1959). *Social Darwinism in American Thought.* New York: Basiller.

Hooper, Barbara (1998). "The Poem of Male Desires: Female Bodies, Modernity, and 'Paris: Capital of Nineteenth Century'" in Leonie Sandercock, ed. *Making the Invisible Visible: A Multi-cultural History of Planning.* Berkeley: University of California Press.

Horkheimer, Max (1947). *Eclipse of Reason.* New York: Oxford

———— (1972). *Critical Theory.* New York: The Seabury Press.

Huizinga, Gerard (1970). *Maslow's Need Hierarchy in the Work Situation.* Broninger: The Netherlands: Walters-Noodhoff Publishers.

Husserl, Edmund (1970). *The Crisis of European Science and Transcendental Phenomenology.* Translated and with an introduction by David Carr. Evanston,IL: Northwestern University Press.

Inglehart, Ronald (1997). *Modernization and Postmodernization: Cultural, Economic, and Political Change in 43 Societies.* Princeton, NJ: Princeton University Press.

———— (1999). "Postmodernization Erodes Respect for Authority, but Increases Support for Democracy", in Pippa Norris. *Critical Citizens: Global Support for Democratic Government.* Oxford: Oxford University Press, pp. 236-256.

Innes, Judith (1995). "Planning Theory's Emerging Paradigm: Communicative Action and Interactive Practice". *Journal of Planning Education and Research.* Vol. 14, No.3 (Spring), pp. 183-90.

Jongmans, D.G. and P.C.W. Gutkind, eds. (1967). *An Anthropologist in the Field.* Assen: Van Gorcum.

Junker, Buford (1960). *Fieldwork: An Introduction to the Social Sciences,* with and introduction by Everett C. Hughes. Chicago: University of Chicago Press.

Kane, Robert L., et al. (1976). *The Health Gap: Medical Services and the Poor.* New York: Springer Publising Co.

Kavafis, P. K. (n.d.). The Complete Poetic Works of Kavafis. Athens: Mermigga Publishers (In Greek).

Kay, Geoffrey (1975). *Development and Underdevelopment: A Marxist Analysis,* London: MacMillan Press Ltd., Chapter 5.

Kemper, Theodore D. (1978). *A Social Interactional Theory of Emotions.* N.Y.: Wiley.

_____ (1987). "How Many Emotions Are There? Wedding the Social and Autonomic Functions". *American Journal of Sociology.* 93: 263-289.

Key, Wilson Bryan (1974). *Subliminal Seduction: Ad Media's Manipulation of Not So Innocent America,* New York: New America Library.

Knorr-Cetina, Karin D., and Michael Mulkay, eds. (1983). *Science Observed: Perspectives on the Social Study of Science.* London, Beverly Hills, CA: Sage Publications.

Korten, David C. (1996). "The Failures of Bretton Woods", in Jerry Mander and Edward Goldsmith, eds. *The Case Against Global Capitalism and a Turn Toward the Local.* San Francisco, CA: Sierra Club Books, pp. 20-28.

_____ (1999). *The Post-Corporate World: Life After Capitalism.* San Francisco, CA: Barrett-Koehler Publishers and West Hartford, CT: Kumarian Press.

Koutoulas, Diamantis (1988). *The Imperial Policies of Byzantium against Greek "Ethnics" (4th-6th-Centuries A.D.).* Thessaloniki: Dion Publishers (in Greek).

Krueger, Richard A. (1994). *Focus Groups: A Practical Guide for Applied Research.* Second Edition. Thousand Oaks, London and New Delhi: Sage Publications.

Kuhn, Thomas (1970). *The Structure of Scientific Revolutions.* 2nd Edition. Chicago: University of Chicago Press.

Lakatos, Imre and Alan Musgrave, eds. (1970). *Criticism and the Growth of Knowledge.* Procedings of the International Colloquium on the Philosophy of Science. New York: Cambridge University Press.

Lappé, Frances Moore and Joseph Collins (1977). *Food First: Beyond the Myth of Scarcity.* Boston: Hougthon Mifflin Co.

Larsen, Stein Ugelvik (2000). *The Challenge of Theories of Democracy: Elaborations over New Trends in Transitology.* Social

Science Monographs, Boulder. Distributed by Columbia University Press, NY.

Lasch, Christopher (1979). *The Culture of Narcissism: American Life in an Age of Diminishing Expectations.* N.Y.: Warner Books.

Lauria, M and R. Whelan (1995). "Planning Theory and Political Economy: The Need for Reintegration", *Planning Theory*, Vol. 14.

Le Bon, Gustave (1897). *The Crowd: A Study of the Popular Mind.* 2nd Edition. New York: Macmillan.

Lederer, Katrina, ed. (1980). Human Needs: *A Contribution to the Current Debate.* Cambridge, Mass.: Oelgesch-lager, Gumm & Hain, Publishers.

Leiss, William (1974). *The Domination of Nature.* Boston: Beacon Press.

(1976). *The Limits to Satisfaction: An Essay on the Problem of Needs and Commodities.* Toronto and Buffalo: University of Toronto Press.

Lentricchia, Frank (1983). *Criticism and Social Change.* Chicago: University of Chicago Press.

Lethbridge, David (1986). "A Marxist Theory of Self-Actualization," *Journal of Humanistic Psychology*, Vol. 26, No. 2 (Spring), pp. 84-103.

(1989). "Cultural-Historical Dimensions of Self-Actualization," *Nature, Society and Thought*, Vol. 2, No. 1, pp. 19-29.

Lindblom, C.E. (1965). *The Intelligence of Democracy.* New York: The Free Press.

Linder, Staffan B. (1970). *The Harried Leisure Class.* New York: Columbia University Press.

Lippmann, Walter (1922). *Public Opinion.* New York: Harcourt, Brace & Co.

Louch, A.R. (1966). *Explanation and Human Action.* Berkeley, CA: University of California Press.

Machado, Luis Alberto (1980). *The Right to Be Intelligent.* N.Y.: Pergamon Press.

Macpherson, C.B. (1962). *The Political Theory of Possesive Individualism: Hobbes to Locke.* London: Oxford University Press.

Mander, Jerry (1978). *Four Arguments for the Elimination of Television.* New York: William Morrow & Co.

and Edward Goldsmith, eds. (1996). *The Case Against the Global Economy and a Turn Toward the Local.* San Francisco, CA: Sierra Club Books.

Marcuse, Herbert (1964). *One Dimensional Man: Studies in the Ideology of Advanced Industrial Society.* Boston: Beacon Press.

Marx, Karl (1971). "On Production Relations" in *The Grundrisse*, edited and translated by David McClelland. New York: Harper and Row.

Maslow, A.H. (1970). *Motivation and Personality.* Second Edition. New York: Harper and Row.

McChesney, Robert W. and John Bellamy Foster (2003). "The Commercial Tidal Wave", in *Monthly Review*, Vol. 54, No. 10 (March), pp. 1-16.

McClelland, David (1961). *The Achieving Society.* Princeton, NJ: Van Nostrand.

McCoy, Alfred W., with Cathleen B. Read and Leonard P Adams (1972). *The Politics of Heroin in Southeast Asia.* New York: Harper and Row.

McDermott, John (1969). "Technology: The Opiate of the Intellectuals", *New York Review of Books,* Vol. 13, No. 2, July, 31, pp. 29-35.

McInnes, Neil (1977). "The Politics of Needs - or, Who Needs Politics", in Ross Fitgerald (ed.), *Human Needs and Politics.* Elmsford, NY: Pergamon Press, pp. 229 - 243.

McKeown, Thomas (1976). *The Role of Medicine: Dream, Image or Nemesis.* London: The Nuffield Provincial Hospitals Trust

McNeil, William H. (1976). *Plaques and Peoples.* Garden City. N.Y: Anchor Press.

Meier, Richard L. (1962). *A Communications Theory of Urban Growth.* Cambridge, Mass: MIT Press.

Meyerson, Martin and Edward C. Banfield (1955). *Politics, Planning and the Public Interest.* Glencoe, Il: Free Press.

Miller, George A., Eugene Galanter and Karl H. Pribram (1960). *Plans and the Structure of Behavior.* New York: Henry Holt & Co.

Moretti, Franco (1987). "The Spell of Indecision", in *New Left Review.* 164 (July-August), pp. 27-33.

Mother Jones, "Cancer Soars Near Nukes" (1978), Sept./Oct., p.10.

Mussen, P., ed. 1970. "Piaget's Theory". *Carmichael's Handbook of Child Psychology.* New York: Wiley, pp. 703-32.

_____ and W. Kessen, eds. (1983). *Handbook of Child Psychology.* Vol. 1. N.Y.: Wiley.

Myrdal, Gunnar (1960). *Beyond the Welfare State: Economic Planning and Its International Implications.* New Haven: Yale University Press.

Natanson, Maurice (ed.) (1963). *Philosophy of the Social Sciences: A Reader.* New York: Random House.

Navaro, Vicente (1978). *Medicine Under Capitalism.* New York: Neole Watson.

―――― (1980). "Work, Ideology and Science: The Case of Medicine" in *International Journal of Health Services,* Vol 10, No 4, pp 523-550. No. 3, pp. 395-424.

Needleman, Martin L. and Carolyn Emerson Needleman (1974). *Guerrillas in the Bureaucracy: The Community Planning Experiment in the United States.* New York, London, Sydney and Toronto: John Wiley & Sons.

Noble, David (1977). *America by Design: Science, Technology, and the Rise of Corporate Capitalism.* Oxford: Oxford University Press.

Nord, Walter (1977). "A Marxist Critique of Humanistic Psychology," *Journal of Humanistic Psychology,* Vol 17, No. 1. (Winter), pp. 75-83.

Norgaard, Richard (1994). *Development Betrayed: the End of Progress and a Coevolutionary View of the Future.* London & New York: Routledge.

Norris, Christopher (1999). "Truth, Science and the Growth of Knowledge", in *New Left Review.* Vol. 210, pp. 105-123.

Norris, Pippa (1999). *Critical Citizens: Global Support for Democratic Government.* Oxford and New York: Oxford University Press.

Pateman, Carole (1970). *Participation and Democratic Theory.* Cambridge: Cambridge University Press.

Patrushev, V. D.(1970). *Aggregate Time Balance of a Nation (Economic Region) and its Role in Socio-Economic Planning.* Novosibirsk: Siberian Dept., USSR Academy of Sciences.

Peattie, Lisa (1970). "Community Drama and Advocacy Planning", *American Institute of Planners Journal,* Vol. 36, No.1, pp. 405-410.

Pettit, Philip (1975). *The Concept of Structuralism: a Critical Analysis.* Berkeley & Los Angeles: University of California Press.

Phillips, Roland L. (1975). "Role of Life Style and Dietary Habits in Risk of Cancer among Seventh Day Adventists". *Cancer Research,* Vol. 35 (Nov.), pp. 3513-3522.

Piaget, Jean (1950). *The Psychology of Intelligence.* San Diego, CA: Harcourt Brace Jovanovich.

―――― (1968). *Structuralism.* New York: Harper and Row.

Pierce, John C., Mary Ann E. Steger, Brent S. Sted, and Nicholas P. Lovrich (1992). *Citizens, Political Communication and Interest Groups: Environmental Organizations in Canada and the United States.* Westport, CN and London: Praeger.

Popper, Karl (1945). *The Open Society and Its Enemies.* London: Routeledge and Kegan Paul.

———— (1959). *The Logic of Scientific Discovery.* New York: Harper and Row.

Preteceille, Edmond and Jean-Pierre Terrail (1985). *Capitalism, Consumption and Needs.* Trans. Sarah Matthews. Oxford: Basil Blackwell, Publishers. First published in French as *Besoins et Mode de Production: Du Capitalism en Crise au Socialism.* 1977. Paris: Editions Sociales.

Quine, W.V.O. (1953). "Two Dogmas of Empiricism", in *From a Logical Point of View.* Cambridge, MA: Harvard University Press.

———— (1960). *Word and Object.* Cambridge, MA: Harvard University Press.

———— and J.S. Ullian (1970). *The Web of Belief.* New York: Random House.

———— (1981). *Theories and Things.* Cambrifge, MA: Harvard University Press.

Quinn, Daniel (1995). *Ishmael.* NY: Bantam Books.

Rainwater, Lee (1970). *Behind Ghetto Walls: Black Families in a Federal Slum.* Chicago: Aldine Publishing Co.

Rapoport, Anatol (1957). "Lewis F Richardson's Mathematical Theory of War", *General Systems Yearbook,* Vol. 2.

———— (1960). *Fights, Games and Debates.* Ann Arbor: University of Michigan Press.

Ray, Paul H, PhD and Sherry Ruth Anderson, PhD (2000). *The Cultural Creatives: How 50 Million People Are Changing the World.* NY: Three Rivers Press.

Rein, Martin and Donald Schon (1993). "Reframing Policy Discourse" in Frank Fischer and John Forester, *The Argumentative Turn in Policy Analysis and Planning.* Durham and London: Duke University Press.

Ringen, Knut (1979). "Edwin Chadwick, the Market Ideology and Sanitary Reform: On The Nature of the 19th Century Public Health Movement". *International Journal of Health Services,* Vol. 9. No 1, pp. 107-120.

Rogers, Everett M. (1962). *Diffusion of Innovations*. New York: The Free press of Illinois.

Roszak, Theodor (1968). *The Making of a Counterculture: Reflections on the Technocratic Society and Its Youthful Opposition*. Garden City, NY: Doubleday & Co.

Rueckert, William H. (1969). *Critical Responses to Kenneth Burke*. Minneapolis, MN: University of Minnesota Press.

Runciman, W.G. (1997). *A Treatise on Social Theory*. Cambridge: Cambridge University Press.

———— (1998). *The Social Animal*. London:

———— (1999). "Social Evolutionism: A Reply to Michael Rustin", in *New Left Review*. Vol. 234 (July-August), pp. 145-153.

Rustin, Michael (1999). "A New Social Evolutionalism", in *New Left Review*. Vol. 234 (March-April), pp. 106-126.

Salovey, Peter and David J. Sluyter (1997). *Emotional Development and Emotional Intelligence: Educational Implications*. N.Y.: Basic Books.

Samater, Irbrahim M. (1984). "From 'Growth' to 'Basic Needs': The Evolution of Development Theory", *Monthly Review*, Vol. 36, No. 5 (October), pp.1-13.

Samuels, Frederick (1984). *Human Needs and Behavior*. Cambridge, MA: Schenkman Publishing Co., Inc.

Sandercock, Leonie (1998). *Towards Cosmopolis: Planning for Multicultural Cities*. Chichester, New York, Weinheim, Brisbane, Singapore and Toronto: John Wiley & Sons.

Saussure, Ferdinand de (1959). *Course in General Linguistics*. Ed. C. Bally and A. Sechehaye. Trans. W. Baskin. New York: Philosophical Library.

Schiller, Herbert I. 1976). *Communication and Cultural Domination*. White Plains, New York: M.E. Sharpe, Inc.

Schumacher, E.F. (1973). *Small Is Beautiful: Economics As If People Mattered*. New York: Harper & Row.

Schutz, Alfred (1962a). *Alfred Schutz, Collected Papers, Vol. I. The Problem of Social Reality*. Maurice Natanson (ed.). The Hague: Martinus Nijhoff.

———— (1962b). "Choosing Among Projects of Action". In *Alfred Schutz, Collected Papers*, Vol I.

———— (1964). *Collected Papers II. Studies in Social Theory*. Edited and introduced by Arvid Broderson. The Hague: Nijhoff.

_____ (1966). *Collected Papers. III. Studies in Phenomenology and Philosophy.* Edited by Ilse Schutz, with an introduction by Aron Gurwitsch. The Hague: Nijhoff.

_____ (1970). *On Phenomenology and Social Relations.* Edited and with an introduction by Helmut R. Wagner. Chicago: University of Chicago Press.

Segall, Marshall H., et al (1966). *The Influence of Culture on Visual Perception.* Indianopolis: Bobbs-Merrill Co.

Shapere, Dudley (1974). " The Paradigm Concept", in *Science.* Vol. 172, pp. 706-709.

Shapiro, David and Cecile Shapiro (1977). "Abstract Expressionism: the Politics of Apolitical Painting", in Jack Saltzman, ed., *Prospects: An Annual Review of American Cultural Studies.* Vol. 3, pp. 174-214. New York: Burt Franklin

Shin, Doh D. and Wayne Snyder. (1983). "Economic Growth, Quality of Life, and Development Policy: *A Case Study of South Korea", Comparative Political Studies,* Vol. 16, No. 2 (July), pp. 195-213.

Shirk, Martha (1978). "Job Site Danger". *St. Louis Post-Dispatch,* Sept. 17, p. 1F.

Shirky, Clay (2000). "Beyond Alchemy", in *Feed Magazine,* August 21.

Simmel, George (1959). "How Is Society Possible", in *George Simmel, 1858-1915: A Collection of Essays, With Translations and a Bibliography,* Kurt Wolf (ed. and trans.). Columbus: Ohio State University Press.

Simopoulos, K. (1993). *The Pillage and Destruction of Greek Antiquities.* Athens: (in Greek).

Sites, Paul (1990). "Needs As Analogues of Emotions". John Burton, ed. *Conflict: Human Needs Theory.* N.Y.: St. Martin's Press, pp. 7-33.

Smith, Brewster (1973). "On Self-Actualization: A Transambivalent Examination of a Focal Theme in Maslow's Psychology", *Journal of Humanistic Psychology,* Vol. 13, No. 2 (Spring), pp. 17-33.

Sokal, Alan, and Jean Bricmont (1998). *Intellectual Impostures: Postmodern Philosophers' Abuse of Science.* London: Profile Books, Ltd.

Soper, Kate (1981). *On Human Needs: Open and Closed Theories in a Marxist Perspective.* Atlantic Highlands, N.J.: Humanistic Press.

_____ (1985). "A Difference of Needs", *New Left Review,* No. 152, July/Aug., pp. 109-119.

Springborg, Patricia (1981). *The Problem of Human Needs and the Critique of Civilization.* Winchester, Mass.: Allen & Unwin.

St. Louis Post-Dispatch (1977). "Ex-POWs Healthier than Peers". Nov. 13, p.4K.

——— (1978). "Women's Drug Aduse Described as Epidemic". April 24, p. 4A.

Steinmetz, George, ed (1999). *State/Culture: State Formation after the Cultural Turn.* Ithaca, NY and London: Cornell University Press.

Stonier, Tom (1992). *Beyond Information: The Natural History of Intelligence.* London, New York, etc.: Springer-Verlag.

Strasser, Stephen (1963). *Phenomenology and the Human Sciences: A Contribution to a New Scientific Ideal.* Pittsburgh: Dusquesne University Press.

Streeten, Paul, et al. (1981). *First Things First: Meeting Basic Human Needs in the Developing Countries.* Oxford University Press.

Svara, James H. (1994). *Facilitative Leadership in Local Government.* San Francisco: Josey-Bass, Publishers.

Szalai, Alexander (1966a). "Differential Evaluation of Time Budgets for Comparative Purposes", in Richard L. Merritt and Stein Robban (eds.), *Comparing Nations: The Use of Quantitative Data in Cross-National Research,* New Haven: Yale University Press.

——— (1966b). "The Multinational Comparative Time Budget Research Project". *American Behavioral Scientist,* Vol. 10, No. 4, December (also appendix).

——— (1966c). "Trends in Comparative Time-Budget Research". *American Behavioral Scientist.* Vol. 9, No. 9, May

——— et al (1972). *The Use of Time.* The Hague: Mouton Publishers.

TenHouten, Warren D., et al (1973). *Science and Its Mirror Image: A Theory of Inquiry.* New York: Harper & Row.

Theodorides, H. (1981). *Epicurus: The True Perspective on the Ancient World.* Athens: Kollarou and Sons, Inc. (in Greek).

Throgmorton, J.A. (1993). "Survey Research As Rhetorical Trope: Electric Power Planning Arguments in Chicago" in Frank Fischer and John Forester, eds. *The Argumentative Turn in Policy Analysis and Planning.* Durham and London: Duke University Press, pp. 117-144.

Torff, Bruce and Howard Gardner (1999). "The Vertical Mind - The Case for Multiple Intelligences". Mike Anderson, ed. *The Development of Intelligence.* Hove, East Sussex: Psychology Press, Ltd., pp. 139-159.

Tratner, Michael (1995). *Modernism and Mass Politics: Joyce, Woolf, Eliot, Yeats.* Stanford, CA: Stanford University Press.

Turner, Mark and David Hulme (1997). *Governance, Administration and Development: Making the State Work.* West Hartford CN: Kumarian Press and Houndsmills, Basingstoke, Hampshire: MacMillan Press, Ltd.

Turshen, Meredith (1977). "The Impact of Colonialism on Health and Health Services in Tanzania". *International Journal of Health Services,* Vol. 7, No. 1, pp. 7-35.

UNESCO (1966). *The Multinational Comparative Time Budget Research Project.* Report for the Sixth World Congress of Sociology. Evian, France. Vienna: European Center for Research in the Social Sciences.

Von Neuman, John and Oscar Morgenstern (1947). *Theory of Games and Economic Behavior.* 2nd edition. Princeton, NJ: Princeton University Press.

Wachs, Martin, ed. (1985). *Ethics in Planning.* New Brunswick, NJ: Rutgers University, Center for Urban Policy Research.

Waldon, I.(1977). "Increased Prescribing of Valium, Librium and Other Drugs -- An Example of the Influence of Economic and Social Factors on the Practice of Medicine". *International Journal of Health Services,* Vol. 7, No 1.

Wallerstein, Immanuel (1999). *The End of the World As We Know It: Social Science for the Twenty-First Century.* Minneapolis and London: University of Minnesota Press.

        (2002). "New Revolts Against the System", in *New Left Review,* 18, (Nov.-Dec.), pp. 29-39

Watson, Patrick and Benjamin R. Barber (2000). *The Struggle for Democracy.* Toronto: Key Porter Books.

Weigert, Andrew J. (1970). "The Immoral Rhetoric of Scientific Sociology", *The American Sociologist.* May, pp. 11-119.

Whillock, Rita Kirk (2000). "Age of Reason: The Electronic Frontier Confronts the Aims of Political Persuasion", in Alan B. Albarran and David Goff, eds. *Understanding the Web: Social, Political and Economic Dimensions of the Internet.* Ames, Iowa: Iowa State University Press, pp. 165-191.

Williams, Roger J. (1971). *Nutrition against Disease: Environment Prevention.* New York: Pitman Publishing Co.

Williams, Thomas Rhys (1967). *Field Methods in the Study of Culture.*

New York: Holt, Rinehart and Winston.

Wilson, Edward O. (1998). *Consilience: The Unity of Knowledge*. New York: Alfred A. Knopf.

―――― (2002). *The Future of Life*. New York: Alfred A. Knopf.

Wilson, John Oliver (1980). *After Affluence: Economics to Meet Human Needs*. San Francisco: Harper & Row, Publishers.

Zisk, Betty H. (1992). *The Politics of Transformation: Legal Activism in the Peace and Environmental Movements*. Westport, CN: Praeger.

Zographou, Lily (1983). *Antiknowledge: The Crutches of Capitalism*. Athens: Grammi Publishers (in Greek).

Information Forum. http://
www.ipso.ccc.be/infoforum/
www.paecon.net
pae_news@btinternet.com
http://www.forumsocialmundial.org

AUTHOR INDEX

SUBJECT INDEX

An Uncertain Grave

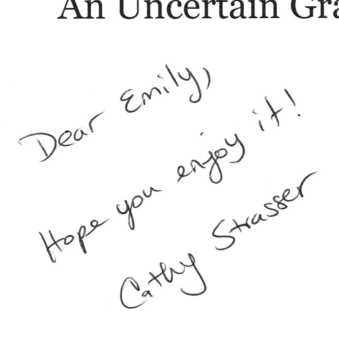

Dear Emily,)

Hope you enjoy it!

Cathy Strasser

An Uncertain Grave

by

Cathy Strasser

Oak Tree Press Hanford, CA

Oak Tree Press
Publishers Since 1998

For information, address Oak Tree Press, 1820 W. Lacey Boulevard, Suite 220,
Hanford, CA 93230.

Oak Tree Press books may be purchased for educational, business, or sales
promotional purposes. Contact Publisher for quantity discounts.

First Edition, August 2014

ISBN 978-1-61009-152-7
LCCN 2014945671